BOOKS BY LEON HALE

Turn South at the Second Bridge
Bonney's Place
Addison
A Smile From Katie Hattan

Easy Going

LEON HALE

Easy Going

Illustrations by Ancel Nunn

SHEARER PUBLISHING

Bryan, Texas

1983

Published by Shearer Publishing

Copyright © 1983
by The Houston Post

Illustrations © 1983 by Ancel E. Nunn

Library of Congress Cataloging in Publication Data

Hale, Leon.
  Easy going.

  Selected articles from the author's column in the
Houston post.
  I. Title.
PN4874.H218A25 1983   814'.54   83-19575
ISBN 0-940672-10-3
ISBN 0-940672-11-1 (lim. ed.)

Manufactured in the United States of America
FIRST EDITION

For Becky, my girl-child, whose laughter
has been music to me

Contents

Foreword

All the stories in this book were selected from my column in *The Houston Post*. As soon as the book comes out, I know what will happen. Somebody will hold it up and shake it at me and ask, "What's your favorite piece in here?" And I won't be able to answer.

But if you forced me to, right now, I would go ahead and pick the piece in Chapter III, about going to Troup to buy a dozen country eggs from Melba McConnell. And she didn't have but ten on hand. So I had to stand around the yard for half an hour and wait for Melba's Rhode Island Red hens to lay two more. The world's freshest dozen eggs. I loved that.

On another day, though, my favorite piece might be the one about eating with the cowboys at Aunt Kate Hudgins' table on the Nash Ranch, in Chapter VI. Or it might be the one about Uncle Luby Morrow's recipe for chicken and dumplings in the same chapter. Another time it might be my friend Mel's story about catching the pass and speeding downfield toward a touchdown he needed to make in honor of Flora Kessler. That one still makes me grin a good bit. It's in Chapter X.

Not all these pieces are good for grins. Some give me a deep sadness. In Chapter III you'll find a story about Pete Locklin, who was my friend. That story appeared in the paper on March 19, 1978. Almost exactly a year later Pete Locklin died, of lung cancer. He was forty-one. He was a special man.

John Rotan (also Chapter III) is gone too. He was the nature-loving old gent who lived in a fine handmade shack in the woods of Tyler County. John died alone in that shack, which doesn't make me so sad because that's where he wanted to be. He'd been in a nursing home and didn't like the sounds. He couldn't hear any hoot owls, so he came on home.

Other things have happened that I'm not grinning about. They're not told in the book because the columns have not been updated. Except for minor editing the pieces run the way they did in the paper. So you won't know, without reading this foreword, that Scheller's Place is closed. Scheller's is my favorite country tavern in all this world, or was. It was at Glen Flora and it's mentioned in the book several times. Pud Joines, its owner and operator, is retired now and Scheller's is no more and as a result, Texas is not as interesting a state as it was.

There's an awful temptation to redo these pieces and try to make them better. But I would never get them all done so let them go as they were in the beginning. You'll find things to argue with, I expect. Somewhere I said that a chicken snake is harmless. Since then I've been taught by Richard Wharton, who lives at Joaquin and knows plenty about snakes and chickens both, that the chicken snake can inflict a painful bite. So it shouldn't be called harmless just because it doesn't inject venom. I can see that's true. Moral: Don't mess around with chicken snakes.

In Chapter I, in a piece I did in '77, I set up a yowl about the price of a motel room being thirty dollars. And in that same piece I seem to have discovered that breakfast in that motel's restaurant can cost five dollars. I want you to know that I still think thirty dollars for a place to sleep one night and five dollars for one breakfast is too high. But in '77 I thought such prices were outrageous. Remember I am the guy who in '68 denounced the motels of San Antonio for raising their prices to twelve dollars a night just before that city's world's fair opened.

In Chapter X the Houston Rockets, a professional basketball team, appear to be winning most of their games. That was in '81, before they set records for losing the following season. And in Chapter XIII, the country songs mentioned as current seem mighty dated. The reason is, that piece was done in '77.

And now, it's thank-you time. Thanks to *The Houston Post*, owners of the material in this collection, for permission to reprint the pieces. And to Suzanne Comer, the book's editor who did the selection and organization of the columns. And to Ancel Nunn who produced some fine illustrations, and while he was recovering from a coronary, at that. And finally thanks to Babette Fraser who, riding at fifty miles an hour about twelve miles east of Port Arthur, saw that *Easy Going* would make a pretty fair title.

Leon Hale
June 1983

Easy Going

{ I }

"Hello, highway . . ."

Driving north out of Burnet on U.S. 281, up to Lampasas, Evant, Hamilton, Hico, along the west edge of the Grand Prairie. The land is open and sweeping and makes me feel good.

It always does when I come this way, because this is going-home country for me. In some ways it is harsh territory but it is the place I began and I still love it. Don't you? Doesn't everybody love where they started? I never heard one person say, "I was born at Such and Which and grew up there and I hate it." Maybe it would be like saying you hate your mother.

I watched my first sunrise in 1921 right on up this highway at Stephenville, and was raised a little way on west in the Cross Timbers country. If I had found steady work, I would have stayed . . .

I get the old going-home feeling when I can look out the window at half a square mile of range and there's one lone tree in the middle of it and a dozen cows crowded beneath it, sopping up shade.

The Grand Prairie isn't always what you think of when you say prairie. I mean it's not anything like as level as the Gulf Coast Plain around Houston. Sometimes it bulges up into hills and ridges it's all right to call mountains.

And their slopes at this season are gray or beige in the distance and patterned with cedar elms and Texas oaks spotted here and there in the most artistic spacing.

This is a country with stinging lizards and mountain boomers and horny frogs and rattlesnakes and tumblebugs.

And sudden creek bottoms shaded by pecans. Little old streams you can spit across except in wet times. They'll have slick rocky bottoms and clear water and orange-bellied bream and finger-long catfish with poison fins.

And broom weeds, and sunflowers in the ditches beside the

road. Johnson grass that'll head out not a foot and a half tall. And gnarly live oaks, been sucking a living out of rocky places for sixty years, and not yet twenty feet high.

Grasses with names like grama and curly mesquite that hunker close to the ground. These old drouthy-looking ranchers like to grab a sparse handful of that stuff and shove it at a visitor and grin and say, "Mouthful of this got more strength in it than half a bale of that high-growing stuff down yonder on your coast. Tell me a cow can starve to death down there, standin' belly-deep in grass, that right?"

Rock ranch houses with screened back porches, built about 1927 by people who still live in them. People who don't like air conditioning. And maybe in all that time they haven't planted a tree around the house.

"Plant a tree? What for?"

"Well, for shade."

"Shoot. That's why we built the house, for shade."

A country where people are apt to say "thuh SEEN-in" for "this evening" and they mean before dark. If they tell you to come thuh seen-in don't you go over there at 8:00 P.M. They libel to be in bed aw-reddy.

Well-done steaks. Hard-fried eggs. Light bread and serp and flat biscuits brown and smooth on top. And overcooked turnip greens that get a little gritty after you've already put 'em in your mouth and it's too late.

Good-natured farmers, faces so wind-burned their skin is actually scaly and it hurts 'em to shave, so they don't much.

Country women with grating nasal voices—"Ever-thang's warshed and arned"—and the loveliest of spirits and the most generous of hearts. "Yawl make out your supper now."

I can't see that the Grand Prairie or the Cross Timbers has changed much, except in the towns. I've always thought of the towns as flat and bleached out. Everything built one-story, and so many buildings of that white native rock.

The smallest country towns are still that way but places like Hamilton and Lampasas don't look natural to me now. Too much new construction, and trees are bigger now and this makes the towns greener and less harsh and helps kill the bleached look.

Another thing. The people look fatter to me. Better fed. I used

to think of them all as being lean. But then that was in a lot leaner
time.

At Smithville lately I picked up a hitchhiker who gave me a hard-
luck story. First one I've heard in a good while. They just don't tell
'em the way they used to.

This fellow was maybe thirty and he was going to Harlingen,
so I didn't help him along very far. Just to La Grange, and then he
needed to cut south on U.S. 77.

Said a friend of his had run off with his car in Austin. They
were staying in this motel and the friend borrowed his car to go see
a girl and never did come back. Said he waited two days and then
it took all his money to pay out of the motel and so there he was
afoot, and broke.

Said he was going on home and wait for the friend to bring his
car back. He didn't seem too upset about it.

He kept talking about being hungry. Said he hadn't had anything to eat in more than twenty-four hours. So when we got to La
Grange I gave him a buck and he asked me to let him out at a
hamburger stand. Said that hamburger was sure gonna taste good.

Which shows he hadn't done much time on the road, being
broke and hungry. A fellow with experience at being hungry is not
going to spend eighty cents of his last dollar on a hamburger, not
when he's in La Grange and riding his thumb to Harlingen. Man,
that might take two more days.

I remember about ten years ago I picked up an old boy hitch-
hiking out of Waco and he put the hard-luck story on me for
two dollars. It wasn't a bad story and was worth maybe twice
that much.

He'd been working in the oil fields out around Midland and
Odessa and a length of casing rolled off a truck and hit him. Broke
his leg in about six places, and he'd been laid up in a hospital three
or four months and they'd operated on his leg twice.

He had a lot of other details I forget now, but I remember it
wasn't a bad two-dollar story. I think his wife divorced him while
he was laid up, something like that.

He showed me the scars on his leg from the surgery. They
looked way too old to me, but it is bad manners to challenge a
story a guy is telling for only two dollars.

He took my name and address and said he would send me the money. Of course I didn't expect to get it, and I didn't, either.

Anyway, what I was going to tell you, he talked about how he would spend those two dollars. Said it wasn't going to be in any cafe. Instead he'd go to a grocery store, and buy bread.

Said he'd look for a big store that might have day-old bread they'd sell cheap, and by drinking plenty of water with it he could keep going two full days on one loaf of bread.

Of course drinking lots of water is standard practice among really hungry people, or anyhow it *was*, back in times when hunger was more common. You take now, you run across a fellow claims to be hungry and give him fifty cents and he's apt to go buy a beer with it. People don't know anything about being hungry any longer.

No, I never did go hungry myself, not really, but I've been around people who were, and I paid attention.

When I first began traveling it was fairly common for hitchhikers to be hungry and broke and I learned a good deal from them.

I remember a fellow I picked up out at Sweetwater one night. He showed me how to make a three-course meal out of a bowl of chili. This was back when they gave you all the crackers you could eat when you bought chili.

First he would eat about half the chili plain, without anything. Then he'd fill the bowl back up with crumbled crackers, to make a sort of chili-cracker dish. He'd eat about three-quarters of that, fill the bowl again with crumbled crackers and—while the waitress wasn't watching—dump about half a bottle of ketchup over it and stir. That gave him a ketchup-cracker course, with a vague chili flavor. Which might not sound too good to you but it would if you were really empty.

He'd drink about a quart of water with all that. Said it made him swell up inside like he'd had a Thanksgiving dinner.

Coming down through East Texas on a pretty day, looking for things I like.

I love to drive through the Piney Woods just at the end of a long wet spell, the first day the sun has been out in a week. Because then the light is so bright and shadows so deep and when you stop along the road there is this faint aroma of wet pine in the air and it's such a clean smell. Not as heavy as wet cedar but somehow cleaner.

A white rural mailbox with a name on it that I like: Myrtle Pride.

Seems peculiar it's so noticeable in a year when nature has put so much natural color in the woods but there is a lot of non-natural color in East Texas. Well, look, at that little clothesline of wash, strung yonder between the corner of the house and a maple tree in the yard. There's a woman's blouse matching almost exactly the brilliant orange of the maple's leaves.

And the cypress down there on the creek matches up with the russet shirt, and the clothesline even sports a multicolored shirt that looks like a sweetgum in the fall, showing red at the top and getting lighter on down below, to pale orange on the bottom branches.

Other non-natural colors that leap out. The red, white, blue, and yellow plastic ribbons left by the oil exploration crews, and the splashes of paint that the timber companies put on their tree trunks to mark boundary lines.

Another sign I like: "Shawnee Prairie Missionary Baptist Church. Welcome."

A buzzard on a fence post, holding his wings way, way out to get the sunlight under there. Feels good, you can tell.

Two young Brahman bulls, standing all isolated in the center of a pasture, taking turns licking one another's ears.

You see so many new houses in the Piney Woods now. I'm not talking so much about the rambling brick jobs on cleared hilltops, surrounded by three hundred acres and a whitewashed fence. I mean small houses, sometimes not even painted yet, and close to the road so you know not much land comes with them.

They're little two- and three-room wooden places with tricycles in the front yard. So these are young folks most likely from the cities, come out to see if they can make it in the country. And, so they can afford it, driving to work every day in Lufkin or Diboll or Jasper or maybe even down to Orange or Beaumont or Houston.

You can look at how the new little houses are placed in their clearings and tell they're meant to be added onto, later, when things aren't so tight.

Then mailboxes. I notice a good many what I guess you'd call distinctive rural mailboxes in East Texas, that weren't there fifteen or twenty years ago. Mailboxes with roses painted on them, or in the shape of birdhouses.

They're significant to me because I think they represent in a dependable way the movement of so many people from the cities to the country. I will bet forty dollars that if you took a survey of fancy rural mailboxes, 98 percent of them could be traced to city folks lately moved to the country.

Not many long-time country folks care to have frills on things that have always been simple and plain. It's just like those white wooden fences. They're pretty, and they cost, but if you handed a million dollars to some old farmer been barely making it all his life on an East Texas sandhill, the last thing he'd ever think to put up would be a white wooden fence.

Something I like to do on calm winter days in the woods is stop and sit and listen, to whatever there is to hear. Pick a day after a wet spell, when women get out and rake leaves and try to get them to burn and the smoke travels straight up.

You hear crows must be two miles away, and crickets by the zillions, and the flutter of little birds, and there is a very loud noise that you *don't* hear—the roar of chain saws, because the ground's too wet and the loggers and pulpwooders can't work.

A pretty day at Bellville, and I went by and picked up Franz Zeiske at the Bellville *Times* and we took one of our customary late-afternoon rides along a couple of those lovely old Austin County country roads.

We've been taking country-road rides that way ever since I met Franz on a dove hunt in September of 1946. Since that day we've both quit shooting things, although I don't know that we deserve so much credit for the change. Likely neither of us could hit anything anyhow.

If you happen to travel in your work, you know how a traveling person needs special friends scattered over his territory. They help make working for a living the pleasure it was meant to be.

It's getting harder and harder to stay on dirt roads for very long in Austin County, and of course almost anywhere else it's the same. Twenty years ago Zeiske and I could roll for two hours, slow and easy so we could see the deer and the birds and so Franz could identify all the trees, and we'd never have to worry about hitting asphalt.

But the other day when I picked him up, Zeiske had to pause and think a while before he decided where we ought to go to drive a few miles off pavement.

Our favorite run used to be the old road between Cat Spring and Bellville. Now it's blacktop and it's just not the same. I don't much like it anymore. You go slow enough to see anything and a truck runs up your tailpipe.

This time we took a dirt road going generally north off of State 159 a few miles west of Bellville. I don't know exactly where it leads. You shouldn't have to worry where a country road goes. Just let it surprise you.

I know a lot of people don't like to ride in the country in winter because everything looks dead. It doesn't look dead to Zeiske and me. We like it in winter as well as summer. The earth looks so trim in February, when it's taken a few good freezes. The lines that separate land areas are so clean, and close-cropped meadows look so rich and smooth, like expensive carpet.

I mentioned that, about the frost-bitten meadows, and it pulled from Zeiske a few lines out of the considerable bank of classical poetry he can draw on:

"The melancholy days are come, the saddest of the year, of wailing winds and naked woods, and meadows brown and sere."

It's not sad to me, though, not here in February. The sad time to me is November, when the falling and the withering take place. By February the naked woods are scoured clean by the wailing winds and trees take on an undecorated dignity that I like.

Those lines Zeiske quoted (I know because I asked him) are from William Cullen Bryant's "Death of the Flowers." You needn't be surprised that a country newspaperman, which is what Zeiske is, can quote Bryant. He came up in a family that set a great store by gentle learning. Here he is, on a country road a few miles out of Bellville, giving to me and the birds and the trees his favorite verses from John Greenleaf Whittier:

"Dear Lord and Father of mankind, forgive our foolish ways, re-clothe us in our rightful mind, in purer lives Thy service find, in deeper reverence, praise."

Certain brands of churchgoers will know those lines of Whittier's were set into a hymn of great beauty.

On a country road or wherever, Zeiske uses as much correct English as any man I ever met. He is the only gent I know who can produce the phrase "visible ostentation" when he's talking about the way a buzzard flies.

On that country ride, we saw a curious cloud formation and it inspired Zeiske to comment that it was "an odd vista." I can't name another resident of rural Texas who would say to a close friend that anything made an odd vista.

I think of what I would have said about that phenomenon, and I expect it would have been something like, "Hey, look at those clouds. Isn't that funny?"

So Zeiske's odd vista may be better. But I know, as he does, that I will never be able to say it.

Greetings from a place I like a great deal. I am in the upper right-hand corner of the old Calvert Hotel. I slept here last night.

Every now and then I get fed up with the twentieth century so I get out of it and go back into the nineteenth for a while. I know several places in Texas where I can do that, and this hotel is one.

The hotel is white frame and two stories tall and faces on Railroad Street in the little town of Calvert. Which is on Highway 6 about ten minutes north of Hearne. Which is about twenty minutes north of Bryan.

I used not to like Calvert but now I love it. I used not to like it because it seemed to be dying and sad. Then the antique shops came. All along the highway the shops opened in the store buildings that had been empty.

No, I am not hung up on antiques and in fact I know almost nothing about them. But I like the kind of people who operate antique shops. And I like the effect they have on little towns when they concentrate their businesses as they have in Calvert. The town doesn't look sad any longer. It looks older, but happier.

In the middle 1960s before all the shops came, this hotel was closed. It pleases me that it is open again as it ought to be. I am in favor of old wood frame hotels staying open. I would run for office on that platform. As the ages of hotels go in this state, this one qualifies as plenty elderly. The first planks of it were nailed up in 1872.

Business here on weekends gets to booming. But on this week-day it's a trifle slow. Counting myself, the total number of guests who slept under this roof last night was one. Which is why I got the only room in the house with twentieth-century plumbing. If you are the only customer signing the register, you get your pick of the pickings.

Right now, at ten o'clock in the morning, as far as I know only one other person is on the premises and that is Philip Atkins, who owns the place. He is in his apartment up front, surrounded by books and bills and other paper things. I have seen no maid. No desk clerk. No bellhop. No groundskeeper. No house detective. No maintenance man.

After I checked in yesterday a carload of prospective guests rang the bell—you have to ring the doorbell to get attention—but Atkins didn't like the look of them. Sent them on down the road to Hearne.

Atkins tells me I slept in an 1850–model Dutch pine painted bed last night. I care little for such things, except that they do represent my retreat into the nineteenth century. I have an old wooden telephone, but it is hooked up only to the wall. There is no television. No radio.

When I leave the century I have been assigned to, I don't mind taking along a few comforts I would otherwise miss. That plumb-ing I mentioned, yes. And the air conditioning. I don't mind that.

The other rooms have bowls and pitchers but no running wa-ter. Community baths are located at the middle of the hall. Are you able to see the guests shuffling in bathrobes and slippers along the hardwood hall, carrying their towels and their shaving mugs and their toothbrushes, going to the facilities?

Atkins insists they enjoy doing that. Maybe that's because it's a little like acting in a movie set in the 1890s.

I can tell you are worried about oversleeping, since there are no phones for wake-up calls. But never mind. Every morning around 6:30 a Southern Pacific freight comes growling and whooping by about fifty steps from the front porch and wakes everybody up.

From my window I can see the railroad that this street got its name from. Just the other side of the tracks are the buildings on the highway, which is Main Street where the shops are. I am looking at the back sides of the buildings. I suspect the ends of the older ones have been switched, that they once faced on the railroad. Atkins has a map from about 1918 that seems to support this notion. Map shows the highway running in front of the hotel, along Railroad Street.

This hotel is a bookish sort of place. In the hall are nine shelves loaded with books. Novels, biographies, self-help books, travel books, all kinds. Rule of the house is that if a guest starts reading one of the books, he or she can take it on home and finish it and keep it.

Well, I have got to pack up and get along. I am testing the hotel's library rule. Since I got here I have read a little way into four different books, to see how many of them I will be allowed to take with me back into the twentieth century.

The Lower Rio Grande Valley in the middle of summer:

Bright sun, white-hot and glary.

Deep green citrus orchards, like square miles of ornamental shrubs.

Thirty or forty brown-skinned boys, playing baseball barefooted in a vacant lot.

Lines of tall palms on the horizon. Even a cornpatch, mature and brown in mid-July, is glamorized by a line of palms in the turnrow.

Two women with full grocery sacks, waiting at a bus stop.

Bi-winged airplanes, flying low and slow over the Valley's greenness. Spraying cotton.

The small white cafes sitting at the edge of the citrus groves, and all called El Ranchito.

The penetrating whistle of locusts. The Valley, around McAllen especially, has a surplus of high-whistling locusts this year. Not the old lazy, buzzing cicada most of us associate with hot summer, but one that produces a high-pitched whine that can actually hurt the ears when thousands of its associates join in. Some in McAllen say they can't stay in their own yards because of the racket. Nature's noise pollution.

Stacks of Mexican *pan dulce* on the bread racks in cities like Brownsville and Edinburg.

Patches of sunflowers rising out of Johnson grass beside the roads.

White-wing doves, making soft love-sounds in a pecan tree. Beautiful. Nature apologizing for the locusts.

Signs like "Juan's Exxon."

Signs that say "Fresh Orange Juice Ahead," even when there isn't any.

The almost incredible spread of huge new shopping centers near the Rio Bravo, showing the increasing importance of northern Mexico retail trade to the Valley's economy.

The great stocks of expensive merchandise in near-border stores: radios, stereos, tape recorders, televisions. They end up in Mexico, most of them.

Miles-long beds of oleander and bougainvillea bordering a Valley highway.

Rows of mechanical cottonpickers, like military tanks primed for battle, waiting on their season.

Grain trucks, maize siphoning from under their tarp covers, roaring down U.S. 83 toward Brownsville and the ships.

The beauty and peace of a comfortable-income residential area in a Valley city. All that tropical greenery. Mangos growing by the front step.

At the international bridges on the river, the constant movement of pedestrian traffic. Down at the tip of the state they like to say, in the way all of Texas exaggerates to make a point, that Brownsville and Matamoros swap populations every day. If anything ever happened that would close the Texas-Mexico border and shut off that flow, cities on both sides of the river would flat dry up.

At sundown, a young housewife in Reynosa standing in her doorway, sprinkling the street with a garden hose to settle the dust.

At the bridge, an old woman wearing a head scarf opens a big paper sack while a Mexican customs officer peers in to see what she bought in Texas.

In Matamoros, what a short distance you go to reach a street where almost no English is spoken or understood. Sometimes just one block off the tourist drag and you can sure practice your Spanish. Those who say that "the border is not really Mexico" are just repeating what somebody once told them.

Then, in a sprawling new supermarket on McAllen's booming 10th Street, a big sign which seems to sum up all the contradictions of Valley life: "Your food stamps stretch further at Kroger's."

About two hours ago I woke up in a motel that's about four shades plusher than the kind I generally sleep in. And now I am just sitting here looking out the window, trying to get my money's worth, and wondering what my father would think of this place.

The first fit he would have would be over the price of the room here. It is going to be somewhere between twenty-five and thirty dollars. It is against my religion to pay thirty dollars for a place to sleep one night, but the cheaper place on down the road where I normally stay is full up on account of a singing convention, or some such.

My father traveled for as much of his life as he possibly could, and quit only when he wasn't any longer able to make a living on the move. This place would astonish him.

He was constantly sticking over the edge of financial disaster and so he took accommodations that weren't what you would call highest grade.

But even on days when he was flush, he stayed in the same kind of places. One reason was, at least in his last years on the road, he traveled with a scrappy little fox terrier named Danny McShane, after the professional wrestler.

And he refused to stay in a place that wouldn't take the dog. He would go in carrying a cardboard box that the dog slept in. By day the box held the dog's equipment. His blanket, for instance, and his rubber ball, and his spare harness, and the old brown shoe that he would grab by the lace and sling round and round, growling fiercely.

My father thought that was cute, and felt everybody else

ought to think it was too, although many did not, especially when the dog did it in hotel and motel lobbies while they were trying to read the paper. That was when people sat around in lobbies a lot.

So you see why he didn't stay in the best places.

How he would howl, if he found out I paid nearly thirty dollars to sleep here. Why, thirty dollars would have made the monthly payment on his old Willys Knight he traveled in, with a couple bucks left over to rent a hotel room.

If he had come along with me on this trip, right now he would be pointing to the coin slot by the side of one of the beds, and asking, "What's this?" Well, it is one of those bed shakers. You can feed fifty cents into the slot and it makes the bed vibrate. Supposed to relax you.

"Good night nurse," he would say, about that. It was his favorite thing to say, when he was amazed. "Good night nurse." I don't know where he got that.

Then I would let him discover the steam treatment that they've got in the bathroom here. I have not used it because I'm afraid it might scald me. But you adjust certain valves, and get in the shower and close the door, and you get steamed some way. I believe this is supposed to be good for you. The steam machine would bring out another couple of good night nurses, I expect.

So would the two kidney-shaped swimming pools, with automatic cleaning devices that float around and scour down the walls without direction or interference by human hands.

One thing he would like, there is a lot of clear floor space in this room. He used to complain a little that the small rooms he got in those second-rate places did not have enough space for that dog to sling his old shoe around.

That exercise did require a good bit of room. Counting dog, and lace, and shoe, it needed about a six-foot circle of floor space, otherwise the shoe would bounce off chair legs and walls and mess up the dog's timing.

Rather than have that happen, my father would go down in the lobby and have the shoe-slinging there. It used to embarrass me when I was with him. Sometimes I would keep over by the desk, and lay low, and try to pretend I didn't have any connection with the man or the dog either.

But the prices. They would be the most astonishing to him

now, in a place of this sort. Just a while ago I went into the dining room and had a standard breakfast of two eggs with sausage and toast and orange juice and a couple pats of butter and half an ounce of strawberry jelly. And coffee.

Time I gave just the customary tip to the waitress, that breakfast ran me almost five dollars. Good night nurse.

A few hours ago I was chugging along the highway near Brenham and the radiator in the old station wagon threw a leak, and spewed out a fog of that evil-smelling coolant and antifreeze that they put in cars now.

Well, of course you can't go wandering around the state with a leaky radiator, not in one of these late-model Detroit marvels most of us are driving. You got to get into dry dock and do something about it that's expensive.

In the beginning, and even after it was clear that cars would replace wagons and teams, a leaky radiator was just barely worth a notice. One of the things that radiators did was leak, the same as windmills squeaked, and dogs barked, and babies cried, and wagons rattled. Drivers stopped now and then and put water in the radiator, so the plume of steam would stop coming out of the cap.

But now there is a sign beneath the hood of my car telling me I must not put water in the radiator. Put engine coolant only, the sign says. And if any steam comes out, it smells like the devil's halitosis and means something sinister and costly.

So the station wagon is in a Brenham radiator shop, and I am sitting here in the house of a friend, waiting for the radiator shop people to call and give me whatever bad news I've got coming.

But I am not poor-mouthing. If I've got to have radiator trouble I'd as soon have it here as anywhere. I have sat in this place before, and I am at peace here.

Leaky radiators and similar routine disasters don't really bother me much any longer. I used to fume and boil about such events, which prevented me from going where I had set out to go.

Finally I saw—it took me so many years—that it didn't much matter if I got there or not. What I saw there, or heard, or wrote about it, would not change one line in the history of the world, and so why stew about it?

If you want the truth, I had rather be here than where I was going anyway.

This place is several miles out in the country, and nobody is here but me and a hound by the name of Old Dog. I hear him scratching under the house.

A tranquillity lies over this place today. It is not always here. I have sat here in violent storms and gusting winds, dry and hot and unpleasant, and I have been too hot here and lonesome and mosquito-bitten.

But today it is tranquil. Quiet but not silent. Never silence. Today there is just the right combination of quiet and of sound, so that they enhance one another, and the quiet is made deeper by the sound, and the sound richer by the quiet.

Birds. Crickets. Grasshoppers, popping in flight. Bees and wasps and the jingle of Old Dog's collar buckle when he scratches under the house. A car on the road. An airplane, its sound traveling so far ahead of its passing, and lingering so long afterward.

You find things out about yourself in quiet, thoughtful places like this. What things? Well, things like the changes taking place within yourself. Changes in interests and values and dreams and regrets.

For instance. All right, not so many years ago I fretted so much that I would get old and die and never see the world I live in. I was afraid that I would never get to know islands in Polynesia, or mountain villages in Asia, or walk among the ruins of Egypt, or stand on cliffs and look into the fiords of Scandinavia.

I have retreated from all that now. I would still like to go but it no longer worries me. I have gotten interested in things much closer to where I've always been.

Just outside this window is a little meadow where I can count two dozen kinds of wildflowers, and I am interested in things like that, which so many others consider small and unimportant. Within two hundred yards of this house are woods and gullies and water and bushes and trees hiding ten thousand mysteries of nature, and I am interested in those. Things I've been around all my life, and didn't pay attention to.

So I am narrowing, I'm afraid. Right now, to me, the most pressing monetary matter in the universe is, how much it'll run me to get my car out of that radiator shop in Brenham.

It's two o'clock in the morning and I'm rolling down U.S. 59 below Lufkin, headed south, going slow and sleepy, sipping on a paper cup of coffee from an all-night cafe back in Nacogdoches and keeping awake by listening to a radio show aimed at truck drivers.

This program holds me, has me leaning forward, straining to hear when I go into low places. The signal fades in the creek bottoms because it's coming out of New Orleans and it's not real strong for listeners roaring through Redland and Diboll.

The show gets pretty cornball but I keep tuned, I think because I am so aware of the audience, of all the others listening. Well, sure, I can see them, hear them, smell their fumes. Yonder come three, four of 'em in a covey, through Corrigan, over there in the northbound lanes, their shapes described by the lights on the trailers.

Then here's a listener closer by, passing me now, the sides of his great trailer looming up, I can't even see the roof of it. He's downhill, doing seventy, maybe more, and I imagine I see him sitting way up there in that cab the size of a bedroom, listening just the same as I am to ol' Porter Waggoner moanin', "Thuh add-mish-shun tew this place . . . is a teardrop awn yoar face. . . ."

Don't you suppose there's a network of all-night stations carrying this show? Because the commercials are bought by truck stops in Florida, in Oklahoma, in Ohio, in Tennessee, in the Carolinas. None of your deodorant or paper didy ads. Everything they sell on this show is for you-know-who—CB radio, secondhand rigs, oil filters, crankcase additives. Even a truck stop in a little old Mississippi place maybe an hour above New Orleans on I-55 will buy time on this great show, to lure those boys in the big rigs to stop there where "the people are a little bit friendlier . . . the prices a little bit lower."

Sometimes musical commercials, special written for rolling stock. One'll come on with a guy warbling, "Hello, highway, don't you know me? Come on, highway, take me home. . . ." Then the pitch.

The records are Waggoner and Charley Pride and Loretta Lynn and like that. "Man what a man my man is. . . ." Lyrics for lonesome old boys a thousand miles from their women. Fodder for their fantasies, don't you suppose?

Special dedications, too. All right, a gal writes in—or calls?—and she wants "Birds and Children Fly Away" for ol' Leroy Wilkins, in an eighteen-wheeler out of Savannah and right about now he ought to be rolling across Tennessee. "How 'bout it, Leroy, are yuh listenin'?"

Once in a while a commercial is fun. I can't give you the script exactly but there's one comes on with a highwayman stopping a truck and he sticks a pistol in the driver's stomach and demands his entire rig, truck, trailer, and all.

Trucker says why man, you don't need to hook no rig, all you gotta do is go to Such-and-Which Sales twenty minutes east of Texarkana on I-30 and the prices they got on tractors and trailers there, they're so low it beats stealin'. And the highwayman says, "Let me write down that address. Here, hold my pistol. . . ."

And it's just funny, I don't know why. Maybe because it's 2:00 A.M. and you can see truckers over twenty states sitting behind their wheels and grinning at it because there's not anything else to grin at.

Then highway weather forecasts. Okay, if a driver's running from Oklahoma City to St. Louis on I-44, you think he cares what the weather's gonna be like in the Oklahoma Panhandle or North Missouri? Why no, he wants to know if there'll be rain or fog on his highway, on I-44, at Tulsa, at Joplin, at Springfield. And that's what he gets—highway forecasts dependable for forty-eight hours, so the man says.

Must be dozens of country songs been written lately, special for truckers. "Take me to Ohio. Tell me where she's gone. Take me to Ohio. Can't you hear my song?" And, "I'll be there before the next teardrop falls. . . ."

Then there's this one they're spinning now at about 3:15 and I'm getting close into Houston. It's called "Doggone, That's Just My Truckin' Luck" and it's about this ol' boy been on the road a long time and up ahead he sees a hitchhiker with pretty blonde hair waving in the breeze and he figures now that's just what he needs, to keep him awake. So he stops to pick up the hitchhiker— and all that blonde hair, well, you know, it's growing on a boy. "Doggone, that's just my truckin' luck."

It's the middle of the morning on a calm quiet day and I have followed an impulse and a country road and now I'm stopped under a live oak tree somewhere off U.S. 77 between La Grange and Schulenburg.

The countryside has an unreal quality about it. Still, full of curious echoes, expectant. Something is about to happen.

A rain shower. A blue-gray cloud has drifted in from the northwest and covered all the sky that I could see early this morning when I woke up in La Grange. I may have to fold up and take cover before I finish.

I find this spot a very good place to be right now. I'm a little bit lost, since I can't tell you exactly where this oak tree grows, or what people call this country road. But that's all right. I do think there's a benefit in being lost occasionally. It leads a person away from the routine matters that keep his mind employed.

This is a Sunday morning. Maybe that's why this place reminds me of being in church. Long ago, church was like this, had this same atmosphere. The echoes, the hushed expectancy, the other-world quality.

Maybe you know it. In church services there are pregnant pauses, such as just before the choir is going to sing an anthem, and any small sound is hollow and magnified and echoey. Like a cough from the back row. The scuff of shoes. The stage whisper of a child, asking its mother a question. Even the knock of an elbow hitting the back of a pew.

It's that way here, now, in this deep calm.

Across the road and down the slope and maybe a half mile away I can hear somebody hammering, driving nails. I had to get out my binoculars to find who it is, working like that on a Sunday morning, and it's a fellow building what looks to be a pigpen. But he is not genuine country. What I mean, he's wearing shorts and a red cap. A real country person doesn't wear shorts while building pigpens. But let it go.

The thing about it is, when this fellow in shorts swings his hammer, I see it strike against the board but I don't hear any sound until he has drawn his hammer back to the top of the stroke. And then I hear the blow. Whap-whap. Twice like that.

A bobwhite quail has come to sit on the top of a fence post a little way down the road. He makes his call, which doesn't really sound anything at all like bob white but let that go too. There is that same curious delay. He hollers, and nothing comes out of him for a full second.

This live oak is a really old party. It's not so big but size and age, in trees, are not closely related. This one stands on a rise, so that its roots must wander about and search for moisture, and in drouthy seasons it likely didn't grow at all. So it may be older than other live oaks three, four times its size that grow in low country and good soil.

I hear chimes, from somewhere. Maybe from the farmhouse behind me. Now and then the music floats in, distant and delicate and sort of celestial-sounding. They're the kind of chimes that women hang in breezy doorways, or from mimosa limbs in back yards.

But now, suddenly, the entire mood of the land changes. The wind comes. Thunder grumbles. The birds stop singing. The doves go charging across the sky in that frantic way they have, as if they must get somewhere, home and safe, before whatever is about to happen starts happening.

A cool freshness sweeps across the country road, and behind it come the first drops of rain. Yonder goes a ground squirrel, skittering over the road, in a great hurry the same as the doves. I've got to fold up, and find the way back to the highway.

II

Home to the Country

Over the past year I've fallen way behind in the matter of getting lost on country roads. Getting lost in the country that way is an activity I consider entirely worthwhile.

Last weekend I made up a few miles but I didn't get nearly as much done as I ought to have. I started out of Greenvine, which is in Washington County a short drive southwest of Brenham. Along in there close to Klump and Latium.

I didn't plan to get lost. It's no good if you plan. I had stopped at Greenvine to read the historical marker about the Greenvine Gas Discovery. That happened in 1879. A farmer named William Seidel was drilling a water well and when he'd punched down to 106 feet, whoosh, here came a stream of gas out of the hole.

Don't you expect *that* caused a stir around the drill site. A lucky thing Seidel wasn't smoking, else it could have caused something besides excitement. The story is that gas from that well was piped to a nearby farmhouse and this most likely was the first domestic use of natural gas in Texas.

I was already headed sort of west toward the Fayette County line so from Greenvine I kept in that direction and inside of a mile I was reasonably well lost. I count myself lost if I am on a country road and don't know where I am going to end up. You don't have to be lost in the sense that you'd turn around and go back, or ask somebody where you are. Asking directions spoils the game.

The first thing you notice when you get onto country roads just now is that there is a pretty good drouth going on. Stock tanks are low, and a lot of the small ones are nothing but bog holes. There is a thirsty, short-grass look to the land. Of course you don't expect the countryside to be blooming at this season but it is hard to find a patch of anything green. You'll see the cows grazing down the bottoms of ravines, where water last collected and a little moisture is keeping the grass going.

Still headed generally west on a hard-packed gravel road that takes frequent ninety-degree turns around the corners of farms.

You can see and identify objects so far away at this time of year, when vegetation is short and the earth is gray and dull and the trees have given up their leaves. Do you see that line of small white thingamajigs way over yonder near the crest of that hill? Must be two miles away. Do you know what those are? Beehives, six of them all in a row.

Then a half mile this side of them, and a little to the south, that sloping meadow-like field seems to have widely scattered white flowers blooming in it. They are white hens, though, just chickens, ranging on that slope, grazing and looking for grasshoppers.

I especially love the part of Texas that lies between the Brazos and Colorado rivers, and one reason is that it still has farmers who let their chickens run loose, and scratch in the dirt, and catch bugs the way God meant for chickens to do. I like to see them out there doing that.

You go to East Texas and see how many chickens are running free in the woods. Most of them are all cooped up in long narrow hen houses, and don't even have any straw to sit in and lay an egg, and when they get old they will pass on into chicken soup without ever scratching in the dirt or meeting a rooster.

Curving around fencelines still, up and down modest hills, across narrow wooden no-rail bridges. The remains of gardens show up now and then, still green somehow. Sometimes the powerful perfume of a hog house boils into the car window. Hoo boy, but that's rich.

Well, look where we have come out. Over on Highway 237 in Fayette County, at the old LaBahia Cemetery. A very nice spot where I have stopped several times before, coming off 237 from the other direction.

LaBahia Cemetery is not at all a sad place. I like it because the gate is always open and the grounds are kept in perfect condition, so neat and clean. Never an aluminum can or a hot dog wrapper or a paper sack. And they have benches under the trees and it's good to sit there late in the day and watch the sun go down.

Next time I intend to stay lost a little longer.

One of the customers has written to ask whether people in the country still go to storm cellars when the weather threatens.

I would say some do. I haven't heard anybody talk about spending the night in the storm cellar in a long time but a good many cellars are maintained. Once in a while you'll even see a new one, so I have to believe that people use them.

But generally, Texas rural people don't run from the weather the way they once did for the reason that they are better informed about it. In early times when a bad-looking cloud boiled up on the horizon there was a tendency to head for the storm cellar just to be on the safe side. Now people can switch on the radio and get the forecast, or even watch the weather person on TV show a radar picture of where the weather is and where it's going and talk about how severe it's apt to be.

So a lot of storm cellars aren't kept in a state of readiness any longer. I see them full of old furniture, stored, or cluttered with junk and draped with spider webs and not looking too inviting.

I guess anybody who spent much time in the country in the early half of the century has storm cellar experiences to talk about. I always hated to go into the things. I had the feeling I was gonna get snake-bitten down in there.

Because we were always going at night, and it was sort of scary.

Stormy weather wasn't as frightening in the day as it was at night. In daylight the family weather authorities would stand on the front porch, or out in the yard, and study the sky and maybe they would announce, "We don't need to go to the cellar. It's circling around us to the east. I doubt we'll even get a shower out of it."

But at night, when the thunder and lightning came, the weather authorities weren't so confident. They couldn't judge what they couldn't see and they played it safe. "Better wake the children up, Maude. Let's go to the cellar."

The cellars I remember were mainly the crude type. Just a rectangular hole, about six feet deep, with timbers laid over it. Then the timbers were covered with the dirt that came out of the hole, and usually there was an air vent sticking out of the dirt mound, looked like a stovepipe.

Some cellars had fancy improvements but the ones I knew best had dirt steps that tended to wear and crumble and when the family went down there in a rush you were likely to sort of slide down, or tumble.

The cellar door was heavy, and mounted in a crude frame, and it lay very low, not far off horizontal, and a lot of the women couldn't even lift it. They used to say, about a growing boy, that he was getting up pretty strong because he could already lift the cellar door.

The inside of the door had latch chains or ropes on it, and it would be chained or tied down when the family was in, so the storm couldn't open it and siphon everybody out.

A curious notion existed among us then about the nature of tornadoes. (We called 'em cyclones.) I try to make my memory say that the idea lived only among the children, but it did not. Because even the most respected family weather authorities demonstrated this belief:

That a tornado could be a crafty, silent enemy that seemed almost to stalk its prey. That it appeared sometimes to hide, like a beast behind the barn, and spring out at its victims. That even after the dark clouds passed, and the wind lay, and the rain stopped, and the skies brightened, even then the tornado might pick that moment to rush out—SWOOP!—and carry all hands away in one terrible instant.

Stories were told, on warm spring nights when lightning flashed in the northwest, about such things, and how they had happened in other places, not so far away.

So when we emerged from the storm cellar, we would come out watchful and quiet, and stand around the door a while, waiting to see if anything was going to attack.

But there were jokes then too, about those who were 'fraidy cats about storms. We'd laugh and talk about Maude, how she'd run to the storm cellar every time the sun went behind a cloud.

There were stories, too, about those who refused, ever, to run from storms. Grandma, remember? When everybody else got up in the middle of the night and ran for the cellar, Grandma would make her little speech again. She'd say the Lord could send a cyclone and carry her on home if he thought it was her time, but she wasn't running to that hole in the ground and get eaten alive by

spiders. Then while the elements raged outside, she would roll over
and go back to snoring.

Grandmaw Gray died last night.
How'd she die?
With a mouthful of rye
And one foot in the sky.

Grandmaw Gray is the name of a game children once played, long
ago when the games youngsters loved didn't require $37.50 worth
of store-bought equipment.

Any number could play. The leader would make that an-
nouncement that Grandmaw Gray had died. The players would
ask how she died. Then the leader had to describe the conditions
under which the poor old soul departed, as in the example above.

The players were obliged to try to look the way Grandmaw
looked. That is, they would pooch out their cheeks as if they had a
mouthful of rye, and stand on one foot with the other leg held stiff
and high.

The idea was to see who could stay in that ridiculous posture
the longest without laughing or falling. If a player laughed, the
leader declared him eliminated.

I learned to play Grandmaw Gray out on West Grove Street in
Lufkin one morning last week. Edmund Winston was the one who
taught me. After Winston retired not long ago, he got to thinking
about those old games he played when he was a country boy at
Moscow. He made a list of them.

Some on his list are familiar to me. Mumblety peg, which we
used to call mumbley peg or just mumble peg. Red Rover. Farmer
in the dell. Ante over, or Annie over as we said.

But some of Winston's games I never heard of, like that
Grandmaw Gray. Then he remembers one called stink pot. Little
house on the hill. Flying Dutchman. Even one known as Ransom
Ransom Tee-i-oh.

Flying Dutchman was a racing game similar to drop the hand-
kerchief, except two couples raced, in opposite directions, around
a circle of players.

Children played a great variety of chase games in those times,
and some featured elaborate ceremony. Little house on the hill,

Winston explained, was a charades-type game. One group would approach another and this exchange would take place:

"Where you from?"

"New York."

"What's your trade?"

"Lemonade."

"Show your wares."

Then the charade would be acted out and when the answer was guessed the actors ran and the other side gave chase. Many of these chase games were a form of early courtship, in which the boys chased the girls and vice versa.

For example that Ransom Ransom game began with a chant, "Ransom ransom tee-i-oh, off we go to Mexico . . . ," then there was something about shutting the eyes and turning around three times, to get dizzy, and the boys then tried to catch the girls in a chase.

All these games had many variations in their names and rules, from place to place. Winston said about that stink pot game, "It was played at Center Grove, but never caught on at Moscow." Center Grove was about ten miles from Moscow.

Stink pot was a variation on hide and seek. The person who was "it" would catch the hiders and put them in a pen or a stink pot until everybody was caught. We played a similar game we called sheep board down, in which a player still free could slip in and free those who had been already caught.

Winston has a game called base on his list which is also similar. Fox and dogs was another chase game, in which a swift runner was chosen to be the fox. He was pursued in the woods by the others, who were required to bark.

One of the roughest games Winston remembers was wolf over the river. "It was football," he said, "without a ball and without a helmet or pads or any protection."

In wolf over the river a youngster would do what amounted to some broken field running through a gang of pursuers who were required to catch him and pat him three times on the back. Most times, to do that, they had to tackle him.

Or *her*. Winston remembers that a lot of those country gals played those rough games, right along with the big boys, and some of them could flatten a guy, too.

Edmund Winston and his wife live in a sort of country-looking house there in Lufkin. It's got hound dogs in the back, and a tree house and swings and an old dinner bell for the grand-children to play with, and Winston seems to be having a good time being retired. I wish you could have seen him showing me how to play Grandmaw Gray, standing there with his jaws pooched out and one leg in the air.

Maxey Brooke is a chemical engineer, retired. He lives down at Sweeny and he writes letters. It may be that Brooke has been writing to *Post* columnists longer than any other subscriber.

Most of the Brooke letters I have received over the years have been about words. He is a word lover from away back.

Last weekend I was in Sweeny and met up with Perry Johnson, who is a letter writer himself, and he took me to see Maxey Brooke.

Even when he came to the door wearing a pajama top for a shirt, Brooke still had the look of a scholar. He wore the pajama top because he has been laid up with shingles.

You may know that shingles is a fairly common disease. It is also an interesting disorder from the standpoint of words. According to my dictionary its name is kin to a medieval Latin word, *cirgulus*, meaning "belt." It's related also to the Latin verb *cingere*, meaning "to gird."

If ever you had shingles, you won't have any trouble remembering that the breaking out of the skin is apt to follow a path of nerves, often around half the torso. Like a belt, or like the girth or cinch of a saddle.

There in his living room on a quiet Sweeny street, Brooke grinned and remembered the superstition once held by country people that if shingles traveled all the way around the body, the patient would die.

"Friend of mine, J. R. Waldby, is ninety-two," Brooke said. "He says the remedy for shingles used to be to kill a chicken and put its blood on the body."

That got us onto the subject of old-timey cures and remedies. "I remember about this time of year," Brooke said, "my parents would give me what they called a blood thinner. My mother believed in sassafras tea and my father preferred cream o' tartar and sulfur. So I'd get a dose of both. I must have had the thinnest blood in Ottawa County." (Which is in Oklahoma, where Brooke grew up.)

My feeling about most of those old country cures is that they showed the durability of the patient. A youngster had to be tough to withstand the treatment.

"When a child would get to looking puny," Brooke went on, warming to the subject, "he'd get a round of calomel. Then a dose of castor oil to wash the calomel out."

(I am a survivor of those early calomel wars myself. I have just now noticed in the dictionary that the word calomel has a peculiar history. It springs from the New Latin *calomelas*, meaning "beautiful black." How anybody could connect beauty with calomel is mysterious. Dictionary explains the medicine was developed from a dark powder, which is where the dark comes in.)

"For chiggers," Brooke said, "you applied a mixture of bacon grease and sulfur. For a cough, for the croup, the treatment was a spoonful of cane sugar, wet with kerosene."

You see what I mean about surviving the treatment? A young mother of present times would be appalled at the idea of feeding a child kerosene. But plenty of children, even little babies, used to get it. I don't know, maybe that's why the infant mortality rate used to be so high.

(You want to know the origin of that word "croup"? Dictionary says it's probably one of our sound imitative words. Imitating, that is, the sound of coughing. Croup, croup, croup.)

Brooke can remember going to school with children who wore asafetida (sometimes spelled asafoetida, and often pronounced something like "assfedity"). They wore it in stinky little bags tied around their necks. Purpose of this was to ward off colds and coughs.

I never saw children wearing the bags but I have smelled asafetida. Whew! There's a theory about the effectiveness of that stuff: It did, in fact, tend to protect the wearer because it smelled so rotten nobody with a cold would come near enough to pass off any germs.

Spider web, applied to a cut, to stop bleeding. "Yes, I've heard of that," Brooke said, "but I never saw it done. I've seen a wad of chewing tobacco held on a wound to stop bleeding."

How about earache? "Blow tobacco smoke in the ear," Brooke grinned. All right, I remember that one. You'd see an old grandfather on the front porch. He'd take his pipe out of his mouth and reach out and draw a child's head close and give the kid's ear a dose of smoke.

For toothache? "Oil of cloves," Brooke said, "applied on a piece of cotton." And then there was the bark of the tickle-tongue tree. Prickly ash, that is.

How about a treatment for boils? "A flax-seed poultice," Brooke remembered. "Boil the seed, wrap it in a cloth, and apply it to the boil. That was supposed to draw the poison out. If you didn't have any flax, you could apply a mixture of bread and milk."

We got into a discussion on how to spell "risen." Dictionaries available wanted us to spell it "rising" but I never heard it pronounced anywhere near that way. A risen (a boil) was always a risen and not a rising.

In summer in the country, seemed to me that you always had some member of the family going around with the awfulest old sores, boils, carbuncles, whatever. You'd notice a guy sitting down real slow and careful and you knew what his trouble was—a boil on his behind.

"You don't see so much of that now," Brooke said. "I assume because of improved hygiene. Or better nutrition." Let's hear it, then, for better nutrition. I have known even small boils, rising up in strategic places, to lose critical athletic contests, or destroy love affairs.

"Treatment for heart trouble was foxglove," Brooke said. Which made sense because the foxglove plant turned out to be the source of digitalis.

"For nosebleed you put a penny under your tongue," Brooke recalled, "and for colic you used paregoric and alcohol."

It took me ten minutes in the dictionary to learn how paregoric ought to be spelled. Elsewhere I may have misspelled the names of other medicines we talked about. If so, I will hear about it pretty soon in a letter from Maxey Brooke.

Something that interests me is the way people in the country give directions when they are steering you to a place you've never been.

Through the years I have received some really beautiful sets of directions in the mail. I wish I had saved them all, along with the maps that often accompany them. I love a homemade map.

I had a nice set of directions just recently in a letter from Minnie Hickman, who lives out of Corrigan on Route 1. She was telling me how to find a house called the Old Farris Place.

"That house sets on a high hill about one and one fourth miles north west of the small town of Corrigan . . . go the Union Spring Cemetery Road until you cross Bear Creek, turn left on the first dirt road, cross a small bridge on a spring branch and go straight up the hill."

I went directly to the house following those instructions, after I asked where Union Spring Cemetery Road is. One thing I liked about Minnie Hickman's directions is her use of the old expression "go the Union Spring Cemetery Road."

Lot of the older country people still say "go" a road rather than "take" it. I used to hear, "The Unity Bridge is no account so go the Old Foster Road."

Not many people are skilled at giving directions, and even fewer are any good at following them. I had a nice set of directions over the phone recently from Fred Dahmer who lives at Uncertain on Caddo Lake. He said turn left at the beer sign, coming into Uncertain from Karnack. The beer sign was big and red neon and plenty obvious. Then he said turn right and cross the little bridge at the orange house that isn't finished yet. Then turn left again and watch for a gray station wagon under a carport. Directions worked beautifully.

I liked that "orange house that's not finished." A good giver of directions will use landmarks that way that a stranger can't miss. I mean even in Houston an orange house would be distinctive.

A poor giver of directions will often assume that just because a thing is familiar to him, it is also familiar to a person who has never before been anywhere near it. This seems strange but it's true.

I have had somebody say on the phone, "You just come right on out by the pens." And I would ask, "What pens?" And the giver of directions would seem to scold me. "Why, the *stock* pens, by the railroad, all along there by the railroad."

His tone was saying, "My law, those pens have been there for seventy-five years. How could you not know about the pens?"

Well, of course the reason I didn't know about the pens is that I never saw them before. But a poor directions giver will not count that an excuse.

I have learned to be suspicious of the distances that people quote in giving directions, unless I already know them to be good navigators. A person will say on the phone, "Turn east on the second shell road after you leave the main highway." That sounds plain but I always want to know how far it is from the main highway to that second shell road, so I ask, and the answer will be vague. "Oh, I'd say it's a mile and a half or two miles." When it may be fully four miles, or not even one mile.

Then other times you get people who will quote you distances down to the tenth of a mile. "Check your odometer," they'll say (notice they know it's an odometer and not a speedometer), "and turn north on a blacktop that's three and seven-tenths miles from the courthouse square."

Some folks will mislead you by giving too much detail, too many checkpoints.

"Come west on 226. You'll pass a schoolhouse and a football field. Then over to your right you'll see the stacks at the power plant and a string of trailer houses. Go on past there and you come to the auction barn. Take a left on down to the pipeline crossing. There'll be a rig drilling off to the west, and . . ."

Then they'll tell you about a rock house with a tall TV antenna, a bunch of red cows, a long chicken house "must have ten thousand fryers in it," a sign saying Cedar Hill Cemetery, and a shack with some junk cars in the yard. It sounds like the house you're looking for is two counties away when it's not but a mile and a quarter from town. Some directions givers just like to tell you everything.

As a general rule you get more detailed directions in the east and central parts of the state than in the west and south.

I've always enjoyed stopping, say, in Encinal and calling a ranch and hearing a drawly, friendly voice say, "Why don't you run out to the house a minute. Just come east on 44. Name's on the mailbox."

Which may be all the directions you'll get, and if you don't ask you won't know that from where you are to that mailbox is twenty-seven miles.

In the Hallettsville-Shiner-Gonzales area recently I got acquainted with another rattly old country-road bridge I hadn't seen before. For such a short bridge it certainly has a lot of character.

It's an iron bridge with a sign, "Load Limit 7 Ton." It's floored in timbers just loose enough that they make the proper rumble when a car crosses. I rolled over slow, and turned around and went over again a little faster, and parked.

Pretty soon here came a flop-hatted fellow in a pickup. He went across a bit faster than I did and those timbers made a different sound, a little higher pitched. I hung around a while and finally I got a young gent with long yellow hair in a black sporty car. He drove over the bridge pretty fast and the timbers made another sound still, higher pitched than the pickup made, and a couple of loud pops that the slower speeds hadn't produced.

So it became clear that this old bridge can almost be played, like a piano, that it produces a range of sounds and pitches depending on the vehicle crossing and how fast it's traveling.

What I want to do is go back there with my tape recorder and sit around on the bank of that little creek and record that old bridge, see how many tunes it will play during a day's duty. I'm afraid that one of these times we'll realize suddenly that no more rattly bridges exist and nobody will have preserved that old country sound.

In fact, I have lately been thinking about a lot of sounds that I want to get on tape before it's too late. I'm serious about it, yes, and I have made at least a partial list of them.

Early on the list is the braying of a mule, or a jackass. I don't believe mules, or jackasses either, are about to become extinct but I sometimes go an entire year without hearing a mule sound off. Oh, it's a grand thing to hear. I bet we have native Texans fully grown who never have heard a mule sing. True, it may not be anywhere as beautiful as the mule thinks, but it's country music that needs preserving.

Also I want to record a small Texas church congregation singing *Just As I Am*.

And the sound of a freight, a steam locomotive train, off in the distance, going CHUH-chuh-chuh-chuh-CHUH-chuh-chuh-chuh. And the whistle, blowing lonesome on a cold night.

Then I want to record a steel-tired wagon going over a rough road, and the sounds of the harness and the trace chains.

An old hen, clucking to fourteen baby chicks.

A woman churning, with a crock churn and a wooden dasher that makes that steady, down-in-a-well sound pattern. Clonk, she-clunk, she-clunk, she-clunk.

A norther moaning around the corner of the house in January.

An egg, being cracked on the rim of an iron skillet, and dropped into grease so hot that it comes out with brown lace around its skirt. Which isn't the best way to fry an egg but I was old enough to vote before I knew there was any other way.

The sound of a cow being milked, when the first few streams hit the bottom of the bucket. Now that's a sweetheart of a noise, and I can't think of a sound any more countrified.

The strange whir a bullbat makes when it pulls out of its high dive.

Scissortails chattering on a telephone wire.

An ancient windmill clanking and clattering in a steady breeze.

The mating call of a big bullfrog on a still night.

The creaks and pops that a house makes when it cools off at night.

A whirlwind going through a corn patch in August. I love that one. I can hear the dry stalks rattling and feel the dust stinging my eyes and blasting needle-like around my face. We used to lie in the middle and look up and see how high the whirlwind took the corn shucks.

The metal buttons of your overalls going clackety-clack up and down the rub board on wash day.

Ice in a tow sack being crushed with a hammer, to go in the ice cream freezer.

The pot-rack, pot-rack of guineas.

The come-and-get-it grunt of a big old sow as she plops down to give dinner to her litter of pigs.

Rain hitting the leaves of a magnolia tree just outside a bedroom window.

A hound's tail going thump thump thump on the front porch.

Sheets on the clothesline, popping in a gentle wind.

Ice being dropped into tea glasses.

A ripe watermelon, splitting when the knife is stuck in it.

A gruff voice mumbling a blessing before a meal:

"Heavenlyfatherblessissfoodtoourbodiesandforgiveoursins-amen."

When I get all my sounds recorded, I might get a composer interested in basing a symphony on them, and we'll all go down to Jones Hall to listen. I can already hear the kettledrums and the bass viols, and maybe the bassoons, creating the sound of a pickup rolling across that old iron bridge on Sandy Fork.

When people move from country towns to big cities, one of the many things they have to get accustomed to is that it takes such a lot, in a big city, to make up an Event.

Country-town folks are used to getting details on public happenings, good or bad. They want to know the complete story about anything that makes a noise, breaks glass, or gives off smoke.

Such as fires, and car wrecks, and shootings.

Right now I am sitting here in a multitude of about two million people and in the last two hours I have heard sirens four times. It isn't likely I will ever find out why those sirens were blowing.

If one of them was on an ambulance going to a car wreck, even if somebody was killed in the wreck it won't get but six or eight lines in tomorrow morning's paper. Unless of course the party killed happened to be prominent for one reason or another.

In my time I have lived in country places where I would never sit still while sirens sounded. I would go and see what was happening, and get all the details I could, and then hope somebody asked me a question about the event so I could report.

I think it would be good if the big-city papers just once in a while would pick a routine disaster and report it the way country weeklies used to do it. Some country editors could cover a minor car wreck, say, in such an interesting style. I always loved the way they did it.

Such a report would go something like this:

At 3:30 P.M. on Tuesday afternoon Lucy Dell Peyton and Leroy Townsend crashed together at the corner of Mulberry Avenue and

East Main, causing $780 worth of damage. Lucy Dell was taken to the hospital where she suffered a broken arm and six stitches above her left eye. Leroy was not hurt except for his blood pressure going high. His mother was riding with him, receiving a bruised right shoulder.

Lucy Dell was driving her daddy's dark blue '74 Pontiac and traveling south on Mulberry, going to Erma Thatcher's house who is making her wedding dress. Leroy and his mother were in his '62 Ford pickup that he delivers eggs in from out at Murphy's Chapel, going west on Main.

Lucy Dell and Leroy came to the intersection at about the same time and Leroy struck her a solid lick on the side and back toward the rear. We could hear the crash at *The Messenger* office four blocks away.

When they hit, Lucy Dell spun around and one of her hubcaps flew off and landed all the way up on Isom Darby's front porch and knocked over two pot plants. Lucy Dell then skidded into the telephone pole so when Lorene Darby went to report the accident the phone was out of order due to Lucy Dell knocking the wires loose.

Debbie Pool, that's Maynelle and John Pool's next to youngest girl, ran seven blocks to the hospital to say the phone wasn't working and Leroy and Lucy Dell had run together. They let her ride back in the ambulance.

Police Chief Henry Atkins said it looked to him like it was Leroy's fault but he has not filed charges against him. He said Leroy will have trouble enough anyhow, paying damages to the front-end of his pickup. Clayt Boyd at Clayt's Garage estimated damages to the pickup at about $300.

Barton Peyton, Lucy Dell's daddy, said he had insurance on the Pontiac although $200 deductible on collision.

Leroy said it wouldn't have happened except he was looking at a liver-spotted dog going north on Mulberry and didn't see Lucy Dell coming. He has been trying to buy that bird dog a good while, which it belongs to Dan Whitmore and runs loose around town a lot.

Lucy Dell spent one night in the hospital. She said the worst part was she would have to put off her wedding. It has been reset for August 15. She is engaged to Carlos Singleton who played fullback three years for Consolidated High School. Dr. Moresby said Lucy Dell's cut over her eye was clean and the stitches won't make a bad place. That is good because she is one of our prettiest girls, being runnerup year before last at the Alfalfa Fiesta Queen Contest.

At press time Wednesday the telephones on the west side of town were still not fixed yet.

"Mr. and Mrs. Orland Shepherd from Waco visited Sunday in the home of Mr. and Mrs. Sam Bright on the occasion of Verna Bright's birthday. Her grandsons James Shepherd and William Ray Shepherd cranked two freezers of homemade ice cream. They had a half inch shower . . ."

That's from a clipping that somebody sent me, out of a small-town newspaper, evidently up in Central Texas somewhere. The sender didn't identify it.

Obviously the clipping is from the column of what we used to call a country correspondent. Every small-town weekly newspaper would have a correspondent in all the rural communities the paper served, and each week these correspondents would write about who was sick and who had died and who had visited and why, and generally what the weather had brought.

Of course a lot of small-town newspapers still use the country correspondents. Sometimes one will whip out a jewel of a paragraph that deserves to be saved and distributed wider.

It would make a good project for these people who collect Texas folklore to read a few bales of country papers and select correspondent paragraphs that need preserving. I wanted to do that myself one time but it turned out to be about like milking forty cows by hand. Too much work.

Back in the '50s and '60s somebody used to send me a paragraph now and then that a woman named Opal Hughes wrote in the Seminole *Sentinel*. I suspect, because of the way she said things, that Opal Hughes had fans a long way from Seminole, which is up yonder near the New Mexico line between Odessa and Lubbock.

Recently it pleased me to find out that Howard Peacock, up at Woodville, has been an Opal Hughes reader for years. He never has even been to Seminole as far as he knows but he subscribed to the *Sentinel* just to read what Opal Hughes would say next. He saved a good many of her best paragraphs and has let me borrow a few of them. I think most of these are from back in the '60s.

"Mr. and Mrs. R. C. Pattie are fine but have lots of good and bad days," Opal Hughes wrote one week. "Mrs. Belle Whitaker is doing as good as she can."

"Mr. Jim Golden has good health for his age."

"The Doodle Bug Fellows are drilling holes in this country now. . . ." A reference to oil exploration activity.

"Talked to another old-timer, Mrs. A. L. Duff, Sr. She says she is doing just fine and washing her fresh tomatoes."

Correspondent Hughes seemed at times to be giving a person a subtle scolding: "Mrs. Ruby McHaney came to church but her husband did not get there."

Or offering medical advice: "We hope Earl went to the doctor today at Andrews."

Many of the country correspondents used to mention themselves in the third person. For example, here is Opal Hughes on Opal Hughes: "Mrs. Opal Hughes went to see her sisters in Lamesa. . . . While there Opal Hughes attended to business."

Here is one of Howard Peacock's favorite Hughes paragraphs: "Mr. Raymond Sinclair has been real sick. He is Chester Sinclair's father and he lives at Pittsburg, Texas. Chester was called to the bedside of his father. While there they fished a little."

"Gene Allen is sporting a new secondhand pickup."

"Mrs. Noble Fox is doing pretty good."

"Josie Fox was in the cafe last Sunday but could do very little work."

You want to know how Opal Hughes knew that? It was because: "Mrs. Opal Hughes went to Josie's Cafe for Sunday dinner."

The result of a hail- and windstorm: "Homer Whitaker said he had 100 or 150 acres of freshly planted feed blowed out."

Here's an Opal Hughes medical bulletin on a local gent: "The doctors removed one malignant tumor off one lung and the other lung was serious. They will give him cobalt treatments. If his condition is not too serious he will live."

Let us close with a report on how Karl Hughes is doing: "Karl Hughes is doing fine and as usual, passes his time off good."

Last week I had some business in Jefferson County and when I finished with what I was doing I drove twenty miles into Beaumont to get a shoeshine.

I never thought I'd drive that far to get a shine but this was a special one. Several months ago I was moaning here that I no longer had a satisfactory place to get shines the way I used to, and that had created a little vacant spot in my life. Because shines to me always had to do with a lot more than shoes. I loved the ritual of going to the barbershop for a shine, and the smell of the polish, and the drawly joshing of the men.

And a shine made me feel good. Relaxed me. It was like getting a foot massage. But I had not bought a shine at a barbershop or anywhere else in about five years.

When I said that in the paper, one of the customers wrote that I ought to go to Beaumont and buy a shine at the Mirror Shine and Shoe Repair, as it is one of the last old-fashioned shine shops in the state.

Well, if there's anything I love it's patronizing an old-fashioned kind of business, or taking part in any activity that's fading and will probably disappear forever pretty soon. So twenty miles for a shine didn't seem excessive.

Mirror Shine is in the 200 block of Crockett Street in down-town Beaumont. That part of town is now a curious blend of old and new, of progress and decay. I'm not sure which I like better.

No, I don't mean I'm in favor of cities decaying. But there's something about the buildings around Main and Pearl and Crockett that reminds me of the first cities I knew. Places like downtown Fort Worth in the 1930s—austere and substantial and important and unfriendly and exciting.

I stood awhile at Crockett and Pearl and got the feeling a streetcar might come groaning and cracking and sparking along pretty soon. I wish one had. I am lonesome for trolley rides, too, the same as for store-bought shines.

Mirror Shine is right in between Tip Top Chili and Papa Joe's ("Biscuits, Gravy, & Coffee—$1.49"). The old Annex Apartments are in that block. But the drive-in windows of a modern bank are just across the street, and a high-rise of some kind is going up a block or two back east toward the Neches.

The interior of the shop suggests an antique place. Here is the reason, a sign near the cash register: "We Buy Used Furniture." So while you wait for a shine you can shop for a baby bed, or an old popcorn machine, or a chest of drawers.

Halfway back, on the right, is a battery of shine chairs mounted on a platform. Four broad-armed seats with built-in ashtrays. All four were occupied and two more men waiting. Two shinemen were working. So this would take a while. The system is that you sit in one of the waiting chairs and when a shine chair is available everybody moves up one seat. I sat down and the familiar shoe-polish smell came to me, and the sound of a shoe repairman working drifted up from the rear.

For the waiters-in-line, dirty-eared *Hustler* and *Playboy* magazines are provided. They are more recent numbers than they appear. The pages have just about had the ink looked off them. And here was a big whisk broom with straws more than a foot long, the kind once used in barbershops to brush hair off customers climbing out of chairs. I did not see the brush used in the shine parlor.

While you get your shine you may study the artwork framed and hung on the wall before you. A remarkable gallery. George Washington's portrait. A village blacksmith print. Jesus Christ at prayer. A Charles Russell-looking print of U.S. cavalrymen charging. Misty mountain scenes out of Middle Europe. The front cover off a piece of sheet music, with Rudy Vallee's face on it. The song was "Springtime in the Rockies."

Nobody wanted to talk. The man next to me was spending five dollars to get two pairs of high-topped shoes shined. He remembered when downtown Beaumont had "twenty-five or thirty" places to get a shine and he thought this one was the last place left. He thought in another ten years store-bought shines will exist only in the memories of old men.

At one point I was distracted by an astonishing photograph in that *Hustler* magazine and my heel slipped off the footrest. Made me remember that getting a shine at the barbershop was once a measure of growing up. That is, you were adult if your ankles were strong enough that the shineman didn't have to hold your heel on the footrest.

Took forty-five minutes to get my shine and with the tip it cost $2.35. Real nice shine, though.

Two Texas institutions I enjoy are country churches and country taverns.

A few of the customers have accused me of spending more time in one than I do in the other. If that accusation is fair, it is because the one stays open more days of the week than the other.

People who never visit churches or taverns may have bum notions of what goes on in them. I sometimes hear some curious opinions expressed as to the kind of folks you meet in these two places.

A tavern is not populated entirely by drunks, as some imagine it is. All the folks in a tavern are not drunk any more than all the people in a church are devout.

Drinking beer, or whatever, is not even the principal reason people go to taverns. Because they can buy it cheaper at the store and drink it at home or under a shade tree somewhere and save money.

They go to taverns mostly for company, because they are lonely. Yes, I think many people go to church for the same reason. In fact I see several curious similarities between churches and taverns.

Down at Wharton the other afternoon I was sitting in Augusta and Ben Holeske's place, listening to Ben carry on a conversation with his little brown dog Mitzie, when it struck me that Holeske's is different from any other tavern I have ever visited in Texas.

No, I don't mean it is unique because of the conversation between Ben and the dog. I know a number of taverns where the proprietor talks to dogs, although I admit I can't name one offhand where the dog answers as well as that Mitzie does.

No, what's different about Holeske's is that it used to be a church. When the church folks moved out Ben bought the building and changed it up some and made a tavern out of it.

Ben is a fellow with great respect for matters of religion, and he has never put up on that former church house a sign announcing that it is a tavern. There is no sign saying that beer is sold there, or even that a talking dog lives there.

There is not even a sign stating that behind those doors, plugged in and warmed up, is an actual, operating juke box that will play for a nickel.

I am telling you, that machine demands only the twentieth part of a buck to play such tunes as Glenn Miller's "In The Mood," and "String of Pearls." Also Pee Wee King's "Tennessee Waltz," and Johnny Long's "In Old Shanty Town," and others you may remember playing on a genuine nickelodeon.

Ben keeps that old juke in there out of respect for the past, the same as he keeps an antique pinball machine that also lights up for a nickel.

To me, a nickel juke box is far more marvelous than a little brown dog that carries on long conversations. But then a great many people go to Holeske's to hear her talk.

Your most successful taverns will often have little side attractions that way, to draw crowds. And of course you see successful churches doing the same.

A talking dog? Really?

Oh yes. Ben's dog can count, in fact, in four languages. And do standard arithmetic, such as add, and multiply, and subtract. (I didn't see her divide but then I never cared much for division anyhow.) And she can read paper money. Tell you the difference, I mean, between a $1 bill and a $5 and $10, and a $20 as well, I hear, but when I was at Ben's nobody had one to show her.

She is just an ordinary brown dog. Ben says she is really a police dog but doesn't resemble one because she is wearing a disguise.

On the average of about once a month I spend a few hours sitting around somewhere in a country store, just visiting and listening and watching who comes in. I am obliged to limit myself on country-store sitting because I am hooked on it, and unless I'm careful I might end up doing it full-time.

In December I stopped at Henry and Lorena Randermann's place, out on Route 2 from Brenham toward Navasota. Henry Randermann is an old-fashioned type of country man who can witch up a water well with a peach limb, and kill you a hog the old-style way when a cold snap comes, and cut it up just right, and make a batch of blood sausage.

From what I hear he is also the sort of fellow it won't do to fool with, as the saying is, meaning if anybody wanders in off the road and tries to get smart, why Henry will not mind bringing out the baseball bat he keeps behind the counter.

People who are in business in lonely spots along our highways now are very much aware that a lot of strange characters are on the loose in this state, and they keep a close eye on folks they don't know.

For example when I stopped out front of Randermann's the other morning Lorena Randermann was in there alone tending the store, and I could see her come to the window and give me a good inspection as I got out. I suppose if a person seemed suspicious enough she would then have time to latch the door and look closed. She told me when I went in she had just heard about a fellow getting shot as he was opening his store, and it had made her jumpy.

A good thing about sitting around Randermann's in winter is that they've got a Birmingham Box 36 in there. Which is a wood stove, and a big one that will take a stick of wood three feet long. You don't see those just anywhere now. You talk about a hot fire, you get that baby roaring and it will scorch a tomcat sleeping a yard away.

So many country stores in Texas have now become combination stores and taverns, and will stay open till maybe ten o'clock at night. Or as long as anybody is sitting in there playing dominoes, or discussing what the world has come to.

"They sit and talk and drink beer and have a game or two," Lorena Randermann said. "We used to do that in private homes, you know, but not so much now."

There's all manner of entertainment in country stores that you might never have thought about. There at Randermann's if things get dull you can always take the phone off the hook and listen to what's being talked about on the party line. Seven other phones, besides the store's, are on that line.

Tickles me sometimes about these city folks who fall in love with the country and can't stand it till they move out there, and lot of 'em don't think about the conveniences they're giving up. Then they get in the country and their phone, for instance, is on a line with a flock of other parties. And it becomes a problem even to get the line to make a call. And forever afterward they've got to be careful what they talk about on that line if they don't want it known by everybody in the county.

Mrs. Randermann tried to make a phone call when I was there in the store and the line was busy and finally she broke in, the way we used to do in the country, and called out, "May I have the line, please?" But whoever was talking wouldn't give it up.

Then somebody went off and left a phone off the hook. When

that happens it puts the line out of whack for all eight parties. To get something done about that you may have to get in the car and go to a neighbor's house. For example, the Randermanns can go to Cecilia Hensen's down the road and call the operator and say a phone is down on the store's line. (Hensen is on a different party line.) Then the operator can put a tone on that line and usually the party whose phone is down will hear it, and hang up, and get things back in operation.

A water witcher?

Well, I guess we do have a lot of new customers moved into this part of the country who never have met a water witcher. We got a lot of water witches in Texas, everywhere. Mostly men but a few women.

All they are, they're just people who are gifted at locating underground water, by the use of some kind of divining rod. Some use a peach limb, some willow, some say it doesn't matter *what* kind, long as it's got plenty sap in it.

Say you're one of these folks just moved to the country, or you're fixing up a weekend place, and you need a water well. Okay, you can hire you a water witcher to witch that well up for you.

He'll walk around out there until his stick starts pulling, and then he may get down on his knees and let the stick tell him how far down the water *is*. It does that by bobbing up and down, a bob for every foot of depth to water, or whatever unit of measure the witcher uses. Then he marks the place and that's where you drill your well.

Oh sure, I've watched 'em do it, dozens of times. Does the stick really move? Sure it does. What *makes* it move? I don't know that. It won't move for me. I've tried it and tried it and nothing happens. Because I just don't have the gift.

Some people swear by water witchers, and some don't believe in them at all. Most of the water well contractors I've talked to don't believe in them.

The water witcher, he doesn't seem to care whether you believe in him or not. All he knows is, his stick moves, and tells him things, and he can show you all those good wells he's witched, and what more proof would anybody ask for?

"I've got a seventy-one foot well I witched for myself," Henry Randermann said, "and it never has given me any trouble. I've even got artesian wells not but eight feet deep."

Reason he talks about depth that way, the water witchers generally feel that well drillers dig deeper for water than necessary, in order to make more money. The drillers will argue you blind about that. So there you are.

But you want to know what the Number One Main Thing people in country stores talk about? It's money, what things cost. What a can of beer costs, or a pound of coffee, or a used car, or an acre of this land the city folks have been buying up, and driving the price up on. They speak of this in tones of disbelief.

Here's Rip Sheffield, a customer, sitting by the stove talking about the medicine he has to take. "The bottle of pills I was paying six dollars for at the drugstore a year ago cost me twelve dollars now." Now I agree with him on that. Something's got to be wrong when that happens.

Before I left, just to see what they'd say, I asked if anybody around there would sell off about five acres of that pretty country. "Yeah, we'll sell it to you," Lorena Randermann said. Then she laughed. "But you'd sure have to pay for it. We've found out from these Houston people what to charge for things."

Lesser's is in downtown Chappell Hill next door to the bank but you don't need to think it's not a country store. Groceries, dry goods, hardware, the works. The nails are offered in boxes in front of men's shirts. The floor has some wonderful waves and warps that peak at the center of the store, near the cash register and the wood stove and the Star Brand Shoe bench. If you poured out a bucket of water there, half of it would run toward the front door and half toward the back, where Harry Lesser holds court.

He is head storekeeper and Chappell Hill justice of the peace. Lesser was writing in his criminal justice docket when I walked in. The entry showed that a young fellow from Persia, a student at Brenham's Blinn College, had just paid $17.50 to learn that a Persian driver's license is not any good on U.S. 290.

"I was born in this store, in the back, in 1894," said the judge, adjusting a hat he wears at all times, whether he is dispensing justice or slicing cheese. "I've never been out of the store except once during World War I and again in 1950 when I had two major operations."

Now through the front door came Maggie Simpson Newsom Reeves, to buy a few groceries from Judge Lesser's son Phil. She came back to sit a while and said she'd been a customer in that store for sixty-five years.

"Look at this." That was Phil, holding up a round metal object. "A six-inch damper, two twenty-five. Isn't that awful? Hadn't been long ago a six-inch damper cost seventy-five cents."

His father said, "Doesn't seem many years ago to me that it cost two bits."

People come every day into Lesser's to buy dampers and stovepipe. I noticed a small lightweight wood stove, priced at $15.95.

"Some of these city slickers come in here," the judge was saying, "and want to know how I could stay so long in a little town like this. I tell 'em I just didn't know any better.

"But I've seen these country fellows around here sell a farm, and go to town, and work like the devil until finally they get enough money to buy back the same farm they sold."

Now came Sadie Schaer and Mildred Shaver, from the canasta party breaking up in the Old Rock Store just the other side of the bank. They're sisters, and have lived at Chappell Hill all their lives. "We used to play together right out here in the street," Lesser said.

I wandered up front and read an old "We Fit Your Feet" sign, slogan for Lesser's shoe department. The judge grinned at the sign: "Old man Jesse Crockett used to come in here and read that sign and twist it around. He'd always say, 'We give your feet a fit.'"

Strangers will wander into Lesser's looking for beer. "I tell 'em they've come to one of three business in town that doesn't sell beer. The only other places you can't buy beer are the post office and the bank."

Here came Eddie Elegan, and paid Lesser some money he owed. "A personal debt," Lesser said. Country storekeepers, the ones who've been in business a long time, nearly all do a little private money-lending that way.

I asked Elegan how things were going with him and he said, "I just lost a spare tire off that old truck. Seems like I'm havin' bad luck some kinda way."

The Old Rock Store, little way up the street from Lesser's, was built in 1869. The local historical society has the building now and uses it as a community hall.

Sadie Schaer said I ought to "go in the Rock Store and see the hanging." Not certain what that meant but Lesser and I went up there to look. Turned out to be a hanging stitchery, two of them, covering the walls of the building. They were sewn by Chappell Hill women and the scenes stitched onto the material give the town's history.

Lillian Smith was there to talk about it, and so was Aline Winfield who told me something about Chappell Hill I didn't know, that those green hills around there that I love so much used to be covered with cedar trees. "It was brown cedar," she said, "what they call pencil cedar. Several of the fine old homes around here are built of it."

We went back to the store and Phil was having a little rush before closing time. I stood around and watched the Lessers sell groceries.

"Look at my Depression scales," the judge said, weighing a stack of potatoes. What he meant was that the way the scales are marked is somewhat out of date. They range from half a cent a pound and go no higher than sixty. So if something costs $1.20 a pound, Lesser weighs it and checks the sixty-cent mark and doubles the result. "Some items we have to triple, and some quadruple. Like on bacon, that was more than two dollars not long ago."

What I wonder is, what grocery item even in Depression times sold for half a cent a pound.

Now came Billy Bryant of the Texas Highway Patrol to file a complaint with the justice of the peace. He just went to the back and wrote it out. Most of the fines are paid by mail, and nearly all are the result of traffic violations up on U.S. 290. Lesser said he collects fines averaging about $200 a day.

Before the store closed James Parker came in and bought that little $15.95 wood stove. The stovepipe and the other stuff that came with it ran the price to $24. Lot of homes in the Chappell Hill area are heated still by wood that way.

Before I left, Lesser talked some about his father Phillip who had the store when the judge was born. And about Will Taylor, who once ran the icehouse there in Chappell Hill.

"I remember my father asking Will Taylor one time," Lesser said, "what he did with all that money he made selling ice. And Will said, 'I buy more ice.' And that's pretty much what you do in this business too. You take the money you get selling groceries, and you buy more groceries."

In my growing-up times long ago, an exciting event in the country was the cutting of a bee tree.

The excitement was in the risk taken by those who did the cutting, or who just stood around and watched. The risk, I mean, of getting stung several times by angry honeybees. Also exciting was the element of mystery—not knowing whether the tree would yield several gallons of honey, or only a little dab.

A few days ago I went up to Buffalo to see a bee tree cut again, and I found it exciting as ever. And I met a couple of honeybees who didn't mind refreshing my memory of how it feels to get popped on the scalp.

Some of the younger customers may not know that colonies of wild honeybees live here and there in the woods. They are mainly in hollow trees, where they store their honey and raise their young. It is an old custom for country people to cut such trees, and get the honey, and capture the bees and domesticate them.

Jack Ellison is the reason I was able to return to the past and see another bee tree cut. He is a lawyer at Buffalo, the Leon County town there on Interstate 45, about halfway between Huntsville and Corsicana. I was sitting in his office one day, taking up his time and keeping him from the practice of law, when the matter of bee trees came up. He said he would try to locate one, and I agreed that if he did I would come back and watch somebody cut it. Provided they would let me watch from a safe distance.

I imagined it would be hard to find a bee tree, but it wasn't. Ellison put a classified ad in the Buffalo *Press*, asking if anybody had a bee tree they wanted cut. In a short time he had located seven of the things. He selected one on the property of Ruby Coburn on Highway 75 south of Buffalo. I thought it was a good choice for somebody who doesn't know any more about bees than Ellison. It is surrounded by open territory handy for running. And there was the paved highway nearby, so we could jump in Ellison's pickup if necessary and outdistance even a swarm of mad bees.

John Peterson and Elmer Parker came to do all the work. They are both beekeepers there in Leon County and know about such things as cutting trees and capturing queens and robbing hives.

They equipped themselves as follows for the work: Put on their screen-wire hoods over their hats and pulled on heavy gloves. Stuffed their britches into their boots, because nobody wants a honeybee flying up his pants legs. Fired up their smokers, those little bellows-like cans that puff out smoke. Smoke has a tranquilizing effect on bees.

The tree was a post oak about two feet in diameter near the base, where the hole of the hollow was. Before the cutting began, the bees were coming and going out of the hole and not paying us the least attention.

Cutting such a tree often serves a variety of wants. Ruby Coburn mainly wanted to get rid of those stinging bees, which were not far from her front door. Parker and Peterson wanted the honey but not as much as they wanted the bees. A colony of bees has a value. Then Ellison and I, we just wanted to watch. As I remember, any time a bee tree was cut you always had a good many watchers standing off in the shade.

Using a chain saw, Peterson first cut a plug out of the side of the tree, hoping to expose the honeycomb. This failed to locate any honey.

But it sure stirred up a lot of bees. Peterson said he had never seen so many come out of one tree. Parker pretty near burned up the fuel in his smoker, puffing away at those bees.

Ellison and I tried to stay close and watch by closing the windows of his truck and driving up near the tree. When that truck was built I don't think air conditioning had been invented. Pretty soon the temperature in the cab would reach about 160 and we'd have to back off for air. Once Ellison turned on the heater and I swear it felt cool.

When Peterson and Parker got the tree down, they gathered a large dishpan of honey from the hollow. There was a great deal of comb but most of it old and dark. Peterson said some of it looked a dozen years old.

When the tree fell and split, the bees flew a wider circle and one came and landed in my hair and stung me on the scalp. The next time I attend a bee-tree cutting I intend to be hooded up like a member of the Klan.

It was so hot. Peterson did most of the work. He took a little break while Parker poked around in the mass of bees at the base of the stump. He was looking for the queen bee. If he could find her and stick her in the hive they'd brought, the bees would follow her inside and could be captured and taken home.

Peterson took his hood off, and bees came immediately and landed in his hair and stung him. He reached up and calmly plucked them off. He said a honeybee likes to sting you in the same spot another one has popped you a little earlier.

About a minute after he said that, one came and stung me within a quarter of an inch of the spot that the first one did. Evidently bees schooled in hollow trees are taught that two stings delivered at the same place produce discomfort equal to four stings in widely scattered localities. A matter of concentrating the fire power. "All right, you turkeys," says the squadron leader, "let's tighten up the formation."

Parker came walking up, covered with bees and talking to me. He said he had been stung even through his gloves but it didn't hurt much. He said some folks believe bee stings are good for arthritis. I wanted to talk to him more about that but I don't much care to interview anybody who has got mad bees all over him.

When bees buzzed my ears I would go to ducking and fanning the air and going north in a hurry. Parker said for me not to run or fight because that would make it worse. I felt that advice was a little hollow, though, coming from a gent standing there in a hood and gloves and a little smoke pot in his mitt.

Peterson and Parker discovered that most of the honeycomb was down in the hollow roots of the tree. Peterson's chain saw went on the fritz then and we knocked off. I checked with them later on. They had returned and gotten another dishpan of honey and thought they'd gotten the queen in their box. So I suppose the enterprise was successful, although some big bee trees will yield eight or ten gallons of honey.

Ellison never did get stung, unless you want to count that he had to pay for the ad in the Buffalo *Press*. Once he was attacked and took to fleeing and flailing the same as I did. I called out and told him not to run or fight, that he should stand his ground and keep calm. But I guess he didn't hear me.

"No, I didn't build this mill for profit," Lorenza Driver said. "I'll never live long enough to get my money out of it. I built it because serp making draws a lot of company, and we love that."

At that moment he ought to have been happy, then. Because

the rain had stopped and a fire was swooshing beneath his syrup pans and the cane juice was bubbling and that sweet steam rising up, and I guess a hundred folks or more had come to watch Lorenza Driver make syrup.

Driver is a tall and thin man, with big round gentle eyes and a friendly little grin for everybody. He lives in the Odell community of Angelina County, out east of Lufkin and Huntington toward Sam Rayburn Lake. And that's where his syrup mill is.

The day I was there, Driver and his helpers were making syrup from a cane crop raised by H. D. Matthews, who lives a little way west of Lufkin. He was firing the pit while his cane juice was being cooked.

I hadn't been to a country syrup making in a long time. Back during the '50s and '60s I thought syrup mills were going to pass completely out of the rural Texas scene. But now they've made a comeback. When I was at Driver's I heard of four mills in Angelina County alone.

Some say the reason for this is the high cost of sugar but my guess would be a greater influence is this strong interest in old-fashioned things that has lately spread over the entire nation.

For country folks, going to the syrup mill was once a sort of adventure. The children always wanted to ride along when their folks hauled cane to the mill. It was an exciting, sweet-smelling place, and the young ones would get to drink some of that cane juice and it was good.

Syrup making has not changed a lot from the way I remember it. The main way is the source of power. Driver's mill—that is, the machinery that squeezes the juice out of the cane—is run by the power takeoff on a big tractor. The old mills were mule-powered, like the early hay balers.

Everything else is pretty much the same. You need a lot of help to make syrup. Especially skimmers.

When the juice bubbles out of the mill a lot of green scummy-looking stuff is on it and this needs to be skimmed off. You always have four or five folks standing around with skimmers, dipping and shaking.

The skimmings are generally fed to livestock. The old syrup makers used to keep hogs to eat the skimmings. When that stuff would ferment, those hogs would sometimes get wobble-legged drunk on it. Maybe you've heard the old saying, "Drunk as a syrup-mill hog."

Driver feeds his skimmings to his cows. They stand at the fence and fight one another for it.

A syrup-making setup comes in two basic parts. The mill where the cane is juiced, and then the pit and the pan where the juice is cooked.

From the road I expect Driver's setup is mistaken for a barbecue pit sometimes.

Making syrup is a simple process, but you've got to have at least one man on the job who really knows what he's doing. He'll be the one on the plug. That is, he is standing at the low end of the pan and he decides when a batch is ready to run off and he pulls the plug to let the finished syrup drain out.

The cooking pan is long and narrow and has a baffled bottom to guide the flow of the juice. Raw juice goes in the high end and moves slowly through the maze of baffles, cooking all the way, giving off clouds of steam. The syrup maker decides by color and consistency when it's time to pull the plug. Good ones always have long experience behind them, and are highly respected for their skill. Driver told me, "I've been foolin' with serp a long time. I imagine forty years."

When it comes out of the cooker the syrup is strained through burlap into a tub. Then the bucket brigade comes in, and pours the finished product into syrup cans.

So all you do in making syrup this way is to cook just the proper amount of water out of the juice. Nothing is added. Quality of the syrup depends on the quality of the cane, and the skill of the syrup maker.

I had a little visit with Matthews, who raised the cane being processed.

"This is Cuban sugar cane," he said. "For makin' serp I put it above all the old Texas ribbon canes that there are. It'll give you a better yield, and make you a better serp."

Only thing Matthews will use to fertilize his syrup cane is cottonseed meal. He won't put commercial fertilizer on it. "I don't want any kind of nitrates on my cane. It'll ruin your serp. Make it so strong it'll burn your mouth."

There are certain little threats to a person's health that it's good to know about when you go to a syrup mill. One, you can get stung. Bees are always hanging around syrup mills. Or you can get your hands burned, trying to pick up a harmless-looking bucket of fresh syrup. Mister, that can stays hot a long time.

Or you can get sick, from drinking too much cane juice. Satan himself couldn't devise a more desperate nausea than a country boy can suffer under these conditions. He's already sick from that juice, and now he's got to ride home five miles over rough road in the bed of a steel-tired wagon.

I stayed at the mill until Driver ran off a batch or two and called Matthews up to the peg for a tasting. They each dipped a finger into the cooled sample, and stood tasting and smacking and looking at one another, and then Matthews said, "Now that's good serp."

Driver nodded. "I think so," he said.

As a general thing, people born in Texas do not stay all their lives where they begin.

They go to other towns, other states, even to other nations, and it is getting harder and harder now to find a Texan who stayed put.

In the country towns where I spend so much time, I have heard it said for so long, "Our young people can't make a living here. There's nothing for them to do. So they leave."

But they don't all leave. You see that husky fellow drinking coffee on the first stool at the cafe counter? He is one who stayed, in a little town that hasn't got a population of five hundred. I know something about his history.

He grew up about three miles out in the country, on a thin-soiled farm that made a creepy, stooped old man out of his father by the time he was fifty-five. Four children were born and raised on that place. Three boys and a girl. The baby of the family is our friend sitting yonder on the cafe stool.

He was born in '27. So he's what—fifty-two now? When he came out of high school in '45, his older brothers were already gone. One gone forever, the eldest. Killed in '44 by a Japanese booby trap on one of those islands in the South Pacific.

This family was always known around here as hard-working, bootstrap kind of people. Quick-minded. The sister got a scholarship and toiled through college and taught school four years before she married the basketball coach.

The "middle boy" got through college too, with one of those engineering degrees, and he has spent his time in Houston working for an oil company. He is talking now about taking early retirement. He's fifty-four.

His older brother getting killed in the Pacific might have had something to do with the younger boy's decision to stay home. Some say he couldn't leave his grieving mother.

Anyway about a week after he came out of high school he hitchhiked the fifteen miles over to the nearest "big town." Never mind which one. It had eight thousand folks then.

He went to work there in a little two-man auto repair shop. He became the third man, just a helper. He's always been pretty good with machinery on the farm. And loved cars.

He picked up an old trashed-out truck, and at night they'd let him work on it in the shop, and use the tools. He overhauled it for transportation, and for two years he drove it back and forth from the farm, to work in that garage.

His older brother came out of college and went on into Houston to be a speck in the multitude. His sister had a baby, and the basketball coach quit coaching and took up selling insurance.

One of the mechanics in the garage got so he couldn't lift anything, or grip a wrench. Arthritis, they said. So he checked out, and our boy became a partner in the shop. Took on a little debt. People began to talk about him. "He's a good boy. Do you a good job. And one thing for sure, he don't know nothin' about stealin'."

On his twenty-fifth birthday, he went to the bank and borrowed $10,000 and opened a little garage of his own in his hometown, just a half mile down the highway from the high school he attended.

He is still there. He has never expanded. Never taken a partner. He has stayed there and worked on cars, and he will fix lawn mowers when he gets a slow place, and chain saws, and even vacuum cleaners, and he'll do welding, and a little blacksmithing, and people say, "I don't know what we'd do without him."

When he was twenty-six he married the girl who was in the stands at the football stadium on the greatest night of his life. He was eighteen. Playing in the line, a tackle. Rushing the passer.

Threw up his arms and tipped the ball and it fell crazily into his arms and he lumbered sixty-seven yards, untouched. The winning score. Nothing in his experience since has been as sweet.

The girl who watched him perform that marvel is the mother of his three children. And the grandmother of his five grandchildren.

They still go out on Saturday nights to the dance at the community hall. He takes off four days a year in November and kills a buck on a lease he shares down at Pearsall with six friends.

Their big year was '76. To celebrate the Bicentennial he closed the shop for two weeks, and they went. To Washington, to New England, to New York City. And talked when they returned about how good it was to be home again.

Home is a white house they built on their share of the farm. The old mother, after the father died, partitioned the place. Each of the three children got sixty-two acres.

The one with the engineering degree? He's building a house on his sixty-two acres, too. Gonna come back, when he retires. The daughter, who married the coach, she wants to do the same. She hasn't yet convinced her husband. But she will.

Then they'll all be back where they started, and you won't be able to tell the difference between the ones who went, and the one who stayed.

III

Uncommon Folks

Back in early August I saw Buckshot Lane down at Rockport, where he has a beach house. He said if I'd come by his home in Wharton sometime he'd tell me how he burned the Kendleton Bridge on U.S. 59.

The burning of that wooden bridge on the San Bernard River is, I believe, my favorite Buckshot Lane story. He burned that bridge on purpose when he was constable of Precinct 1 in Wharton County. He didn't admit doing it for ten years.

He did it because he thought the bridge *needed* to be burned. He says now, more than forty-five years afterward, he still thinks he did the right thing.

The burning of the bridge is one of dozens of Buckshot Lane stories that would be worth telling again. I say again because they have been told so often, over and over. In this newspaper. In others. In magazines.

T. W. Buckshot Lane (that Buckshot is not a nickname) was sheriff of Wharton County from 1941 to 1952. He became probably the most famous sheriff in the country.

Even *Saturday Evening Post* wrote up Buckshot Lane. *Life* magazine twice did picture stories on him. *Time* magazine had him. *Readers Digest* had him. Several crime magazines had him.

Mainly I think because he was good copy. Little old round-eyed sheriff, five feet seven and 145 pounds, carrying a .45 inside his shirt where it didn't show, not even wearing a big hat or cowboy boots. What kind of Texas sheriff was that?

A mighty hard-working and imaginative one, to begin with. Also one that got in trouble sometimes. Also one that was just full of sand.

He had Pete Norris in the Wharton County Jail that time, when Norris was known as Public Enemy No. 1. Lane let him out of the cell to make a phone call in the office. Norris pulled a gun he had hidden. The sheriff said, "Now don't shoot me, Pete," and went for the gun and there was a wrestling match and the gun went off and a slug burned a path up the side of Lane's face. But he got the gun, and Norris went to the hospital, and the word got around—don't mess with that little old dried-up sheriff down at Wharton.

Buckshot Lane introduced the polygraph, the lie detector machine, to Texas. He built a countywide police radio network when such systems were rare in the country. He learned to fly an airplane and the voters bought him one to fly, "to catch criminals," as he says. Any donor who gave a dollar got his name painted on the plane. There were more than six thousand names on that craft.

Lane for a while wrote a daily column in this newspaper, not just about being sheriff of Wharton County but about anything that leaped out of his fertile mind. He also conducted a daily fifteen-minute radio program on an El Campo station, on which he would notify law violators that he was looking for them. "All right, Jake, I know you whipped a woman last night so you better come on in this morning." And like as not Jake would.

In '52 Lane ran for Congress, and got beat by "a hundred and some-odd votes" and believes now it's the best thing that ever happened to him. Then he ran for state representative. "I spent nine dollars on that campaign." It was enough. He served one term and didn't much like being in the Legislature. Came home and took up public speaking.

He traveled the country on the Knife and Fork circuit, talking about the way he enforced the law when he was sheriff. His key line was, "When the law didn't do what it ought to do, I gave it a little kick."

One of his little kicks was aimed at the Kendleton Bridge.

It spanned the San Bernard about halfway between Rosenberg and Wharton. A wooden bridge, built when the route was a county road. The concrete-rail bridge that replaced it is still there, on the southbound side of U.S. 59. Some people, remembering, call it Buckshot Lane's Bridge.

"When the highway was paved and designated U.S. 59," Lane said recently at his home, "they didn't replace the wooden bridge. And they left it offset. I mean it didn't line up with the highway, and it was dangerous, and it killed a lot of people.

"There was talk about dynamiting the bridge. Actually, I was afraid somebody would try that, and get hurt. This was in 1934. Maybe it was '35. Anyway I was constable of Precinct 1." A little grin right here. "I had taken an oath to protect the lives of the people. Well, that bridge had killed thirteen folks, so I decided to do something about it."

Lane was then selling cars at a Wharton garage. "At the garage I got me a bunch of gunny sacks and some waste (oily rags used by mechanics) and I filled a five-gallon Koto can with kerosene." Koto was a petroleum product popular in the '30s. "I went out to the bridge (at night) and wadded those sacks up and wired them onto the bridge with baling wire in three places. Then I soaked them with my can of kerosene.

"Then I came on back to town and fooled around, so I'd be seen, and about ten o'clock I went back out there. I took my waste rags and dipped them in my gas tank and stuck them onto the gunny sacks and lit 'em. Then I came on back to town and went to bed.

"I hadn't got to sleep yet when a Red Arrow truck driver called me. I knew all the truckers. He said, 'Did you know the Kendleton Bridge is on fire?' I got up and went back out there. The wind had come up and it was sure burning good. Only thing I worried about, I was afraid the railroad bridge alongside it would catch. When I saw that railroad bridge smoking it scared me."

The bridge burned nicely and everybody, Buckshot says, was happy about it.

"Some truck drivers down in the Valley started taking up a collection to help defend whoever got charged with burning the bridge," Lane said. "District attorney here then was Bob Bassett. He announced he'd buy a new suit of clothes for the man who burned that bridge if we could find him.

"The day after the bridge burned I was due to go to Austin so I went on. I saw Homer Garrison (then an official of the Texas Rangers) and he said, 'What are you doing here? I just sent Willie Williams and Evie Davenport (Rangers) to Wharton County to find out who burned that bridge last night. You ought to be there helping.'

"So I came on back, and for about a week around here we investigated the bridge burning." A little pause here in the telling.

"We never did find no leads."

And so the case remained unsolved, and all those years Buckshot Lane was getting famous as sheriff, and doing so much talking, one thing he didn't talk about was who burned the Kendleton Bridge.

He was quiet ten years, until the statute of limitations on arson ran out. "I saw Bob Bassett then," Lane said, "and I told him, 'Bob, you owe me a new suit of clothes.' And he said, 'You SOB, I *knew* you were the one burnt that bridge.'"

Buckshot Lane, still weighing 145 pounds, is now seventy-eight years old and fishing four days a week at Rockport and doing just fine. I'd heard he's made a great bundle in the real estate game. I asked him if he's a millionaire. He said he's not sure. But he figures he's a lot better off than he'd be if he'd gotten elected to Congress that time.

Johnny Barton came out of his house and sat with me under the big bois d'arc tree in the sandy yard. Said he wouldn't mind talking a while. Said he *likes* to talk.

He was wearing striped overalls with only one suspender hitched, and a purple shirt with red, white, and blue designs. He was barefooted, and hadn't shaved that day. Maybe not the day before, either. He grinned and said he wasn't wearing his teeth.

His face showed friendly and intelligent behind that stubble. There was a sharp little light in his eye, too. So here was a plenty alert citizen, just like you'd heard.

Johnny Barton, almost seventy-five, is one of the shrewdest ranchers and land owners and farmers in the Colorado Valley. When he walks into that bank at Bastrop, even wearing the overalls with one suspender hitched, a lot of people get up and say hello Mr. Barton, how are you Mr. Barton.

"Yes, this is Utley," he said, talking about the place on the Colorado River where he has lived all his time. "We're about halfway between Elgin and Bastrop. I was born on this place. So was my father.

"My grandfather was Hugh Barton. He came in here a-huntin' this place ahorseback from Alabama before the Civil War. He was born in 1817. Not many people living that their grandfather was born that far back.

"We were all slow about getting married. Grandpa was fifty-three. My father (John Barton) didn't get married till he was getting up old enough to know better. I was forty-six when *I* got married.

"Grandpa was a cranky old fella. I've listened to a lot of his foolishness, from my father. When he came here before the Civil War he bought some Negro men, slaves, in New Orleans. The first year they just built cabins, and planted a patch of corn, figurin' on getting to work the next year.

"The slaves were all single and they told Grandpa, 'Go back and get us some women.' And he said, 'What kind of women you want?' Well, one would want a long tall woman, and another would want a short heavy one, and Grandpa took down what kind every man wanted, and he went back to New Orleans.

"He took his time, and bought carefully, trying to get what they all wanted. Well, when he brought those women back, and the men got together with 'em, not a one of the men picked the woman Grandpa had bought for him. After that Grandpa always said *nobody* ought to ever try to pick out a woman that'll suit a man."

Many descendants of those first slaves Hugh Barton brought from New Orleans are probably still living along the Colorado.

"I knew one of the women in that original group," Johnny Barton said. "Aunt Becky. She was around here a long time. She couldn't wear shoes, and always claimed a parrot had bit her on the heel.

"When slavery was over, it was the common practice for the Negroes to go to work on a sharecrop basis, and farm with the landowners on halves. At one time we had thirty-seven tenant houses on the place here. Now we've got only three families, because it got so a man couldn't make a living if he didn't farm five hundred acres."

Ever since the Depression, Barton has farmed and ranched, with his father until John Barton died about fifteen years ago. They raised cattle, cotton, and pecans. Most of the farming is done now by the renters.

Johnny Barton attended both the University of Texas and Texas A&M, accumulating enough credits, he told me, for a master's degree. But he didn't graduate from either place.

"They'd tell me, 'You better get your credits in order or you're never going to graduate.' I'd say, 'To hell with you. I didn't come here lookin' for a degree anyhow.' Well, they took me at my word.

"When I left school and went looking for a job, nobody asked me what I knew. They asked me what I could *do*. Well, I could pick peas, and chop watermelons . . ."

He also had a talent for fixing machinery, of all kinds. This set the pattern of his career on the land. Barton is recognized now by pecan growers as the man who did so much of the pioneer work in the mechanization of pecan harvesting.

I meant to tell you, before now, what Barton's place looks like. Take the yard where we sat. It's like a parking lot. Must be a dozen old cars and tractors sitting around there. The bois d'arc we sat under is surrounded by what you or I might call rusting junk. To Barton it's useful stuff, waiting for its purpose to become clear. He won't throw away *anything*.

Chains. Electric motors. Pieces of trailers. Lawn mowers. Buckets of bolts and nuts. Wheels. Gears. Shafts. Fan blades. Metal chairs. Wire. Rope. Saws.

Barton is the only farmer I ever met who owns fifty acres of junk cars and rusty farm implements. The lane into his house is lined with 'em. He talked about why:

"Farming's always been a hard racket. I found out when you buy a new tractor, you wear it out before you pay it off at the bank. So I just decided to buy wore-out ones, and fix 'em up.

"When I was farming I had a lot of tractors. Well, it got to where my renters would be out in the field, and if one wanted to go to the house for a dip of snuff, why he'd crank up one of my tractors and ride it in.

"So I began buyin' old cars, for 'em to drive back and forth from the field. Old wore-out Model A's, mostly, pay just five dollars or ten dollars for one. I wouldn't register 'em so they couldn't be driven to town, just here on the place.

"When I quit farming, I must have had twenty of those old cars. But I got rid of 'em now. These boys would come get 'em to restore 'em.

"But I never owned a new car in my life. Right now I'm driving that '56 Plymouth yonder. I got it from a fellow whose wife thought it was gettin' too old, and he wanted a new one. I drove

it to Brownwood, to the National Nut Growers Association Convention.

"Before the Plymouth I drove that old Pontiac sittin' here. And before that, the Cadillac there. . . . When something gets the matter with a car, I don't sell it because I might need it for parts. So I find a place to park it . . ."

Which has become the Barton philosophy: Don't ever sell a mechanical thing because you might need it for parts. And that's the reason so much of his place is taken up by rusty equipment and worn-out cars. He's even got a couple of bulldozers around there.

Maybe this occurs to you: That if the voice of experience on used cars exists, it ought to be Johnny Barton's. He has bought and worked on and driven scores of them.

And he says: "Any time you buy a secondhand car, you know there's something wrong with it because that's why somebody wanted to get rid of it. So I hunt up what the matter is, and patch it. Get an engine, or a rear end, and put it in. Then I'll drive it until it gets full of plunder."

All right, take the old Caddy there, parked under the big post oak. Barton paid about fifty dollars for it, put a new engine in it and drove it two, three years. Finally it got so full of stuff (plunder, he calls it; mechanical things he collects) he couldn't see out of it very well. So he parked it. Maybe for good, maybe not.

He actually uses old cars for storage. "They'll hold a lot of plunder."

Nearing seventy-five, Barton may not be overhauling many more old cars. Then again he may. Lately he's been threatening to overhaul his own self. He turns on the grin and the light in his eye and says: "I already got me some new teeth. Next I'm gonna get some new glasses so I can see, and a hearing aid so I can hear, and then I'm gonna get me a wig, and then a brand new secondhand car, and I'm gonna take off."

A good many citizens who've been successful are fond of saying that if they had it to do over again they'd do everything just the same way. I've always thought that sounded stuffy, and I liked Barton's answer when I asked if *he'd* do anything different if he had it to do over again.

"*Yes*," he said, "almost everything."

A few minutes' drive up the Guadalupe Valley northwest of Victoria there's a little town called Nursery.

I was by there to see Lester Giese, who's in the cow business. When I drove up he was getting ready to go to the blacksmith, so I got in and went with him.

I hadn't been around a blacksmith shop in a good long while and I'm glad I went because we had a nice visit with Otto Raab. I've met a lot of old-timey blacksmiths in this state and I picked up the idea that I could spot them walking down the road on Sunday afternoon, when they weren't anywhere close to their shops.

Because they tend to be big, and have hammy hands that don't ever look clean. That doesn't mean their hands are not sanitary but they're apt to look the same as a shade-tree mechanic's, with black streaks in the skin creases, and fingernails bordered in dark stain.

But if I saw Otto Raab dressed up for church I would pick him out for a retired schoolteacher. He has a bookish look, and he's not very big, and his hands are long-fingered and slender and almost white. They have a bleached look.

Yet those hands have been doing blacksmith work at Nursery for sixty-two years. Raab is seventy-eight and still working, in a little shop out behind his home. But then I've come to expect blacksmiths to be old and still going. They're mighty slow to quit, the same as country doctors.

Raab began blacksmithing when he was still a schoolboy. He set up under a chinaberry tree in his parents' yard in the country, and something about him people remember is that he always wore gloves. Even on the most delicate work he'd keep those gloves on, and he told me he has put in days out there in the sun when he'd get so hot he actually poured water out of his gloves.

So that's why, I suppose, he has the bleached-looking hands of a preacher. They *are* bleached, from sixty-two years of sweating inside those gloves.

Raab doesn't mind telling you now that he was plenty strong in his prime, whether he looked it or not. "I was a lot of man," he said, grinning to show he expected you to put up with his good-natured boasting. "I could do anything I wanted to do and I ain't awoofin'. Once at a carnival they got me on one of those gripping machines. I competed with an oil field roughneck that weighed 240 pounds. I weighed 165. He gripped 600 pounds on that machine, and I gripped 625."

Now here's a little oddity for your book: In sixty-two years of blacksmithing, Raab has shod only one horse. The reason is, he is allergic to horses. How about that? A blacksmith with a horse allergy. He could even ride in a buggy and when the mare got to sweating, he'd start popping out with all manner of weird symptoms. The only horse he ever shod, he had to give it a bath before he began. Scrubbed that animal with soap and water, the way you'd do your car in the driveway. Once he got the sweat washed off the horse he could go ahead and shoe it without getting sick.

The thing I like the most about old blacksmith shops is that old-timey people come in them, and make old-timey talk. While Giese and I were at Raab's a farmer came in to pick up some plow sweeps that had been sharpened. His name is Dentler.

At the time I didn't think I was going to mention him in the paper and I didn't get his first name. Lots of Dentlers around Nursery, Giese said.

Anyhow, looking back on Dentler's visit to the shop, I can see it was the best thing that happened while we were there. I liked the dignity and the politeness and the caring that was exhibited between these two old friends doing business with one another.

"I'm gonna be hard on you," the blacksmith said to Dentler. What he meant was, the price for the work about to be paid for would be high.

Dentler, a great, round, red-faced man, said, "Well, you ain't the only one being hard on us. It's hard everywhere you go."

"You ain't awoofin'," Raab said. He picked up the sweeps he'd sharpened. They were in a neat bundle. There was some other work he'd done for Dentler. I never did understand what it was. A lot about blacksmithing I don't comprehend.

Dentler complimented the blacksmith on getting the work out so fast. "I thought it would be a month," he said. Raab said, well, he had caught up and done the work in one day.

He took off his gloves and sat in the wooden chair that he built out of the hickory off an old buggy. The shaft and the singletree and the wheel spokes all can be identified in that chair in the corner of the blacksmith shop. The office, really, though it is not apart.

Raab got Dentler a chair and they sat facing one another for the little ceremony, the receiving of the work and the paying of the bill. There was talk about crops and weather. Had Dentler planted his corn yet? "No, I lost the moisture in my black ground. Been rainin' all winter, and now spring and no moisture in my black ground." But not really in a complaining tone. In fact with a little smile.

"Well, I've seen it happen so many times. All winter rain, and a dry spring."

Dentler nodding. He talked about trouble he'd had with the throttle on his tractor. The throttle would not stay in the notches designed to hold it at a constant setting.

"I didn't dare bring it to you," he told Raab. This was in consideration of the fact that Raab's doctor has made him slow down, work only a six-hour day, and Dentler didn't want to overload him with work after he'd already brought all the sweeps to be sharpened.

Raab had in his lap a green ledger where the work he had done for his friend was recorded, along with the price. But he took time to be concerned about the tractor throttle problem. He told Dentler how it could be fixed. He had fixed such things before.

Then at last the price for the work was announced. It was $25.70. If I had to guess I would say that the same work in another place might cost much more. Giese told me later it was true, that Raab doesn't charge enough.

Dentler's visit took about twenty minutes. After he left I began to feel as if I had witnessed a special thing, in that exchange between these two elderly country men. I did not quite know how to tell about it, and don't yet.

Otto Raab's forebears came from Germany. When he started to school in the Levi Sloan community near Nursery, he knew no English. There was one teacher, sixteen years old, to teach nine grades. Raab had a schoolmate who knew both German and English and the friend translated lessons for him, and Raab went through that school, and became a blacksmith, and served his neighbors. I think that's a grand accomplishment, and I ain't just awoofin'.

At Corrigan, the little town on U.S. 59 between Livingston and Lufkin, I stopped and made myself a new friend. She is Doris

Spears, who is fifty years old and stands six feet tall and weighs two hundred pounds and operates a fork lift at the plywood plant in Diboll.

She has promised to let me go with her some Saturday night to Goat Hill, a popular country dance hall in the woods up north of Corrigan a few miles. I have been wanting to pick a weekend and go there to observe the rural nightlife.

It will be a pleasure and a comfort to be in company with Doris Spears, because she used to work there at Goat Hill as floor bouncer. Which meant she saw to it that everybody behaved, and didn't get too rowdy or do any damage.

She was very good at that job, from what I hear. She is good at other things you don't expect a woman to be good at. She can snake logs out of the woods with a team of mules. She can drive a log truck. She is the first woman fork lift operator that plywood plant ever had.

She lives with two pretty teen-age daughters in a mobile home alongside the railroad tracks in Corrigan. When I found the place it was already dark. Doris was mighty impressive when she opened the door and looked down at me. She filled that door. Had on wedge-heeled shoes and her hair was fixed real pretty and I expect from the floor to the top of her hairdo she was six feet two.

"I've always been proud of my height," she said, when I hadn't been there five minutes. "I enjoy being up high, so I can see over everybody."

I started out calling her Mrs. Spears. "Forget that Mrs. stuff. Call me Doris. Some of the kids call me Mama Doris." Lot of the men at the plywood plant call her Big Doris.

I asked her to give me some of her history. "I won't tell you everything," she said, and grinned. "I was born down at Baytown. Old Pelly, really. My daddy decided he couldn't make enough to feed his kids down there so we moved up here to Polk County and went to farming.

"I've been in Polk County most of my life, mostly here at Corrigan. I'm fifty. I don't mind tellin' my age. Godamighty knows how old I am. I was fifty on the tenth of this month.

"I grew up in the Trinity Bottom where that lake is now. I watched the water cover that sand patch, that knoll where we lived. We were about eleven miles below Livingston.

"My daddy and mama had eleven children. I was in the middle. We lived in a house with cracks this wide, and one fireplace. We're Irish and Dutch and Indian. My daddy's eighty-six, and lives in a trailer house at Livingston. My mama's dead.

"I'm the smallest one of the children. I got one brother six feet seven. One of my sons is six feet six and weighs 325 pounds. He's a foreman on the railroad.

"In 1942 I quit school. I finished the eleventh grade. When my brothers went into the service I quit and stayed home and helped my daddy farm. I didn't like housework, and still don't. I didn't wash them dishes there tonight. I didn't want to. I like to be outside.

"Up till I got married I followed in my daddy's footsteps. I plowed. I logged cotton with a mule, pulled a log over it after it was planted to make it come up quicker. When we got a tractor, I learned to drive it. My daddy taught me to do what he did. He taught me how to dance, too, and have a good time. When I got married, he wouldn't let me leave home till my husband came and helped get the crop in.

"I said I wanted a dozen kids when I married. Well, I had six. Three boys and three girls. I really had seven but I lost one."

Doris has been married twice. She said she didn't want to talk about husbands. So we didn't talk about husbands.

One of her daughters is married. The two still at home came in during my visit. Wanda, nineteen, and Sheila, fourteen. Both pretty girls. Here was the group picture, of all six of Doris' children. Every one of them good-looking people. The girls are not especially tall, though.

You can see Mama Doris in all those faces. And you can't help try to visualize her when she was eighteen, and six feet tall, and following along behind a mule in the river bottom. She must have been something to see then. Well, she still is.

Now she was talking about raising her kids, and getting along with them. "We're all pals. I never did make my kids do things. I *led* 'em. I went *with* 'em. My daddy and mama did the same thing. Sometimes my girls had rather go out with mama than have a date. New Year's Eve at Goat Hill I had thirty-three in my party, family and friends. It's not anything for me to feed thirty-five or forty here on a weekend. Christmas Day I had twenty-five. We get along good."

Don't expect to hear any stories about Mama Doris flinging a drunk out the front door when she was bouncer at Goat Hill. "It's always easier to reason with 'em than try to manhandle 'em." Doris talks rough sometimes but friends say she is really a gentle person.

"When I was younger," she told me, "I was stronger than the average man. Couldn't any one man outdo me. Two could, but not one. I was always in perfect health. But I'm not that strong anymore."

Driving that fork lift is far easier than work she has done in the past. "Before I took that job up yonder (at the plywood plant), I drove a log truck, to make a livin' for those kids of mine. I also snaked logs out of the woods with mules, and I taught my boys how to do it, too.

"But I like this job I've got now. I like machinery. That lift keeps me moving, getting on and off, and I move around a lot. Tell jokes. Shoot the bleep."

Before I left, Mama Doris drew a couple of her kids up close to her and let go of a pronouncement: "I don't ever worry, about anything. It don't do no good. I just live from payday to payday. I've got every kind of insurance there is, so I just relax and enjoy it."

When we go to Goat Hill, I'll let you know.

Over the past few months I've gotten acquainted with a fellow named Pete Locklin. He is forty and has inoperable lung cancer.

We get along just all right. Pete's good company. On account of his sickness he's not working now and we've gone around some. He's ridden with me, and we went to a party back around Christmas. We've shared a couple of cool ones, and watched a lot of eight-ball, and talked a million miles.

About love, injustice, war, women, softball (which he loves), religion, work, life, death, time. Sure, we talk about his cancer, if we feel like it. Pete's a strong guy. He is, let me tell you, one hell of a man. I have gained from knowing Pete Locklin.

The past few weeks we've been talking about this story, and whether or not to do it. In the beginning Pete wasn't sure he wanted it done. Then when he decided he did, I decided I didn't want to write it. Afraid I'd mess things up some way.

Pete and his wife Lynn have three little girls. One's a baby born since Pete got sick. The others are old enough to know their father is ill but they don't know how seriously. Pete says never mind, he'll handle that.

So we decided to go ahead. For one thing, when a guy gets into a spot like Pete's in, there's a good chance to help somebody by speaking out. Then, too, Pete wants to hear from old friends.

Being bad sick that way can be such a lonesome business. Some of your friends can't face it, and won't come around. "Then I guess some just don't want to bother me," Pete says. "Well, I *want* them to bother me. I wish they would. We don't have to sit around and talk about how sick I am. But if we do, I'm not going to break down and cry about it."

Pete's a fine athlete. You can go and put it in the bank that he is among the finest softball players in the world, because it's a matter of fact. He played with that old J. H. Rose Trucking bunch that was always going to the world tournaments. Pete went twice himself. The kind of player who just didn't much believe in losing. Well, he's that way yet, about everything. That may be why he's alive right now, I don't know.

Up at Thorndale where he went to school—I was through there not long ago—up there they still talk about the way Pete Locklin could hit from outside. He made all-district in basketball four straight years. And they talk about Pete running the hundred, and Pete pole-vaulting, and Pete quarterbacking the football team. That one year he ran at halfback, even then he called all the plays.

Smart, you bet. Came out of high school averaging better than ninety in his studies. Good-looking too. One of these young fellows just seemed like he had everything going his way. Everything so easy for him.

Went to Blinn College (a 150-pound quarterback), then on to Houston to get married, and then there was a hitch in the Army, travel to Europe and the Far East, and back home to Houston and a job he liked in the steamship business. And back to his ball playing. More travel. Good times, playing ball in tournaments from Mexico City to Connecticut.

Then last July, in Port Arthur, still a plenty tough competitor at thirty-nine, Pete got sick after pitching a ball game. Threw up a lot of blood. Must be that stomach ulcer he thought he had. Better go have it checked.

He'd been having trouble in his chest a good while. Coughed a lot. Smoking too much, he figured. Then the ulcer, or whatever it was, Pete put that down to his hard-charging ways. He was always going full speed. He didn't know any other way.

Some of these softball tournaments are physical and mental endurance tests. Play three games in one night, and get through at 4:00 A.M. and maybe clock two hours' sleep and get up and do it again. And play with pain, sure. Pete was raised with that old athlete's he-man concept—that you may be hurt or sick but you ought to play anyhow. So he did, and lost weight and appetite, and that night in Port Arthur it caught up to him and sent him to the doctor.

On July 25 he was operated on and the cancer was found, a big, fast-growing lung tumor that had already involved vital organs and couldn't be taken out.

Whether this will finally end up one of those stories about a guy beating the odds that the doctors quoted, I don't know. Can't tell yet. But this is what they told Pete, as I understand it: That if he took only the standard treatment for the kind of cancer he had, they'd give him a 50 percent chance of lasting three months. And a whole lot slimmer chance of lasting six months.

"They talked me into their experimental program," Pete says, talking now about M. D. Anderson Hospital. "What it amounted to was giving me massive doses of chemotherapy, just saturating me with drugs, all I could stand." There was also some of that strange surgery involving the bone marrow. Then later on came radiotherapy.

"I had a hell of a sick, rough time," Pete said, the last time I saw him. He grinned, as a sort of apology for even talking about it. "I lost thirty-five pounds, and I went bald, but I got through it."

That was the first week in March, when we last talked. He was looking all right. Hair grown back. Gained a little weight. Feeling pretty well. So he had those three months whipped, and the six months as well. What comes next? Can't say.

"The tumor," he told me, "is smaller now than when it was discovered. It's still there, and I guess it's still terminal, but I'm sure not on any deathbed yet." In fact he talks now about being one of the winners. Five percent or less of the people who have this kind of cancer survive, so he's told. He plans now to be in that select bunch.

You know what that scamp's figuring on? Moving. Gonna move out of Houston to the hills of Missouri and start out fresh. I don't know what they are but he gives off hints on things about his life that he doesn't much like. Says he's been doing a lot of apologizing the last few months.

He's got four sisters. "I've apologized to my sisters for things they don't even remember, or never knew about. I've learned so much about them. But for every pound I've learned about them, I learned a ton about my wife, and myself."

Pete has relatives in Missouri, and owns some livestock with them on a farm up there. That's where he wants to take his family, and start over, and go to church every Sunday, and be a good neighbor to people he's never seen before.

That's why he wants to see old friends soon, before he goes. I've learned that he's a marvel at making you feel at ease. He talks about this: How it's so hard for his old ball-playing friends to discuss his illness. "Because they always kidded each other about pain," he says. "Even if a guy broke a leg, you kidded him about it. Well, cancer is not something you can kid about very well."

Yet he does it himself. He told me about driving across the parking lot of a bank, to avoid a congested intersection near his home. A policeman stopped him, asked him where he was going.

"To M. D. Anderson Hospital," Pete told him.

"Why?" the officer wanted to know.

Pete said, "I got a case of lung cancer I take to them out there."

Policeman let him go on. Said he didn't want to give him more trouble than he already has.

"So that's one thing," Pete said, laughing, "that this stuff did for me. It saved me a traffic ticket."

Pete has his down times. He can drive and get around and see people and that's what he does, when he gets to thinking about good things, as he says, "that take a long time."

Pete's not an ordinary man. There are things about him that ought to be said that I don't know how to put into words. Once in a while he'll open his mouth and preach a sermon in four or five seconds. Like when we were sitting in a tavern the other afternoon, on Dacoma Street off the Hempstead Highway, watching an eight-ball game and talking about the hereafter. To you that may be a strange place to do that. You might be right. Anyway Pete was saying he can't believe that this is it, that I have known in my fifty-six years, or he in his forty, all there is to the human experience.

"This can't be all there is to it," he said. "It's just too short, and too shallow."

Several miles north of Cleveland, up on the East San Jacinto, I turned off the blacktop at the aluminum gate with the wire latch, according to directions, and followed the lane that snakes through the woods to Peerless Ellisor's house.

It's a house with a slick-haired dog that comes out to test you and fig trees in the side yard and black hens with baby chicks scratching and clucking and peep peep peeping. And thin smoke rising out of a flue on the roof.

I went in and sat with Peerless Ellisor and Lottie, who has been his wife for sixty-two years. He told me about the most famous man he ever met, and how he came to be named Peerless, and he told me about the hardest work he ever did and the best mule he ever drove.

The most famous man was General John J. Pershing. The place was the city of Brest in France and the time was at the close of World War I.

"I heard him give a speech," Ellisor said. He sat in a wheelchair, not two feet from a television set that was showing a game program. After the game show was over, another came on, and all the time we visited, the TV stayed on.

"General Pershing was the only man I ever saw who would run his hand over his head, like this, and pull out hair. After he gave his speech he talked to some of us. He called me out and he said, 'What's your nationality?' And I said, 'Colored, sir,' and he said, 'What's your name?' and I said, 'Peerless Garfield Ellisor, sir,' and he said, 'Well, that's the finest name I ever heard. We ought to make you a colonel.' And that's the most famous man I ever met."

He sat up close to a wood stove, in between the stove and the TV set, and told me about that name.

"When I was born (eighty-four years ago) there was an old midwife, a slavery-time woman, came to see me and she said, 'Now that's the kind of baby ought to be named Peerless because he was a fine doctor that worked on President Garfield.' So they named me Peerless Garfield.

"When I was nine years old, I was walkin' to school one day in November, and it was cold, and my feet was frozen, and I went by they house (nodding toward his wife, sitting with her eyes closed the other side of the stove). I heard a baby cry, and I said, 'Santa Claus done brought somebody a little baby.' Well, fourteen years later, I married that baby." A wide grin. "When was that, Lottie?"

"The fourteenth of April in 1918." She spoke without opening her eyes. I had thought she was asleep. I don't think she spoke another word during my visit.

Ellisor is in the wheelchair because of a car wreck several years ago. Then lately he "had to take surgery" so he isn't running any footraces now. But this man has done a mountain of labor in his life.

He talked about some of it, sitting there beneath the lone sixty-watt light bulb in the ceiling. An extension cord descends from that same socket to power the TV set. On the wall behind Ellisor's wheelchair is a print of a three-man portrait—John and Robert Kennedy, with Martin Luther King in between.

"The hardest work I ever did was haulin' crossties. When I was twenty-two I was much of a man. I weighed 204 pounds. I had a contract to haul ties into Excelsior. I drove two black mules, Buck and Bob, and I could load twenty-five ties on my wagon. No, I didn't have any help. I loaded 'em myself. Carried 'em on my shoulder. (Did you ever try to lift a railroad tie?)

"When I would top out a load, those mules sometimes would be pullin' in mud kneedeep, and boggin' down, and that old Buck mule would reach out and get hold of a pine sapling with his teeth and pull out of the mud. He was the best mule I ever drove.

"I used to make four loads a day, a hundred ties, and sometimes at night I'd get 'em to spot me a car on the railroad and I'd gather me some pine knots and make a fire and load my ties at night, by the light of my fire, and that was the hardest work I ever did."

It was time for me to leave. Ellisor wheeled himself to the door to say goodbye. At the last he told me that what he had learned in eighty-four years is that a man must have love in his heart, that the most important thing of all is to have love in the heart.

Lorieto Medina lives on a little farm near a city called Rio Grande, down in the central part of Mexico in the state of Zacatecas.

He is twenty-five years old, well-muscled, strong, healthy. You see intelligence and humor in his round brown face, but he can read and write only a little. He is married and has one child.

In the last five years Medina has not spent so much time at home, because he is a professional wetback. A *mojar*, as he calls himself.

Since his twentieth birthday he has waded across the Rio Grande eight times, to enter Texas illegally and work as a farm and ranch hand.

Many thousands of Mexican citizens do the same. They are generally welcomed by South Texas ranchers and farmers who need labor. The wetbacks need the money.

I talked to Lorieto Medina recently in a hot mesquite-grown pasture near Pearsall. He was with three other wetbacks. They had walked through the brush all the way from Eagle Pass. By highway that's about 115 miles. But they walked mostly off the road, through the brush, to keep from being picked up by the Border Patrol. They had been walking six days when we stopped them.

I was with Silvero Hernandez, who goes by the nickname Kero and has worked on ranches in Frio County most of his life. He is of course a U.S. citizen. I wanted to talk to a wetback and he agreed to help, to interpret.

Hernandez seems able to tell a wetback as far as he can see one. Many ranchers in the Brush Country say they can too, that a wetback always walks in a distinctive way—slow, plodding, looking down, being careful where he steps.

I expect anybody would walk slow after he'd stepped off more than a hundred miles. But some wetbacks walk farther than that.

Ranchers will say wetbacks identify themselves in other and more vague ways. "There's a just a look about them." You hear that often.

Medina and his three companions squatted in thin mesquite shade when we came up on them. Hernandez asked, "Which of you is the smartest?" All four laughed. But three of them nodded without hesitation at Lorieto Medina.

He had no objection to giving his name to a newspaperman but he thought it might not be a good idea to get photographed. So no picture of Medina.

He met his fellow travelers on the road, he said, and had not known them before. They came across the Rio Grande near Piedras Negras, at a place where the water was no more than knee-deep. So there is your answer, if you wondered. Wetback is most often a misnomer. Few of them swim the river.

I've always thought of a wetback as being flat broke. Because I've heard grand stories about how they will walk from 150 miles into Mexico and cross the river and walk another 150 miles into Texas, to find work. Some of these stories are no doubt true but it's a mistake to assume all wetbacks are stricken by poverty.

Lorieto Medina is not broke, I promise you that. He rode the bus from down in Zacatecas State to Piedras Negras, and would have ridden it to wherever he is headed if it weren't for the risk of getting picked up.

Wetbacks travel mighty light. Most carry a small knapsack-type bundle with a change of clothes and some grub. And that evil-looking, dark, rough-cut tobacco.

Medina and his new friends walked quite a bit at night, along the highway. They'd hit the brush when a car showed up. Walking in the brush in darkness is not popular because of rattlesnakes. Many wetbacks do it, though.

They came by way of Carrizo Springs, and went into a store there and bought some food. Hernandez asked what they ate and Medina named three items, as if that was what they always ate while walking: "Sardines, tortillas, and pork and beans."

Do they ever get sick while traveling?

"Yes, but we keep walking."

How do they know where to go to get work?

"A leader, a man who has been here before, he tells us where to go and what to do."

We got Medina taking about his life in Zacatecas. He is one of a family of twelve. He has two brothers who have also been wetbacks. His wife and baby live with his parents. She washes clothes on a rub board. Cooks with wood. Has no electricity.

When he is home Medina farms, raises corn and beans. He is saving money to buy land. Wants to raise cattle and goats. That's why he comes.

People who hire this alien labor say that, almost without exception, wetbacks send their pay home as soon as they get it. It's common for a wetback to keep just ten dollars for his own expenses, for a month.

Medina astonished both Hernandez and me when he told us he was headed for Florida, where he expected to make up to one hundred dollars a day picking peppers and tomatoes.

Did he mean one hundred dollars a week, perhaps?

"No," grinning broadly. "Sometimes twenty dollars a day, sometimes forty dollars. But on good days, one hundred."

He said he has been to Florida four times already. He said he once mailed home 40,000 pesos, over a seven-month period, from Florida. That's $3,200 U.S. currency. Quite a bundle, I expect, in rural Zacatecas.

Medina said he would have to pay "a man" two hundred dollars to transport him to Florida from Texas. Transporting alien labor, delivering wetbacks where they're in great demand, is of course unlawful but evidently it's common. In South Texas such a transporter is called a coyote.

Despite that they're in the country illegally, I find it easy to sympathize with wetbacks. I can't help admire a young fellow who'll walk through one hundred miles of mesquite and prickly pear and rattlesnakes, looking for somebody who'll hire him to do hot hard work that nobody else wants to do.

Wetbacks aren't always cheap labor. That is, now and then one will disappear with something that doesn't belong to him and never show up again. In the Brush Country you're always hearing such yarns. About the wetback, for example, who had never ridden in a pickup when he got into Texas but learned to drive one on the ranch where he worked. One night he drove it home to Mexico.

Others became trusted employees, and stay until one day the Border Patrol picks them up.

Has Lorieto Medina ever been caught?

"Five times," he says, grinning again.

He said the Border Patrol treated him very well. Gave him a ride, all five times, to Del Rio and put him across the river. He turned around and came back.

In Brush Country towns like Cotulla, Pearsall, Falfurrias, Freer, you always hear a lot of wetback talk from ranchers. But something they don't much like to discuss, and that's the possibility that one day they'll see really effective legislation that will make the use of wetback labor too great a risk. Say a $10,000 fine, for hiring one.

That'll be a tough mouthful to swallow, because I've heard dozens of South Texas and Trans-Pecos ranchers and farmers say, "We just wouldn't make it, without wetbacks."

Lorieto Medina said when he comes into the U.S., he stays six to seven months if he doesn't get caught. When he gets ready to go home, he takes a bus to the border and strides back across the bridge. No wading on the return trip.

I've been told some wetbacks will get caught on purpose, when they're homesick. Been in Texas six months, and sent their money home, so they'll just go hiking down the middle of the highway until the Border Patrol comes along and gives 'em a ride to Del Rio. Save bus fare that way.

We were cruising along U.S. 59 above Nacogdoches, headed up toward Garrison. Sam Dement was going to work, and I'd asked him to let me follow along and watch.

Sam is forty-one and tall and limber, one of those drawly, good old grinning boys, a fellow you're apt to like as quick as you meet him. While we drove along he talked about selling magazines.

Dement lives in Nacogdoches and that's how he makes a living—calling on country folks, house to house, selling subscriptions to a farm and garden magazine. He does all right at it, too.

"It's mostly a matter of attitude," he said, about the job. "If I'm down, the people are usually down. If I'm psyched up, so are the customers. It's almost like your vibes arrive at the house before you do.

"When I get down, I don't really try to sell. I just go out and visit with the people, and sometimes things happen. Just like last week, a friend of mine had gone in the hospital with cancer and I was down about it. So I started out to work that day and called on a fellow and just visited, and after a while he decided he didn't want the magazine.

"Before I left I asked him if he happened to have any old batteries around there. He had two or three, and I took those, and we made a deal for a subscription, and that sort of gave me a lift. After that I sold everybody I called on, all day.

"Sure, I'll take batteries, instead of cash. An old battery's worth maybe two dollars, for the lead. I'll take old radiators, too. They've got copper in 'em. And trading stamps, I'll take those. It's just the same as cash. I've got seven old batteries in the car right now."

That's a country tradition, for a farm magazine salesman to accept cash substitutes. Back during the Depression, my father sold farm magazines just the way Sam Dement does, and he'd take in chickens and pecans and syrup, anything he could eat or convert to money.

That's one reason I went along with Dement, to watch. It was a return trip for me. I used to go with my father, to help catch the chickens he'd take in.

Sam had a country map. We cut off down one of those red Nacogdoches County roads and called at a house where nobody was home. A little farther on we found a dairy farmer working on a new barn.

"Need any help?" Sam called, when we stopped. Doggone, that sounded familiar. My father used to say the same thing, holler it even before he got out of the car. "Mornin'. I'm Sam Dement, and . . ."

They talked I guess five minutes, about a lot of stuff other than the magazine. Then first thing I knew the farmer was saying to his boy, "Son, go to the house and tell your mother to make out a check for $7.50."

Dement works, of course, on commission. He's the kind who doesn't want a desk job or the restriction of a salary. He's got to be out and moving and talking and selling. Free is what he needs to be.

"Let's talk to this old fellow." We stopped at a country cemetery. The old fellow had a slinger and was knocking weeds and grass from around a grave. "Need any help?"

Turned out he was already taking the magazine. Said he'd got so he couldn't read much though, eyes so bad. Get that way, he said, when you're *his* age. Seventy-seven.

"Congratulations," Sam said. "A whole lot of people never make it that far."

The old fellow looked at the grave. "Here's one that didn't. My boy. He was fifty." He choked up and wasn't able to talk for a while. But then he did talk, about the son. Gave a summary of his life—his boyhood, his schooling, his work, his death at fifty of a heart attack. I watched to see how Sam would handle that and he did it just right, listening, not saying much, letting the old fellow talk.

"Good therapy for him, I guess," Sam said, back in the car. "Lot of people don't understand how these old folks need to talk about things."

A long time ago Sam started out to be a preacher. He's college-educated, in fact, to be one, but it didn't work out for him. He's been in sales-type work ever since college. His wife Margaret, too. Right now she's gone back to school for an advanced degree, at Stephen F. Austin State.

"Margaret has a great love for learning," Sam said, and he sounded a little like a preacher to me.

"Let's try this trailer house here." We pulled up to a mobile home. A woman was running a tiller in the garden. "Need any help?"

The woman's daughter came from behind the house and they both stopped to look at the sample magazine Sam offered. This time I checked the clock and it took him less than five minutes to make the sale and most of that was spent talking gardens.

"Did you get a good stand on your corn?" Sam asked the woman. She didn't, and Sam said he didn't either. The daughter went in the house and came back with a check for $7.50 and a glass of ice water for Sam.

That $7.50 gets Sam's magazine for five years. At first I

thought that was a special he was running but it's the regular sub-scription rate. Sam just makes it *sound* like a special.

He's a tower of confidence. Watch this, now, he'll say. See that foreign compact pickup truck at that house? That means those people are interested in economy, that they'll buy price, and won't be able to resist five years for $7.50. He was right. The sale took him seven minutes.

Of that $7.50, Sam has to send in only 25 percent to the magazine. So a five-year subscription is $5.50 in his jeans. I stayed with him only about an hour and he sold three, and made $16.50. He said if the job is really worked it's "good for $100 a day."

So you don't need to feel too sorry for a country magazine salesman in a dusty old car. He might be making $1,500 a month, maybe even $2,000.

Another house, this time with a new pickup and a woman in a sunbonnet, working in a flowerbed.

"Need any help? . . ."

Omen is a little country town less than half an hour's drive south-east of Tyler. I stopped there to buy a dozen fresh-laid brown eggs. Also to see the woman who sells the eggs. She is Melba McConnell.

Melba and I have been swapping letters several years so we decided it wasn't necessary for me to address her as Mrs. McCon-nell. Good.

The house Melba lives in was built, she believes, back in the 1850s. It's one of these old dog-run places with a sleeping porch on the back and a well with a pulley and a water bucket. And a path leading out to the privy beneath a huge sycamore.

I guessed Melba to be in her early sixties. A small woman with dark hair and a quick grin. Dressed for outside work. When we got through with the hellos she said, "Come out here and meet my girls."

She was talking about her chickens. "Watch out for the grass burrs," she said, walking to the chicken house. She opened the door and we stepped in and twenty-six of the healthiest-looking red hens I ever met crowded around us.

"Now don't you peck me, sister," Melba said to one of the hens. "Yesterday I got twenty-five eggs out of twenty-six hens. Day before I got twenty out of twenty-six. These hens just started layin'

September 12. They're called Buff Sex Link, or the Golden Cross. Their daddy was a Rhode Island Red rooster and their mama was one of those White Rock hens, with the black feathers around her neck. I ordered 'em out of Pleasant Hill, Missouri.

"These hens have never been out of this house. I'm gonna build you a fence one of these times, girls. They'll lay good for three or four years. I've had 'em to lay for five or six. I've always kept red hens. They lay huge eggs. These need a rooster awful bad but I didn't get one this time. A fertile egg is richer, you know."

Richer in what, I wondered.

"In everything," she said. "When a hen's been with a rooster, everytime she lays an egg she thinks it's gonna make a chicken so she puts more of everything into it, for the baby chick. Least that's what they tell me. Some people want fertile eggs, and won't buy from you if you don't have them. And some won't buy fertile eggs because they don't like that rooster spot."

She took two dark brown eggs from under a hen on the nest. "That makes thirteen I've got today so far. I train my hens so I can reach under them and get the eggs and they won't fly off the nest. Let me show you my house."

We walked back through the grass burrs, beneath a fine Japanese persimmon, loaded with flawless fruit. Past a car shed with an old pale blue pickup in it.

"I bought that truck for $1,240. And ninety cents, I think it was. I paid for it selling eggs. Everybody that comes by here wants to buy it. I tell 'em it won't be for sale until I die, and not then if my son-in-law wants it."

She paused a minute at a climbing rosebush that covers one side of the truck shed. "When this thing blooms it's a solid mass of yellow roses. I love yellow roses. They climbed up and took over part of my clothesline. I just let 'em have it.

"How do you like my swamp maple? Did you ever see a bigger swamp maple in your life?"

At the gate she stopped and looked at the house. I supposed she was getting ready to tell about the house and was gathering her thoughts on how to do it best.

The place is old and needs paint and repair but Melba works on it constantly, patching and tightening it up, and planting pretty things to grow around it. "I can raise flowers, chickens, and hell," she said, and grinned the quick grin. "I live here like the old country folks used to live. I don't have a hot water heater or a flush toilet. I laugh and tell 'em I live primitive, but I do it because I want to. I like it. This house called me, and I came."

She cut a glance at me, I guess to see if I'd react to her answering a call from a house.

"I'm a little psychic," she went on. "I dreamed about this house three and four times a week for nine months. I could see it exactly like it was. I could see the street, the highway, just as they are. That was in '67. When I came here in '68 and walked through this gate for the first time, it was like I was coming home."

The way she found the house, she had gone up in the Tyler region to see a friend, and heard a man describing an old house, saying he was tearing the porches off it. It was her dream house the man was talking about. "If you'll put the porches back on," Melba told him, "I'll buy it from you." That was before she ever saw it.

"I moved here in '68," she said. We had come into the living room, which she's still working on. Walls are lined now with heavy cardboard. "I stayed fifteen months and had to go back to Houston and I didn't come back until '75. I paid for this house selling eggs. I sold eggs in Houston. Had my chickens in the side yard. I was on the Eastex Freeway, at Lauder.

"I started out selling eggs for fifty cents a dozen. Then I went to seventy-five. Finally my customers said they were worth a dollar and just started leaving a dollar and it's been a dollar ever since. Was that a knock?"

She went across the dog run, enclosed now, and through the front bedroom to the door. A woman was on the porch wanting two dozen eggs—just about an entire day's production out of Melba's twenty-six girls.

"Used to be several doctors in Omen," she said, when she returned with two bills in her fist. "This house was built by one of them. He was Dr. N. P. Fowler and he began practicing here in 1852. I figure that's about when the house was built. Sometimes people stop here and talk about how pretty the place used to be, how nice it was kept. I tell 'em it wasn't *me* that let it go to pot.

"I feel about forty-five but I'm sixty-three. I'm an Aquarius.

And a Pisces. I was born on the cusp. And I've got a lot of Irish in me. When people like me they love me, but when they don't, look out.

"I've raised three children and been married five times and that's plenty. I refuse to raise grandchildren. My last husband died two years ago. In '78 I had two heart attacks that almost killed me . . . I've had five operations and nearly died on the table every time so I'm not having any more of those. My health is better now than it's been in years. I believe in God and I believe he intended me to find this place, and I'm happy here."

I gave her my dollar for the eggs I came to buy. Turned out she didn't have but ten eggs, after selling the two dozen to the woman who'd come. Melba said, "If you'll sit back down and wait a little while those hens will lay you a couple more to make your dozen."

So I waited about twenty minutes. We went back out to the chicken house and Melba stuck her hand under a hen on the nest. She turned and grinned at me and brought out two pretty dark brown eggs, still warm. I put 'em in my carton and drove away. Don't think I ever before bought a dozen eggs so fresh I had to wait for the hens to finish laying them.

The last few days I have been living in the woods, at a pretty place in Tyler County that I may tell you about later on. I am there now, typing this report, and I have just got back from visiting my nearest neighbor.

My *only* neighbor, I ought to say. He is John T. Rotan, seventy-three. If we were on a prairie I could see his shack from here. But we are in a heavy forest, a few miles outside Woodville. Rotan has been living in this place for eleven years.

Something deep in my past stirred when I walked up to Rotan's shack. Maybe it was the yard, which is bare and sandy and fresh-raked. With a little pile of trash smoking in the middle, away from leaves and twigs that might catch fire and spread. The kind of country yard that used to be swept, long ago, with a homemade brush broom. Before leaf rakes were known.

Rotan was sitting on the front porch, smoking a pipe. On the rail to his left was a package of chewing tobacco. And makings for roll-your-own cigarettes. I told him I thought we were going to have an early fall.

He nodded agreement. Nobody else was about. Rotan lives there alone, except for the three cats wrestling in the dirt. "I felt it this morning," he said, about the early fall. "When I got up I had to put on a shirt."

But it was 4:00 P.M. then and he had taken off the shirt. A slight man, with a narrow face and grayish hair, wavy and close cut. Outdoor skin, tanned and cured.

On his right breast a rectangular shape, about two inches wide, showed beneath the skin. I could see the wire running over to his heart. A pacemaker. He caught me staring and touched the device with his fingers and moved the skin that covered it. And smiled. "If it wasn't for this thing, I wouldn't be sittin' here."

Frame of the shack is covered with corrugated tin. The eaves have been notched in two places to let saplings, an ash and a red maple, grow up through the roof. An old refrigerator, painted gray, hummed on the front porch by the door. Two kerosene lanterns hung from beneath the porch roof.

"I bought that refrigerator seven years ago," Rotan said, "from a lady who thought it was worn out, I guess. I paid her fifteen dollars and it hasn't missed a lick."

A good-humored sign is nailed above the steps. "Hotel de Rotan." Then a larger sign on the outside wall by the door. "That's in the Bible," Rotan said, and turned to look up at the sign. He hadn't moved from the chair.

The sign shows the words out of Revelation, Chapter 3, Verse 20: "Behold, I stand at the door and knock. If any man hear my voice and open the door, I will come in to him, and sup with him, and he with me."

We sat down. We didn't sup but we did sip a little, and Rotan told me about his dead brother Jack and about his old buddy Ivory "Soap" Swearingen. The three of them built that shack in the woods. Now only Rotan is left.

He talked about the place, and about his life. "I was born and raised in Woodville, and lived there all my life. I ran a cleaning and pressing shop. I used to come out here, long years ago when I was young, to hunt squirrels. I always loved these woods. This is the place I love the most, of all the places I know."

I told him he was lucky to live in his favorite place. Not many of us get that.

"That road you came out on, that's the old Doucette tram line. They ran those little engines, pine-knot burners, and hauled logs out of the woods to the mill up at Doucette.

"I remember the whistles. Stratton Riley was one of the main engineers and he was famous as a good whistle blower. You could recognize his whistle in the night. He could sho' make it go lonesome."

On invitation I took a look inside. I am interested in shacks that people build in woods. Rotan has the basic plumbing. Table. Chairs. Old electric stove. No water heater, though. "I have to take cold showers," he said from the porch. An iron bedstead. A wood stove with a brand new flue.

He came into the shack, moving pretty creepy. "I don't get around so good. When this thing went bad on me (indicating his heart) I fell back and fractured my hip joint, and I don't think I'll ever recover fully."

A nut of some sort, hickory I think, fell on the tin roof with a loud bonk and rolled off. Rotan grinned and said, "Sometimes the flying squirrels work in the trees above the shack. They eat at night, and knock more nuts off than they get, and pecans and acorns get to falling on that tin roof and it sounds like a hailstorm." A racket he likes, I could tell.

I asked about the remains of a chicken pen out back. Rotan said, "When my brother was staying with me he brought some bantams out here, and turned 'em loose in the woods. They didn't last long. These hunters would shoot them.

"So he built this pen and bought a rooster and some hens. But as fast as those hens laid eggs, these big old chicken snakes would come crawlin' out of the woods and swallow 'em (swallow the eggs, that is, not the chickens), and finally the hens just quit layin'." So that was the end of the chicken business. The woods can be tough on certain domestic enterprises.

Rotan drives into Woodville just about every other day, to get his mail and buy groceries. But he doesn't seem to feel the need to go and hunt up people to talk to.

Most of the past year he spent in and out of hospitals. Then when he got his pacemaker and was able to walk again, he went to what he called "that old folks home," a nursing home. Stayed three months. Then got up and left, and came back to his shack in the woods.

I waited around a while, guessing that when he got ready he'd make me a little speech about why—why will a seventy-three-year-old man with heart trouble and a near total disability choose to live alone miles in a forest, in a tin shack that doesn't even have a water heater?

"I love it here," he began. "Oh, I got fussed at, when I checked out of that old folks home. They said, 'Why, you can't look after yourself, and drive that old car, and live out there in that shack.' I told 'em, 'Well, if I die I might as well die out there where I want to be.'

"This place is heaven to me. I can sit right here, and the deer come up and graze around the house, and I enjoy the trees, and at night I listen to the wolves howling back up in these woods, and sometimes they come in close.

"I listen to my birds. To the blue jays and the redbirds, and the raincrows, and the bobwhites. And mourning doves, so sad it makes your heart melt. I love to hear that Indian hen, one of the peckerwoods. Some of the old-timers called that bird the Indian war god. I hear hawks whistle, and deer snort. You ever hear a deer snort? I hear the squirrels barking, and owls, and I can hear little foxes out yonder. Now I'm not gonna hear things like that at an old folks home. All I heard there was moans and groans. I'd rather be here."

I left him then and came back through the woods to the place I'm staying. It's night now, late, and I am sitting here enjoying the concert. Bullfrogs, and a thousand chirping insects, and one big hoot owl back yonder in the direction of John Rotan's shack.

At Giddings I ran into Meredith York, a rancher type who often rumbles around on the back roads of Lee County in a pickup truck.

The reason is, he owns a bunch of land in that county, and keeps cattle, and so spends a lot of time in that truck, looking across fences and checking gates.

I got in the truck and rode with him, almost the whole afternoon, and helped him to look at cows and talk about them. Cows need an awful lot of looking at and talking about, especially during a hard winter like we've been having.

How many head of cattle or acres of pasture York has I don't know, because that's a very private matter and it's impolite to ask about it. But York is the same as most other cowmen I know in that he seems to have a personal acquaintance with every animal that's grazing his grass, and knows its history from the time it was a calf, and likes to talk about it.

Once he stopped the truck on a dirt road at Loebau, a community north and east of Giddings a few miles, and studied an old gray Brahman-type cow standing out in the pasture. She distinguished herself from the other cattle by looking thin and pretty bony, while everything else seemed in fine shape.

York made this short speech about her: "I'm a little bit worried about that old cow. Don't know whether she's gonna make it or not. She's twelve years old. I bought her in 1961, at Sealy, at four o'clock in the morning, and paid $123 for her and her mama. Her trouble is, she raised a bull calf last year. We couldn't get him in, and she kept him too long, and he drew her down. She's looking kinda gaunt."

Cattle people enjoy remembering such things as buying a cow and a calf twelve years ago at 4:00 A.M. The reason for that time, these cattle auctions keep operating until all the livestock brought in is sold, and sometimes that means they stay open all night.

We went on, and crossed the branch where York used to earn nickels and dimes in wet weather when he was a boy. I get a kick out of knocking around with a fellow in country where he was raised, and hearing about the little things he considers worth recalling.

At that branch, York and his brother used to pull stuck cars out of the mud. When the weather got wet they'd keep a team harnessed and wait for somebody to come along in a Model-T, and haul him out. Sometimes they'd just get a bar of candy, from a traveling salesman.

Over the years I've developed a feeling of closeness to the cattle people of this state. I think I understand them, at least better than I understand anybody else you can put into a group. I find myself in agreement with their attitudes about so many things.

For example, York and I got to talking about a friend of ours who has always been very active but whose health has failed now and he's obliged to stay close to home.

"I've got a lot of respect and admiration for that man," York said. "He's always had power but he understands it, and knows how to use it. Lately I've been thinking I ought to go see him, but I'm not sure he wants any company. When an old bear gets wounded, you know, he goes off, stays by himself, doesn't want anybody around him. I believe if I was in his place, I wouldn't want *you* coming around, looking at me . . ."

I feel the same way. But I've had men preach to me that I'd feel different about it, if it was really me who was down in the blankets.

A lot of the ranch land in Texas is controlled by men similar to York, in that they have roots in the soil where their cattle graze. Usually their fathers farmed cotton and corn and raised sons who left the land but eventually came back, not to farm but to ranch.

Such men get a huge satisfaction, it's plain, in seeing their cattle graze on land where their fathers once followed plow mules. No matter how much neighboring land a man acquires on his own, he'll always consider the old fields of the home place special. I think he can sit in a pickup at the fenceline and see his family history out there, and watch his own youth passing up and down those old rows, passing in review.

However, what I enjoy most about Texas ranching men is not what I can tell about them just by looking, but what I cannot. They are full of surprises.

An example is that when I was riding with York, he stopped a minute when we came to the old Lutheran Church at Loebau. The afternoon sun was bright on that white church and the snow hadn't melted off yet and the scene had a sort of religious purity about it.

"I never pass here," York said, "that I don't think of those old lines, 'The curfew tolls the knell of parting day, / The lowing herd winds slowly o'er the lea . . .'"

Do you see what I mean? It's something I love about my state, that you can ride around in a pickup with a man who'll talk in one sentence about an old cow lookin' kinda gaunt, and in the next he'll quote lines from Thomas Gray's "Elegy Written in a Country Churchyard."

Sometimes in this job you need to get up awful early. I rolled out of the quilts at 3:45 A.M. and drove to Bellville to catch John Edwards before he went to work.

Edwards is a conductor for the Santa Fe Railway. At 6:00 A.M. every day except Sunday he takes a freight train from Bellville down to Cane Junction and back. Cane Junction is between Wharton and Bay City on what used to be the Cane Belt Railroad. Santa Fe owns it now, and operates it as a branch line. Train crews still call it the Cane Belt.

After making a flock of phone calls and signing a waiver in triplicate I got permission to ride along with Edwards on his caboose. I've been wanting a caboose ride a long time.

So here we go. From Bellville to Sealy we ride Santa Fe's main line, stretching from Houston and Galveston to Chicago. But at Sealy we'll switch off to the Cane Belt, which is more like old-timey railroading, and that's why I wanted to ride it. We've got three diesel locomotive units up front pulling thirty-nine cars but the Cane Belt is an old railroad and our top speed will be twenty-five and the ride will be wobbly.

At Sealy we clear the main line and the character of the ride changes immediately. We hear the familiar click-clack-click-clack of the wheels, which you don't hear on the main line because its tracks are laid in quarter-mile jointless sections. The caboose pitches and rolls and lumbers and makes grumbling noises.

The caboose is not like I imagined it would be. I pictured it a homey-type place, with bunks for the crew to sleep in, and a stove to cook on, and maybe curtains on the windows. But this caboose is drab and colorless. No bunks. Only seats, with desk-type surfaces for doing paper work. There's a toilet and an oil stove but no cooking is done.

When Edwards gets free of his paper work we go up in the cupola and sit in the high seats and look out over the frost-browned pastures and he explains about the caboose.

"Actually the bunks in cabooses never were for train crews. We used to sleep on them sometimes, and cook, in order to save money. But the bunks were really for ranchers shipping cattle. They'd have to go along with the cattle and they'd sleep on the cabooses.

"Then we used to haul vegetables and fruit in reefer cars (that had to be iced, in times before refrigerated cars) and we'd carry what they called messengers, who went along and iced the cars, and slept in the caboose."

Train crews on a slow run like this develop a detached and yet a close association with the territory they pass through, day after day. The cupola seat is a fine spot to view the countryside and Edwards is interested in everything that goes on out there. He comments as we rumble along.

"I've been watching this old boy rebuild his beer joint. It burned down not long ago . . . This old sharecropper here, he's been trying to scratch a living out of that little piece of land for years, but he just never seems to have any luck."

Going through a town, Eagle Lake I think: "We always take you through the ugly part of a town. That's one thing that hurt the passenger trains . . ."

Now we're at Matthews: "Twenty-five years ago we had a combination coach and baggage car on this job and we carried passengers. We'd stop at every pig trail and footpath. I remember here at Matthews every Saturday we'd pick up twenty-five or thirty colored folks going into Eagle Lake, and the fare was sixteen cents."

Somewhere between Eagle Lake and Wharton: "I want to show you our pets. For four or five years we've been watching a pair of Mexican eagles that nest in a big bush along the fence. Every year they raise one young eagle, and leave, and then come back to the same place."

We rolled past the bush—a big McCartney rose hedge—and the male eagle was perched on the crossarm of a telephone pole and didn't even fly as we went by. We could see the female down in the hedge.

Easing into Wharton: "Here's Reverend Williams' church. We call this Reverend Williams' crossing." Sign at the church reads, "St. James Baptist. Wharton's No. 1 soul winning church."

From high up in that caboose you get some intimate glimpses into back yards, and into the lives of people sometimes. "This is a nice town," Edwards says going through Wharton, looking over back fences. "I've got a lot of friends here that I wave at. Of course I don't know any of their names . . ."

On the return trip I rode up in the engine with the engineer, Gene Hintz, and the head brakeman, Thomas Broyles. I'm standing behind them and we're moving along nearly twenty miles per hour and gaining speed. Hintz is answering my question, saying yes, sure he stops for cows on the track.

"One time down close to Bay City I saw an old Brahman cow charge a steam engine head on. Knocked her down but later on she got up and walked away. Then not long ago we had an old bull on the track we couldn't get rid of. Conductor tried to scare him off with a fusee (railroad flare) tied on the end of a broomstick . . ."

Hintz didn't say it but railroads hate to hit anything. You know what they used to say about a $10 mule, and how there's not anything that'll increase his value like getting hit by a train.

We slow down to creep through Wharton, and between whistles Hintz tries to answer my question about the public attitude toward trains, and how it's changed. He says people aren't interested in trains the way they once were. "Most of them won't even wave at you anymore. When you whistle, some people like it, and some get mad."

He kept glancing at the back doors of some houses we were passing. "There's a little carrot-topped boy along here, three or four years old, that always waves. I don't see him today. The children, they still wave at you."

We move now through the rich farms of the Colorado Valley above Wharton, and Hintz is reminded of his steam engine days. "Used to be a lot of cotton grown along here. The cottonpickers would dance in the field when they heard that steam whistle."

Hintz has been on the Cane Belt a long time. His co-workers tell me he's a fine engine man, that he knows the track, every crooked rail and soft spot and hogback, and knows what to do.

Getting back close to Sealy now. We've crossed the San Bernard bridge and we're groaning over brown pastures and Hintz points out a lone live oak to the west of the track.

"That's where Rexville School used to be. My sisters and I went there during the Depression. Mr. Regenbrecht was the teacher. Used to be sidings here and sand pits where they'd bed the floors of stock cars. Mr. Regenbrecht, he used to pull all the shades on this side of the school building so we wouldn't sit there and watch the trains switching . . ."

Easing on into Sealy, horn blaring and bell ringing. A very fine ride, and I'll tell you something I think I learned:

Gene Hintz and the others laugh about crossing bridges at ten miles an hour and about people not paying attention to their train. But I believe they still feel the excitement and the romance of railroading. They show it in quiet ways.

For example. I was watching Hintz's face when we passed the little girl in Wharton. And I saw him grin. She was standing about forty feet from the engine when it roared by. A pretty little girl of about seven, in blue britches and a bright red sweater, and she shouted. You couldn't hear her but her mouth shaped the words perfectly: "I love you!"

IV

Old-timey Talk

In the back of my notebook I've got a section where I write down country expressions that are trying to pass out of use. I get a satisfaction out of turning back there to see what has gotten into the book since the last time I looked.

Most of the expressions I hear by accident in the country, or on the corner next to the post office in little towns. A lot of them I hear right here in Houston, as Houston is very likely the biggest country town in the entire hemisphere.

A few of the regular customers have begun now to send in an expression when they think of one. I am pleased to get them, and add them to my list right away.

I am getting a few now that I never heard. Maybe they go back further than I do. But more likely they are regional to some other part of the country, and have migrated in here with all these new folks we've got.

Until one of the customers wrote to explain it, I didn't know what it means to say a young woman has been "influenced" by a man. It means he has messed around with her, folks. Compromised her. Perhaps got her in the family way.

So maybe the father of such a gal would go looking for the man, to accuse him of influencing his daughter and to demand that he make an honest woman of her at the altar.

A high percentage of the entries in the notebook trace back to times when people were straining to "talk nice." To keep from speaking of improper matters. So they circled about the bush and found substitute words.

It tickles me that we used to be so afraid to say that a woman was pregnant. We kept on a constant search for substitutes, to avoid saying pregnant. That "in the family way" was one substitute. So many more. And often the substitute expressions were far more indelicate than the very word we were trying to avoid. Some are coarse to the point I would not be comfortable using them here now.

The kind of expression I most love to hear is one that used to be common among my own people, but has almost passed off tongues now. So that it surprises me to hear it again.

Here is one I put in the notebook just last week. "Get easy."

To get easy means to stop hurting. So many times I heard my elders use that expression long ago. "I didn't get easy till about eleven o'clock." "The doctor gave him something to get him easy." "I'm gettin' easy now."

"Gettin' Easy" would make a fine book title, or the name of a country song. Or even an epitaph. If I was obliged to design my own tombstone, I would just as soon have "Gettin' Easy" inscribed on it as anything.

Another recent entry in the notebook is the one about the head swimming. "That makes my head swim."

"My head's been swimmin' all day." It means having dizziness. The expression extended itself finally to mean being confused and perplexed. An algebra problem, for instance, so involved it made the head swim.

I still hear that one, from elderly folks. I wonder if medical schools teach the meaning of such old-timey expressions. Would an intern know what an eighty-five-year-old woman meant if she said her head had been swimming all night? I guess so. I hope so.

I call these country expressions, but they are just old-fashioned, and not exclusively rural. Some on my list are taunting chants that youngsters once shouted at those they wanted to pester. Remember?

"Coward! Coward! Buttermilk soured!"

"Liar! Liar! Tongue's on fire!"

"Tightwad! Tightwad! Sittin' on the fence, tryin' to make a dollar outta fifteen cents!"

Now and then one of the entries is a mystery to me. I mean I won't remember putting it down and don't know where it came from. Maybe it's just a sentence somebody said that I liked, or one I read. Like this:

"A man don't need to be a cook to complain about bad biscuits." The oftener I read that the more it says to me.

But my favorite among the recent entries is that "gettin' easy." I am able to feel such a peace in those two words.

Those old-timey expressions just keep on drifting in from the customers. In the twenty-odd years that this column has been running, the old-timey expressions have brought in more mail than anything else I've ever dealt with here.

Thanks to the customers, I've now got more than a dozen substitute terms that people used for bull. The most recent one I've had is from A. A. Callihan down at Freeport, and the word is guffy. If anybody had asked me where a bull was called a guffy I would have said certainly not in Texas. But Callihan says yes, it was common there in Brazoria County back in the times when people didn't say bull in mixed crowds.

Another new one to me, once used in West Texas, is in this sentence: "We all got together Saturday night and went to a back-reachin'." A back-reachin', according to R. R. and Marguerite Richard, is a dance. I used to hear dances called stomps and foot scrapin's but never before a back-reachin'.

Margaret Jenkins up at Somerville wonders why we have quit saying hind part before, when we mean backward. I don't know why but I'm sorry we did. Hind part before says something that backward doesn't say.

Gretchen Weilburg remembers her folks saying that the ox was in the ditch. I used to hear that a lot. "Can't go to church today. Ox is in the ditch." That one has a Bible origin. Look at Luke 14:15. Jesus Christ is quoted there. "And (he) answered them, saying, Which of you shall have an ass or an ox fallen into a pit, and will not straightway pull him out on the Sabbath day?"

Then we used to hear a lot of smart-aleck answers to casual questions. Suzanne Livingston reminds us of one. Question: "What you doing that fer?" Answer: "Cat fur, to make kitten britches."

Peggy Alderton says her Quaker mother in Indiana used to warn her not to whistle. She'd say, "Nature doesn't like whistling girls or crowing hens."

Two or three customers wrote about the answer they used to hear from people who were asked how they felt. They'd often say, "Oh, fair to middling." You hear this still sometimes. That word middling has a long and interesting history which you can read about in any good dictionary.

Mary English here in Houston contributes a usage that's strange to me. It's "mistrust," used as a verb and expressing doubt. As in, "I mistrust I could spell Constantinople."

Then here is Mary Staley reminding us that when a baby is running around without a diaper it does not have its "hippins" on. "Put some hippins on that child." That's new to me too.

But I certainly know what it means to say that a woman or a girl has "swallowed a punkin seed," which is another expression Mary Staley brings up. It means the woman is pregnant but, at least in my part of the country, not necessarily without benefit of a husband. If she was "in trouble" or "ruined"—"influenced" by the young man—that was a family shame; but if she had only swallowed a punkin seed, no problem, because she already had a husband.

In Galveston, J. L. Hendrikson wonders who knows what an "ugly stick" is. I did not, myself. He says it's just a switch that a parent would use to whip a child that needed punishing. "I'm gonna wear you out with the ugly stick."

Georgia Furrer contributes "a whole squirrel," which is new to me. "I killed a whole squirrel." Meaning the speaker went all out, gave a total effort.

Then Linnie Murray up at Caldwell reminds us to "sit loose" when we relax.

And Faye Winfrey down at Liverpool brings up "right smart," meaning a lot. "That's a right smart of peas to shell in an hour."

Ray Loden sent me a short paragraph spoken to him by a ninety-year-old woman he visited. I think it's so pretty. She told him, "I woke up this morning feeling just tolerable. I thought if I could go to the store it would make me feel better. But I had to lag the groceries home, and now I'm really on a low limb."

Sometimes when I am thinking about these old sayings, one will pop up and mean something so special to me. For instance, Ray Wadsworth of Bellaire writes about this quote: "You've got a hard row to hoe."

Now that figure of speech is common in the Texas tongue. I can sit in country cafes in this state and hear it half a dozen times a day. If I dwell on what it meant originally, I see my father.

I see him helping me chop cotton. One year, hiding from the Depression, we worked a crop for kinfolks who lived out where there was enough to eat. I learned about chopping cotton. I found out what it meant to get to the end of a row with my back aching and my arms barely able to lift the hoe. That's when you turned and looked to see what kind of row you had coming up, whether it had much Johnson grass or not. Because rows in cotton fields vary. The fellow next to you may have a lot easier row than you do.

In those times I had days when I was trying to be big, and my father was watching, to see I didn't overdo. Sometimes he would reach out and chop Johnson grass out of my row. I would complain about him doing my work and he would say, the sweat dripping off him, "Well, you've got a hard row to hoe here."

That's when one of these old-timey expressions means the most to you, when it is chapter and verse right out of your own personal history.

When the customers were sending in those old-timey expressions we've been talking about, I misplaced a letter from somebody who wondered if I remember what a risen is.

Yes, but we have to make clear how we pronounced that word, like this: *rye*-zun. I suppose that is a corruption of rising. A swelling, that is. Risen was once in common use as the name of a painful sore. A boil.

Country kids in my early times were always showing up with risens, probably caused by malnutrition or just plain bad personal hygiene.

When you saw a schoolboy come in walking real straight and stiff, as if he didn't want his overalls to touch him anywhere, and he sat at his desk sort of leaning to one side, you could figure he had risens on his seat. They weren't funny, I tell you that.

When a sore became worse than a risen, we called it a carbuncle. We were scared spitless of carbuncles. Somebody always had an uncle who died with carbuncles. So we were afraid of carbuncles the same way we were afraid of bone felon, lightning, rattlesnake bite, blood poisoning, cyclones, and getting salivated. Any of those were pretty near as bad as drinking sweet milk and eating fish.

I will not confess how old I was before I found out that fish and milk together don't really make a poison deadly as strychnine. That was once such a widespread notion, that if you drank sweet milk and ate fish you would go over in a corner and curl up like a piece of pigskin and die. You could drink buttermilk or eat clabber with fish but not sweet milk.

I have met newly arrived Yankees in Houston who wonder what sweet milk is. You pronounce it as if it's a single word. Think of it as being hyphenated and that helps, and put the emphasis on the front end. SWEET-milk. Whole milk, is all it is. Milk the way it comes out of a cow. As opposed to other milk. Sour milk. Buttermilk. Blinky milk, and so forth.

I don't hear Texans saying sweet milk the way they used to. They've got so they don't even say light bread. But sometimes circumstances pop up that demand the use of the old-fashioned terms.

For instance a couple of weeks ago I was up at John Henry Faulk's house at Madisonville and about the middle of the afternoon John Henry announced he was hungry. He went in the kitchen and poured a glass a little better than half full of milk and then crumbled up a big hunk of cold cornbread in it and ate it with a long-handled spoon.

Cornbread and sweet milk. Hadn't seen anybody do that in so long. Country folks used to eat cornbread and sweet milk that way every day, as a sort of diet supplement. If you got a hunger pain and you didn't think you could last till supper, you ate a glass of cornbread and sweet milk. But it just had to be called *sweet* milk. To say simply cornbread and milk wouldn't really describe what it is, and it doesn't even sound good.

Then light bread. If we have people down here now that don't know what sweet milk is they won't know what light bread is either. It tickles me that light bread now qualifies as an old-timey term, because in my growing-up years light bread was considered citified.

Light bread is what we called store-bought bread. Bakery bread, instead of cornbread or homemade bread of any sort. You handle the pronunciation the same as you do sweet milk, by putting the two words close together and coming down hard on the first one: LIGHT-bread.

We had a neighbor with a bone felon one time, and he was plenty sick. An infection out at the end of the finger, and for years afterward he would tell how the doctor lanced it and did all manner of unpleasant things to it. That word felon still has such a sinister sound to me and even now when I hear it I see a messed-up finger and not a criminal.

Cyclones. That's what we called tornadoes. I didn't hear the word tornado in common use until I was old enough to vote. What flattened the barn was a cyclone. Popular name for football teams, too. The Silver City Cyclones, rah, rah, rah.

Salivation, or getting salivated, meant something entirely different from what dictionaries now tell you. I learned to avoid the term early, after a cousin of mine was taken to the woodshed when he asked at the supper table if salivation wasn't what you got when you joined the church.

What I love to do on a cool fall night is sit in somebody's house in the woods and listen to good old country talk. With everybody all relaxed, and not worrying about what some newspaperman in the crowd is going to print.

So then what becomes the most important to me, and worth listening for, is not so much the stories being told but the quality of the spoken words, their genuineness, their music and rhythm, and their beautiful originality.

Like J. B. Flowers sitting in the living room of the little house where he grew up and talking to his mother and father about some family matter and making a reference to "Glen, Pauline's dead husband."

I don't know who Pauline is, or who Glen was, but I love that expression. "Glen, Pauline's dead husband," and I consider it worth saving and putting in the record.

We were in Liberty County, I guess, but it was dark when I got there and I never did ask exactly where the house is. It's one of those little dim-lighted homes you see in the edge of the woods all over Southeast Texas. I have passed so many of them, and seen the people sitting in there together, and wondered what they were talking about. Sometimes I get to go in and listen.

J. B.'s parents are Paul and Lillian Flowers. Paul Flowers is a woodsman, meaning he gets a large part of his living out of the forest. Meat on the Flowers table is most apt to be squirrel, venison, or pork that was once wild in the woods.

So most of the talk the evening I was there was about hunting, and related matters.

The room is rectangular and the light is overhead, a bulb hanging from the ceiling, a string tied onto the pull-switch. A wood stove in the center of the linoleum floor. Deer horns on the walls. Little ceramic figures on whatnot shelves. Family photos. Pictures of Jesus. Kerosene lamps.

"I hung him on a limb and gutted him," Paul Flowers was saying (talking about a deer he killed one time), "and stuffed palmetto in him to keep the flies off and . . ."

He pronounced it pal-*meet*-uh, which is different from the way books say, but what I figure is that Paul Flowers knows more about palmetto than anybody that ever wrote a book.

He can tell you, too, how to get rid of fleas and you do that by bringing in myrtle bushes, because fleas won't stay where myrtle bushes are. I got down his method of getting rid of rats, too. Like you've got rats in the attic, you take lye and sprinkle it in a little circle, and then pour syrup in a ring around the lye. So here comes the rat and he gets syrup on his feet and then he walks into the lye and the syrup makes the lye stick and the rat's gonna leave out of there, running from whatever's burning his feet.

But I wanted you to hear some samples of the talk.

"I promised him a whippin' if he come back around here." And that wasn't a parent talking about spanking a child, no.

"He shore pitched a fit over that." I guess you know what it means to pitch a fit. It means to throw a tantrum but pitching a fit to me is ever so much better.

"We was sleepin' on the front porch on a pallet."

"I was raisin' chickens around here till J. B. went in the dog business." Dogs are bad about getting chickens sometimes, is what that means.

"You could buy pinto beans then for eight cents a pound."

"Asittin' in an easy chair."

"I struck a lope." Yeah, on horseback.

"Daddy and me went afire-huntin'." You know about fire-hunting? In earlier times before flashlights or even carbide lights, woodsmen sometimes hunted at night by the light of a burning pitch pine. Of course now hunting with any kind of light is considered bad manners by game wardens.

"A big old buck come up and blowed at us. Now that'll sure take the tired out of a man."

"Musketeers? Tellin' you them skeeters so bad you could swing a quart jar and catch half a gallon of 'em . . ."

"So mad he could stomp a mud hole in dry ground."

"Crawled between a pair of outin' blankets."

"What you reckon that preacher thought of me for lyin' that way?"

"I trailed him a little piece through the woods, and direckly I heard them dogs." Isn't that pretty? Paul Flowers said it.

He also gave me another way to get rid of fleas. Just get you some *bois d'arc* balls, and pitch 'em under the house.

The other afternoon on the street in Livingston I heard a girl of about twelve speak up and state, "I never done no such a thang!"

Of course you can hear that expression and that pronunciation in practically any town in this state, and at times it will be coming out of people who know well enough how to pronounce "thing" and they know better than to say "never done no such" also. But that is just a cornball, country usage that insists on surviving.

That was my Cousin C. T.'s favorite way of denying whatever trespass he had committed. He would stand flat-footed out in the yard and swear in the name of all that was sacred that he never done no such a thang in his life, when no less than six of us had witnessed that he *had* done it. I always felt that when he denied his guilt in that special way it somehow amounted to forgiveness for him, and he could then go forth with a glad and clean heart, and do it again.

Cousin C. T. had a good many Tom Sawyer traits. I remember him conning a gang of us into thinking that it was fun to white-wash peach trees. This was long before I ever read about Tom

Sawyer getting the fence whitewashed. When I did read it I wondered if Tom had gotten the idea from Cousin C. T.

Farmers used to whitewash the trunks of fruit trees, I think for insect control, but I'm not certain. Anyhow it was a job that boys could do and Cousin C. T. would be the boss, of course, and have every one of us fighting to get a brush while he sat over yonder and ate grapes in the shade.

Speaking of whitewash, one of the customers has suggested that back when we were dealing here with old-timey expressions, we missed probably the best one there is. It was used to describe the economic circumstances of a person's family. The person would say, "We were too poor to paint, and too proud to whitewash."

It's true that that one says an awful lot, and I wish I had thought it up myself. No telling who did think it up. Tracing the origin of such expressions is about like looking for the fellow who makes up jokes.

Once in a while a customer will pitch an expression into a letter that just flattens me, it's so descriptive, and sounds so fine. Somewhere around here I've got a letter from a woman who was telling me about some domestic matter or other, and she dropped in the observation that her husband "had taken up with a heating pad."

Now I love that. I can see that old boy, hauled up in the sack with a misery in his lower back, and he doesn't want anything to do with *anything* except that heating pad.

That reminds me, at our house we've got a brindle tomcat and last fall he fell in love with a hair piece. This wig sort of thing, such as women sometimes wear, was left out on the dresser and this old cat came soft-pawing around, looking for a place to winter, and when he spotted that wig he fell for it, tooth, claw, and nail.

He moved in with that thing and you couldn't get him to leave it to take his meals. I could go off for three, four days and when I'd get back that old cat would still be curled up with that wig, whispering to it. Finally this spring they had a falling out and split up. He glides on by that thing now and won't even give it a polite nod.

---··❦{ V }❧··---

Shirttail Days

Lately we have had some November mornings of the kind that were once special to me. Warm and wet and foggy, and there is a whisper in the air and it sends me back to November times when we went out wandering, with no purpose except to be free.

We would wake up early and know from the feel that this was a good day for going, and we would wander into the woods and fields and thickets and along the creeks and ravines around our little old town.

Nobody would say, "Let's go wandering." We might simply say, "Let's go to the creek." And we would go, early, and roam all day. We didn't call it hiking, because it wasn't hiking. It wasn't hunting, or fishing, or anything with a name we knew. It was just being free, for an entire day.

The fog would burn away before nine o'clock. We loved to be out in the scrub timber when the sun came through and the light spread over the oaks and made the wet leaves glitter. We never spoke of such things. That would have been an embarrassment. But we watched for the time, and stood in silence to see and appreciate it.

Two of us would go sometimes. Three, maybe. Never more than four. I think it was best when we wandered in threes, and one of us was new, someone who hadn't been along before, and we could show him things we knew about.

Fence rows where coveys of quail were, and we'd flush them out and count them.

Stock tanks with mallards so beautiful and fat. We'd sneak up behind the dam, and peek over, and watch.

We knew places where jackrabbits played in the sand, and pecan bottoms where hundreds of crows would sit in the tops of the trees and talk and argue and laugh, and we knew holes in the

creek we had swum and fished in, and those needed to be checked, and talked about.

But we didn't *do* anything. We didn't have a fish hook or a gun. We'd have a dog but it wouldn't have any responsibility except to circle around and sniff and snort. It wouldn't be any kind of a hunting dog.

We'd go to special spots. A rocky rim at a bend in the creek. A high place, where we could rest and point out things in town, small and dim and miles away.

We'd go into old barns that had lost their houses, and were lately filled with fresh hay, and we'd find owls up in the lofts, and chicken snakes, and valuable things like that.

And nobody cared, not then. If you wandered today like that, it could be risky. It can be dangerous simply going through a barbed-wire fence and walking across a pasture because that's trespassing. To go up to a man's barn, and enter it, well, just don't do it, not now.

But in those wandering times, nobody cared, and we hadn't heard about the trespass law then.

We went entirely empty-handed. I remember once we came across a little bunch of Boy Scouts eating dinner on the creek bank and they amazed us by having so much *stuff*. Packs and hatchets and skillets and food from their mamas' kitchens, and canteens and knives and forks and mess kits.

Maybe we'd have eaten a little breakfast. Probably a couple of cold biscuits with holes punched in them and the holes filled with honey or preserves. But it didn't occur to us on these wandering days to burden ourselves with grub or gear.

We ate pecans, and peaches, and sometimes pears, and berries like red haws, and—where are you going to get a more nutritious meal than that?—nuts and fresh fruit. We drank from springs. That scraggly old country is full of springs. Not gushing springs such as you find at New Braunfels and San Marcos, but seeping, trickling springs.

It was part of the adventure to follow a tiny little trickle to where it came out of the ground, and dig a small pool there, and let it fill, and clear.

We built a fire sometimes but not to cook. We said it was for drying socks that got wet in the creek but mainly it was just for satisfaction. Because a fire is good to be with, and to smell and watch.

I have wanted for so long to go back, and try to retrace those wandering routes we took. Mostly to see how far we walked, and ran, and climbed, in a day. We would get home at dusk, and supper would sure taste good. But I don't remember ever being tired.

A couple of schoolboys who live in our neighborhood came cutting across my backyard, as they do frequently, on their way to the drugstore. They came in the middle of the morning on a Monday, so I asked if they were playing hooky.

Whether they really were playing hooky doesn't make any difference to me, but I wanted to find out if they knew what hooky means. And they didn't.

But they knew what truancy is. Said it means "cuttin' outta school."

I wonder whatever influence caused a pleasant and informal and useful word like hooky to pass away and get replaced by such a stuffy term as truancy.

Back in my old hometown long ago when guys my present age were schoolboys, I had a classmate named Hooky. I don't remember his family name but his regular first name was Raymond, which didn't fit him, so he was called Hooky, which did.

One year at school he sat directly in front of me and I have a clear recollection of his desk. I see it unoccupied, because he was absent so much. I can see his cedar pencil and pen staff poking from the interior of his desk, and I can see the carvings he made, the days he did attend, on the desk surface. He was pretty good with a pocketknife. He filled in his carvings with ink and made them look, as we said then, real spiffy.

"Raymond must be sick again," the teacher would say, when his desk would turn up empty. He had a reputation for being sick a lot but I don't think he was. His house wasn't far from mine and once when he hadn't been to school I stopped to see him at noon, when I went home to lunch.

His mother said, "He's in the storm cellar."

I went out back and raised the cellar door and there was old Hooky down in there, grinning and whittling. He had two coal oil lanterns burning and the dirt floor of the cellar was a great battlefield, with miniature trenches and barbed-wire entanglements and cannon emplacements and trucks and little men he'd carved from apple crates.

The layout was crude, I suppose, but at the time I considered it mighty grand. It was such a fine substitute for going to school. I thought Hooky was the luckiest guy in the county.

He was always inviting friends to play hooky with him. I went with him at least twice, about the time of year when spring began to make classes and books a torture.

The early part of the day, playing hooky was lovely.

Every bud on the trees was a promise of summer pleasure. The dew on the brown leftover grass was jewelry in the soft morning sun. A chicken snake in a hayloft was a huge (and harmless) serpent, to be captured by bold and fearless lunges. Every muddy creek branch was a river of hidden fish. The world was delicious.

But by noon, for me, this magic died. I would begin to feel the grip of guilt and remorse, and to worry about the lie I would have to tell at home. And when the lie didn't stand up, then would come the shame they would make me feel with their lectures and their tsk-tsk-tsks. The prospect of all that wiped away the glories of the stolen day.

But not for Hooky. He had no sense of guilt, in those times. Nor of shame, not about a thing like skipping school. He felt no more shame about it than a cottontail rabbit would about copulating with his mate in the middle of a country road in broad daylight—a natural act, which made him feel good.

On spring days I used to sit in school and stare at Hooky's vacant desk and try to guess which way he went that morning.

One of the kinfolks writes a letter from out west, and happens to mention that my Cousin C. T. is now a minister of the gospel in the state of Oklahoma.

It seems curious to me, Cousin C. T. being a preacher that way. Long ago when we were coming up out in the Cross Timbers, Cousin C. T. was an expert on mischief. Of course a boy staying waist deep in mischief all the time is not any guarantee that he won't make a preacher. It's just that preaching is the last thing I ever imagined Cousin C. T. would be called to do.

It would tickle me to tell his congregation how he used to work his little schemes on us. Well, for example, that business about burning the house down.

(Cousin C. T. came along at a time when parents practiced the custom of calling boy children by a couple of first initials. They didn't name babies as much as they lettered 'em. I always thought it must have been a strain on mothers, to look down at a tiny baby and say sweet things to a pair of initials. Do you expect they said, "Go to beddy-bye, C. T."?)

Cousin C. T. was a leader. He learned to do things early, such as read and write and drive a team to a wagon or a plow. He had a covey of younger cousins who looked up to him. We were his disciples and his fans. And he was forever conning us.

The business about burning the house, for instance. He'd been sent with the wagon to fetch something a mile or so down the road, and two or three of us went along. On the way back he stopped at a vacant farmhouse and announced he intended to burn it down.

Well, when Cousin C. T. said he intended to burn down a house his disciples believed it, just as if it had been read to us out of the Book of Deuteronomy. He swaggered into that house and in a few minutes came out and got in the wagon and took the reins and waited. Pretty soon here came the smoke, curling out of a window. Then he whipped up the horses and off we trotted.

Every quarter mile or two, after we'd gotten out of sight of the house, he'd say, "Boy, she oughta be burnin' good, by now."

A week went by before the disciples found out we weren't really the accomplice to a penitentiary offense. I don't know how he made the smoke. A rag in a can, I guess.

Another time he planned to break the dam on the stock tank. Never mind, he said, he knew a way to do it. All *we* had to do was wait downstream and enjoy the sight.

Oh, he said, it was going to be grand, when the dam gave way and released all that water into the little ravine below. We'd see trees uprooted. Chickens and pigs floating by. Catfish the size of coon hounds. Maybe even an alligator.

We stayed down there till dark, waiting for the flood that never came. When finally we went in and collected our punishment for being so late, there sat Cousin C. T. at the supper table, sopping syrup and grinning at us.

He didn't mind getting you in mild trouble that way, with his schemes.

Remember one time there was a Mr. Brewer, seems like they called him, came to spend Sunday with Cousin C. T.'s family. He rode an old pony with a new saddle. It was the first new saddle most of us ever saw and everybody was standing around it, smelling of it and listening to it squeak.

Came time to wash up for Sunday dinner and I was one of the disciples who shared the honor Mr. Brewer gave us, of taking that pony to the horse lot to unsaddle him, let him rest up for the return trip.

Cousin C. T. went along to give advice. Now then, he said, you want to take the bridle off first. We said it looked like the saddle ought to come off first. No, he said, the bridle.

So off came the bridle and the old pony swung away from us and even the horse lot fence wasn't enough to hide what happened from Mr. Brewer. He stood on the front porch and watched his old pony go down and wallow in the dirt, with that new saddle still on his back.

Everything Cousin C. T. planned seemed to work. I expect he made a good preacher.

The other evening while going through a stack of old newspapers I have from back in the 1930s, I came across a story about a fourteen-year-old girl up in North Dakota who claimed to get messages direct from the Lord in heaven.

This child had a great many folks paying attention to these messages, and doing whatever the messages said to do in cases where they contained orders.

It has always been very hard for certain people in this world to ignore a person who claimed to be tuned in to a divine frequency that way. Even though it doesn't seem likely to be true, there is really no way to know for sure whether it is or not, so some parties figure it is best to keep on the safe side and pay attention.

Which reminds me that when he was twelve years old, my Cousin C. T. received a message from God, revealing that his little sister Bobbie had made forty-eight on a spelling test.

The reason that message Cousin C. T. got from heaven was so effective, his sister Bobbie had just got through joining the church. She was nine, I think, maybe ten. As a new church member she was trying desperately to keep on the right side of everybody, and God especially.

The reason I know that, just the year before I had passed through the same phase. When those of us in that bunch got up about nine, the adults would come around talking to us about accepting the Savior and joining the church. They always said it was our own decision to make, but you were considered a fool to turn it down. Because when you got saved that way, all your sins were wiped out.

The offer to get our sins canceled was plenty attractive, because by that time most of us had acquired an impressive list of transgressions. Telling fibs. Stealing peaches. Coveting practically everything we saw that we didn't own. Breaking the Sabbath and so on along the line.

And for a good while after we were saved, oh, weeks and weeks sometimes, we were careful not to get any additional sins put on the slate.

That was the vulnerable spot Bobbie was in when she found the pocketknife on the way home from school. It was lying in the road. A beautiful pocketknife, almost new. Our adults decided that since the owner couldn't be located, the knife was Bobbie's to keep.

Cousin C. T., from his loftiness as jury and judge over us all, was able to see that no ten-year-old girl had any business owning a pocketknife, especially not one with three blades, a leather punch, and a corkscrew.

So pretty soon he came gliding up in the yard after school and announced he'd cut across the pasture and received a message from heaven, saying Bobbie had made 48 on that spelling test and hadn't confessed it to her mother.

Bobbie gasped, and ran to hide. It was true. Bobbie wasn't any scholar and spelling was a mystery to her. She had been keeping that 48 a secret because if her mother found it out she would sentence Bobbie to a week inside a spelling book.

The next message from the Lord revealed that Bobbie had lost her Bible. True again. The Bible she'd been given when she joined the church was missing. I had a good idea who knew where it was but Bobbie didn't. She knew only that to lose a Bible not two weeks after being saved was pretty near unforgiveable.

I never did learn how Cousin C. T. managed the final step. But one day he showed up in possession of the pocketknife. Judging by the relief on Bobbie's face, I guessed that one of those heavenly messages had shown her the way to get forgiveness, and her Bible back.

What amazed me the most was how Cousin C. T. could work a felony like that and never suffer an ounce of remorse. Just as if he was really getting word from God by every morning's mail.

This boy is about ten, I guess. He's the grandson of a friend of mine. I was in his grandfather's house and we got left alone for a while, this youngster and I, and we tried to talk.

I never have been too good about communicating with small children. Can't think of anything to say that interests them. I asked him about school. About playing ball. About his grandfather's farm. About his brothers and sisters. For answers I got mainly grunts.

So I reached back and asked if he'd gotten a spanking lately. He lighted up and grinned and said yes. I asked why and he said, "For laughin' in church." Said he'd got started laughing during the sermon and couldn't stop and finally his father took him out and warmed his britches pretty good.

After the telling of that, we got along a little better. I yearned to tell him about the time my Cousin C. T. and I had a similar church experience. But I resisted. Children don't generally care to listen to adventures that adults had when they were young, unless they were very, very hairy adventures involving guns and bloodshed and stitches and hospitals and cops.

They're not going to sit still for stories about a locust crawling up the back of Mr. Hancock's neck in church in the year 1934.

I never have even gotten a child to listen to an explanation of why a locust would be in church, in 1934 or any other year. The reason one was, Cousin C. T. took it in.

This was the bug that most of us now call the cicada. The voice of summer. You hear them daily now in Houston, buzzing in the trees. Later on they'll get louder, and more numerous.

What we used to do, we'd catch a locust and put him in a shirt pocket and use him as a maker of racket. They aren't as hard to catch as the public thinks. The only trouble is finding one on a limb low enough to reach. He'll be sitting long-ways on the limb, and you have to slip up on his blind side and you simply pick him off. You put him in your shirt pocket and that somehow calms him, and he'll quit buzzing and struggling.

Something you have to understand is that it's important, to a boy, to have a thing that makes a noise in a place where a noise is frowned on. School. Library. Church. Funeral home. Such places are way too silent to suit boys. It makes them nervous to be in quiet places, the same as it makes adults nervous to be in rowdy ones. Other than size, that is probably the only basic difference between small boys and grown folks.

Anyhow, you put this locust in your shirt pocket, and every once in a while you can reach up secretly and tap him through the pocket and he'll answer with a buzz. B-z-z-z-t, b-z-z-z-t. Oh, it's a fine noise, and carries all over a quiet room.

Cousin C. T. had decided that church was too quiet for civilized folks. We caught a good fat locust and C. T. put the thing in his shirt pocket and went in and sat near the back. We were just old enough that they would let us sit apart from the family. So we got in a rear pew as near empty as possible, so we could whisper, squirm, and wiggle, and stretch out on the seat the way we needed to.

Well, the locust wouldn't perform. Some of them won't. You can tap at them all day and they'll just play possum and keep mum. So the bug was a failure. We forgot about it and turned our attention to a red wasp circling around the preacher's head.

A wasp circling a preacher has possibilities. But it too was a flop, and flew on out a window. So we went back to the locust again and it was gone from C. T.'s pocket. We found it crawling slowly up the blue serge shoulder of Mr. Hancock, sitting in the pew ahead.

It got to his white-starched collar, and went along laterally for a way, then began crawling diagonally up Mr. Hancock's furrowed neck. His hand came back slowly and grabbed the bug and took it down to his lap. The locust gave off one short comment.

"B-z-z-t!"

About 30 percent of the congregation turned and stared toward the back and Mr. Hancock's neck went red as fire and it was more than we could contain. We erupted in half-smothered laughter and we couldn't quit. When we almost got control we would look at one another and erupt again. It's painful, holding laughter in, and sometimes it can't be done. I am not sure children ought to be spanked for it. We were, though.

We always wanted to know whether Mr. Hancock took our locust home in his pocket, but we were afraid to ask.

Once in a while, drifting through a country town, I will notice a setup where they're having one of those little outdoor summer revival meetings.

There'll be a bunch of wooden benches, and a pulpit on a low platform, and wires strung overhead in a jake-leg way with a few 100-watt bulbs hanging down. Maybe there'll be an old piano up front, covered during the day with a tarpaulin.

The benches are arranged in two sections, always, to leave an aisle for the converts to walk down when the invitation is given.

That arrangement hasn't changed in fifty years. I am glad of that. Some things ought to remain the same. So few of them do.

We had that kind of arrangement exactly in the vacant lot on the Somervell County Courthouse Square in what I now believe was the summer of 1932. My Uncle Cleveland Autry conducted a revival there which seemed to last six or eight weeks. Probably it lasted only two but I had to attend every night, which may have given me an exaggerated notion of how long those services were kept going.

Anyhow, the main thing I recall about them, and the thing I think about now when I see a little summer revival setup by the side of the road, is that in Glen Rose that summer I committed the dreadful sin of lying about the Bible-reading contest. I am now able at last to talk about it without pain.

My family was then in Glen Rose, the county seat of Somervell, hiding from the Depression. It followed along and found us anyway but I was glad we went because Glen Rose was an exciting place. It had dinosaur tracks and Saturday night fights and whiskey stills in the cedar brakes along the Paluxy River and it was an educational community in many ways.

My Uncle Cleveland was a Baptist preacher and my folks were Methodist. Still, my mother handed down the commandment that we would all attend every blessed night of that revival.

The reason was, Uncle Cleveland was the husband of her sister, my Aunt Addie Autry. Uncle Cleveland that summer was what they called "between churches," which meant he was out of work. This was a condition he shared with about 75 percent of the male population of Somervell County.

So we went nightly to the revival to support Uncle Cleveland, although of course we sat down near the front to show that we were already saved.

Anyhow, at that revival they had a Bible-reading contest. The idea was that during the day you were supposed to read Scripture, and count the chapters, and that night at the service you stood up and announced you had read twelve chapters, or twenty, or whatever, to see who read the most.

There was no way a boy could beat the girls but I did want to beat a couple of kinfolks of mine. They were my Cousin George Oxford and my Cousin Eugene Autry, the preacher's son.

I was fond of them both because they contributed a considerable amount of the education I picked up in a year's residence in Somervell County.

Cousin George shared with me his enormous warehouse of knowledge about girls, and what made babies, and things like that. He confirmed for me what I had heard earlier behind barns, and in restrooms at school.

Cousin Eugene gave me an appreciation for curiosities and marvels. He did it by shedding his skin one time, almost the way a snake does. What enabled him to do it, he acquired the severest sunburn that ever baked the hide of man in this or other hemispheres. Then one day he peeled, all at once. Just walked away and left his skin in a heap on the front porch. I admired that as much as anything I'd ever seen a person do, and my insides boiled with envy.

I was never able to beat either of those cousins at reading Bible chapters.

If I arose in the service and announced I'd read twenty, George and Eugene would come along behind and say they'd read twenty-two, and beat me. If I'd read forty, why here they'd come with forty-two.

I was determined to win just once, and so one night I blurted out that I'd read eighty-six. I said it before Uncle Cleveland and an

entire Baptist revival and God and—worst of all—before my own
mother, and it was a lie. My defense now is the same as it was
then: I just couldn't help it.

The worst part was, it didn't work. Both George and Eugene
topped me anyhow, with eighty-eight apiece. I wasn't a fast
learner, and it took me several years to understand how they were
able to do that.

It was after midnight and I was passing through Hempstead and I
noticed these two boys. They looked to be around fourteen years
old and they were standing outside a closed cafe.

Not bothering anything, just standing there with their hands
in their pockets. They were in my view maybe five seconds.

Only reason I remember them now, I wondered at the time if
they were doing what youngsters that age used to do long ago in
my old hometown—staying out late just to see how it felt.

I suppose all young people reach a point in their growing up
where they have this terrible hankering to see what the world is
like in the quiet hours when most everybody is asleep.

Forty years ago in that little town where I grew up, kids were
constantly on the watch for ways to keep from going home when
they ought to have. We felt an almost desperate need to experience
what we thought of as nightlife. Which just meant being out late.

An example was the strange time I stood with the preacher's
sons in the doorway of the courthouse until almost dawn. It was a
dumb thing to do.

We had been on a bus trip of some kind. In that little town,
four or five adults were forever gathering up a school bus load of
kids and hauling them somewhere. Like to a sporting event, or a
school or church function. We would sometimes go long distances
and get home really late. The later we got back, the more successful we considered the trip.

It's interesting to me to recall how those youngsters would get
home. I mean the bus didn't deliver them. It would disgorge the
whole gang at some central spot, such as the school or the church
or the courthouse square.

Some parents would come to pick up their kids at the prear-
ranged place, but most of us just walked home. Nothing ever happened to us. What could happen?

On some of those bus trips I used to pal around with the preacher's sons. It didn't hurt my standing to do that because those boys were pretty good athletes and therefore they were held in respect. In that town, nothing would gain a boy respect like having athletic ability. And this is still true today.

A pretty tight rein was kept on those boys at home and so it was a delicious experience for them to be out late, such as after a bus trip. We would walk home slow, and take the long way. But we couldn't stretch things too far because parents were kept informed as to when the bus should get back, and they knew when we ought to be home.

On this one trip I am thinking about, we were real eager about it because it was a long ride and we weren't expected to get back in town until about 5:00 A.M. That was unusual but not unheard of.

Anyway, something happened that we got home early, a little after midnight. You can see the opportunity that opened up. We were let off the bus on the courthouse square about half past twelve, and nobody at home expecting us until 5:30.

Why, we could roam about more than four hours. We hadn't ever been offered such a splendid chance.

The only trouble was, a blamed norther blew in about that time, one of the worst kind, just slightly wet and carrying more dust than moisture so it burned your eyes and stung your hide. It wasn't too wet to keep us from roaming around town but it sure did take the pleasure out of it.

Took me about half an hour of that to get enough, but the preacher's boys refused to go home. It was against their policy to go home when they didn't yet have to. They argued it might be a year before they had another chance to stay out till 5:30. Therefore it would be foolish to go home.

Finally I was able to see the sense in their position. We went back to the courthouse and took shelter in one of the entrances.

And there we stayed, leaning up against that locked courthouse door until almost 5:00 A.M., shivering some, not even talking, sometimes fighting to keep awake. Sure it was dumb, but it was also important.

If those two youngsters I saw at Hempstead were doing the same thing, they can comfort themselves that at least they had a pretty night to get it done.

Going through Hermann Park, I pulled over a few minutes and watched some young fellow flinging a Frisbee, and I thought about the time I almost made a million dollars before I was fourteen years old.

I guess it was in the summer of 1934. One afternoon a little bunch of us was going around the neighborhood, doing our proper duty. That is, we were digging into trash heaps in back alleys, sorting out all the good stuff.

Such as cigar boxes that weren't broken too bad and might be tacked back together. Also bottles that could be taken to a suitable place and lined up and chunked at. Or sometimes we'd find old funny papers we hadn't read.

Also we looked for binder twine. Binder twine was used for securing heavy packages that were mailed, and people would throw it away just as if it couldn't be used twice. We'd tie the pieces together and roll the twine into a ball and save it. We were always needing binder twine.

The best trash heaps were behind the houses of rich folks. By our rules, a family was rich if you found in their trash a baseball bat that was thrown away because it had a crack in it. We would take a cracked bat and put a couple of nails in it and wrap it good with tire tape and play with it all summer.

We had a good bit of territory to cover, working trash heaps that way.

We'd have to check behind the grocery store for apple crates. The thin planks on the sides of apple crates had to be saved because you could strip 'em with a pocketknife to make kite sticks.

Then we'd need to go by the feed store to see if they'd thrown away any tow sacks. Sometimes if they were holey the sacks would get pitched out and we'd get those and sew up the holes and rip out the seams and make seines, to catch minnows and crawdads for catfish bait.

The filling stations had to be checked for old tires and blown-out inner tubes. The hardware store had the best pasteboard boxes, the sturdiest I mean. The shoe shop had leather scraps.

What I am telling you is, we weren't just out messing around. We had stops to make and jobs to do.

But back to the million dollars I almost made. That afternoon in the alley, one of us picked up a coffee can lid and gave it a back-handed flip. It sailed a hundred feet or more, about waist high, and that pleased us. It went along so smooth and slow, like some kind of mysterious little flying machine, and it almost hovered before it settled gently into the dirt.

Right away we saw we had come across something worthwhile. So we dug around and found half a dozen more coffee can lids in the trash. We took them to the vacant lot where we played ball, and we spread out, and all afternoon we flung those lids back and forth, just the way the young folks do now with the Frisbees in the park.

This was a metal lid, not a plastic one. Coffee was sold in a can with a slotted key soldered on top. To open the can you yanked the key off and fitted it onto a tab and peeled away a strip of metal that sealed the coffee.

That summer, an exclusive little gang of us in my neighborhood became expert coffee can lid throwers. I could make a coffee can lid do just about anything those yellow-headed boys in the park make a Frisbee do.

I could make one skip. I learned how to throw one into a high wind at an attitude that caused it to go out there and stop and come back to me, all on the fly. I could catch one behind my back. Throw under my leg. All that stuff I see in the park now.

Where the million dollars comes in, I had a notion that coffee can lids, or something kin to them, could be manufactured as play pretties for boys on vacant lots, and that they might be sold for twenty-five or thirty cents apiece if you painted 'em real nice.

If I had followed through on that idea, I expect I'd have made all the money the Frisbee people have made, which I suppose is a million dollars if not more. The reason I didn't do it, everybody sort of laughed at the thought of manufacturing and trying to sell something that could be fished out of a trash heap in the alley.

Last time I returned to my old hometown, I went wandering around in the mesquite pastures out south of the city limits, and I ran across a pile of broken bricks and burnt planks. There was a familiar feel to the spot, and finally I recognized it as the place where Dude and I dug for the buried money that summer.

We tore the rotten flooring out of that old house, and lugged in picks and shovels and grubbing hoes, and we strained and sweated and dug up all the earth beneath one room, looking for the money.

I can't tell you where we got the story in the first place. I don't even remember all the details. Some old guy on the courthouse square probably told it to us. Told us about the two men that robbed a bank, in a nameless town on out west somewhere, and killed a teller, and headed east. And they were arrested in that old house, right out there in the mesquite pasture south of our very own town. And get this: *The money was never found.*

So what would a couple of bank robbers do with their loot while they were holed up in an old house, waiting for the hunt to cool off? Why, they would bury it, wouldn't they? Of course they would. And that's why we started the search.

We couldn't really have believed it. Not if we'd questioned ourselves. But we accepted the story because we wanted to, and because we hadn't ever dug for lost money, and because it was something we had to do. We were fourteen, maybe fifteen that summer.

I was surprised, seeing the spot again, how close to town the site is. When we carried the tools out there, it seemed like a ten-mile haul. The house was pretty rickety even then. It was burned down, a long time ago, probably by some rancher who was afraid it would fall on his cows.

Dude was the foreman on the job. He drew a diagram, and made X marks at places under the floor where we would dig, on a systematic basis. It was hard work, and hot. We spent a lot of time cooling out, in the sketchy shade that mesquites furnish. The first couple of days we'd talk of nothing but the money while we rested.

Then we got to knocking off in the hot part of the afternoon and swimming in a tank about half a mile away. We started bringing hooks and line, and fished some for perch and polliwog cats, and ended up swimming and fishing more than we dug.

Some days we'd go to the old house and wouldn't dig at all, but just sit around and look at the dirt we'd stirred.

I think what stopped the search altogether was the story we heard about the green walnuts. You could take gunny sacks full of walnuts, with the green hulls still on, and crush those nuts, and pull the sacks through a stock tank, and it would poison the fish and they'd come to the top and you could catch them with your bare hands. Well, naturally we were obligated to try that. Digging for money was important but there were other things that needed attention too.

Finding the walnuts wasn't any problem. But it took time to gather them because green nuts don't thrash so good, and carrying two big gunny sacks full of walnuts a couple miles across a mesquite pasture is hard work, and tires a person out, and doesn't leave him much energy to dig for buried money.

We never did poison any fish. We got waterlogged trying, though. And other things kept interfering. We flushed several water moccasins, and those had to be killed, and inspected. Then we saw an awful lot of big bullfrogs, and for two nights straight we came back to the tank and gigged a few, and slept late, and didn't have much time for the digging. Eventually the tools were needed at home and we had to bring them in, and that was the end of the search.

It's a bleak and lonely spot, there where we dug. I wonder if Dude ever thinks about it. I haven't seen him in twenty years. He is an engineer, for an oil company somewhere. I've lost his trail. But I'm sure that, the same as me, he isn't one bit sorry he shed so much sweat, digging for the buried money that summer.

Any time scarecrows come to mind, I think of the little city of Glen Rose, the county seat of Somervell County southwest of Fort Worth. Long ago my family spent about a year of the Great Depression at Glen Rose, living in a big old barny house outside town, eating red beans and cornbread in winter and blackeyed peas and tomatoes and watermelons in summer.

I walked to school that year along the banks of Paluxy Creek. We called it a river then, and it could sure act like a river when it got on a high rise. A little bunch of us always walked together and had delicious times.

I hated the school at Glen Rose because I was afraid of a teacher who kept a heavy wooden paddle leaning against her desk. But I loved the route to and from school, along that creek.

The Paluxy in those times was the best stream in creation for school kids to horse around on. I am thankful I got to know it.

It was full of great white rocks where we kept hooks hidden, with lines and corks and sinkers, and it wasn't anything to come home from school with a bucketful of bream. The Paluxy had cold springs bubbling out of solid rock banks. It had quiet deep pools overhung with elms and willows. It had rock-bottomed shallows excellent for getting the feet wet in early spring before the water was too cold for swimming.

In some places the rock bottom was slick as soap and we had this game—wade across the creek with your shoes in your hands, just to see if you could do it without slipping and sitting down and wetting your behind.

Where else could schoolboys on their way home step in dinosaur tracks? Where else could they tromp through cedar brakes and happen onto operating whiskey stills? Somervell County was famous for its moonshine booze.

Glen Rose had a lot of characters then, some of them not exactly scoutmasters or Sunday School teachers. Even from those, though, you learned valuable knowledge of deep burning interest. The town also had a supply of gentle and kindly adults who didn't seem very busy and paid attention to youngsters.

The man with the scarecrow, I want to call him Mr. Griffin. Maybe it was Griffith, something like that. He had this big garden along the road where two-thirds of the town's population passed every day, and he always had a fine scarecrow out in the middle of it.

Mr. Griffin—go ahead and call him Griffin—in the hot part of the day would sit on his front porch in a rocker. He wore fresh-ironed khakis with the shirt buttoned all the way to the top. He was a round person, as a general thing. He had pink hide and the smallest eyes, sunk deep into beds of grin-wrinkles. Then white socks, always, and black high-topped shoes with hooks at their tops.

Every two or three days in summer we would go by his house and check his scarecrow, because that thing changed now and then. Mr. Griffin evidently got a boot out of drawing attention to his scarecrow, and he worked at it.

One week the scarecrow would have on a straw hat and ragged overalls, and the next it would have its pants and hat changed, or it would acquire accessories. Like once it had on a baseball cap and an old catcher's mitt stuck on its hand. Another time it showed up as a woman, with a long checkered skirt and a sunbonnet. So it became almost the same as a person to us, and we counted it a huge coarse joke the day Mr. Griffin's scarecrow appeared in the garden without any pants.

What seems curious to me now is this: I can't remember Mr.

Griffin ever talking about whether his scarecrow scared any crows. My personal notion is that it didn't repel anything, but had the opposite effect and attracted human beings.

With the heat turned off at night, some of these mornings lately have been pretty chilly. I've been reminded of how it was to get up early long ago, when the custom was to let the fire die and raise the windows when you went to bed. When you waked up, the house was as cold as the outdoors.

Everybody had his own system of getting out of the quilts in a way that was the least uncomfortable. I used to marvel at my father's style of rising in winter. He was a springer-upper.

He would get what appeared to be almost a running start at it, and hit the hard cold floor three feet from the bed and begin throwing his clothes on in a regular fit of activity. So the very act of dressing was physical exercise that kept him from getting chilled.

He charged everything just that way—food, work, play, all of life.

A younger brother of his, who lived at a much slower pace, taught me his method of getting up on a cold morning and it fit me better than my father's system.

This uncle and I slept a good part of one winter out on a screened porch. Many mornings at getting-up time, the temperature would be below freezing.

He would begin by reaching out of the covers and putting on his hat. Next he would grab his shirt off the cane chair by the bed and he would put it on sitting up, with the lower part of himself still under the covers.

Then came his socks. The reason the socks were put on after the shirt, which seems out of turn, is that it's hard to pull on your pants without exposing your feet to the cold air. That was the aim of his system—to dress without letting cold air hit his bare hide anywhere.

He kept his socks inside the pillowcase, so they were fairly warm. (I later refined this plan by wearing the socks all night, and during especially cold spells, I still do it.)

He put on his pants by lifting the covers at the foot of the bed, poking his socked feet out, and sticking them into the legs of the britches.

So then he could roll the covers back and swing his legs off the bed and stick his feet into his shoes and he would be fully dressed by the time he hit the floor.

In the account of my uncle's rising and dressing you will notice there is no mention of taking off pajamas and putting on underwear. This is because he wore no pajamas. He slept in his shorts and undershirt. Or in a one-piece suit of underwear called BVDs. Or in long johns.

In my early times in West Texas I was not associated with any men who got out of bed and put on house slippers and a robe over pajamas. They were all underwear sleepers and they got up and pulled on their pants.

I expect, at the time I am thinking about, pajamas represented a luxury most men could do without. The same with robes. I am almost certain that my uncle, the one who taught me how to dress on a cold morning, did not own a robe of any kind.

So I grew up thinking that it was a mighty citified business, and maybe even sissified, for a man to mess around the house in pajamas and a robe. It seemed womanish.

The men I knew got fully dressed as quick as they got up because they had things to do outside.

Habits of this kind seem to get into a bloodline. I never have learned to use a robe the way my neighbors do. I see them come out all house-slippered and pajamaed and robed to pick up the paper and they look mighty proper.

I've got a couple or three robes hanging back in the closet somewhere but I've never worn them except in the hospital a time or two. Three robes in the closet should be very handy for these chilly fuel-shortage mornings, but they just don't fit into the system of getting up that I learned out on that screened porch.

Back in my old hometown they used to have what they called summer dances for the young folks. Maybe summer dances are still held in many towns. I hope so.

When the bunch of guys I grew up with got old enough to recognize that girls should be followed around instead of run from, we loved summer dances more than anything. An exception might have been the hay rides.

In our town in those times we had a little group of parents

that helped make our lives sweet and good. They weren't moneyed people but they had not been destroyed by the Depression as so many adults were.

What I mean is the men in this group had kept steady work, as we said, and were making two hundred dollars a month or more—so they had everything they needed and cash left over.

Most had country backgrounds, as the majority of people in our town did, so of course they were interested in doing things considered citified. Such as giving summer dances.

A figure I remember is, you could rent the roof garden of the hotel for twenty-five dollars. Then for five dollars you could get a juke box with all the best Tommy Dorsey and Glen Gray dance tunes. A man with a truck would deliver the juke box and stay there with it the whole evening to keep it working right. A nickelodeon, is what we called it.

The point is, twenty sets of parents could chip in less than three dollars apiece and throw a dandy summer dance, with a big bowl of punch and crepe paper decorations.

The only requirement for attendance that I remember was that you take a bath and dress up. All of us cooperated with a great willingness.

A boy who attended summer dances needed a white linen coat. Jacket, is what they're called now. We called them coats. To us, a jacket was what we now call a windbreaker.

You would get your white linen coat when you were a sophomore and wear it to everything nice that was held in the summer. You would wear it until you graduated from high school. This was why you saw so many guys aged eighteen in white coats with the sleeves coming to an end about halfway between the wrist and the elbow.

Even guys who never danced would dress up and come to these summer dances and stand around and talk and watch.

I liked the girls in our town a lot better in summer than in winter. They were at their best at a summer dance. Not much else was going on around town and they were happy to have an excuse to doll up and look pretty. So they glowed, radiated, beamed.

They were also more likely to be sincere and genuine. You take a real pretty girl in winter, she was always politicking about one thing or another. She wanted to be elected to this or that, so when she smiled at you you didn't know whether she liked you or just wanted your vote in the Class Favorite election. In summer, the signs given off by girls were less apt to be phony.

Another reward of the summer dance was that you got to meet new girls. Somebody always had a flock of cousins visiting from other towns. These had a special appeal to us, in the way that imported merchandise is always appealing to consumers.

The romances that bloomed at these affairs had outward appearances of being fierce and serious but they seldom lasted long. One summer an exception arose, and shocked us. A member of our bunch startled the entire community by hauling off and marrying one of the prettiest girls, who had a year to go in high school.

The effect of that was extraordinary. I personally felt resentment, and then a deep sadness. It was as if I'd lost two friends, that from then forward they would be different people, and never come to the summer dances again.

It was early afternoon of a bright fall day, and I was drifting around Glen Rose, hunting for places I could remember from the year I spent in that town long ago. It was 1930, I think, and part of '31.

Something about a little old frame building on the courthouse square tugged at me, as if I'd been in it. It's a tailor shop, and has the best old-timey look. Two four-paned front windows and the door open so you could look in from the street and see the shop's one light bulb hanging from the ceiling.

Under the bulb, working at the press, was a white-haired gent wearing roomy dark pants and a shirt to match his hair. And two-toned tennis shoes. When I went to the door and he turned to look at me, I knew him.

I don't mean I could call his name. But I knew him in the vague and teasing way that tells you, when you see somebody from deep in your past, that you were once around him, listened to him talk, watched him do things.

"My name's Deason," he said, and spelled it. "Soda Deason."

I asked him if he ever played baseball at the old field over the other side of the Paluxy, there across the road from where my Uncle Ray Oxford lived; there where my Cousin George Oxford and I carried water for the team; and got paid by Rabbit Darnaby, who played center field, with the gate receipts in the great hip pocket of his uniform and you could hear the money jingling when he ran to first base.

Deason grinned and said yes, he played there, and umpired some when he got so he couldn't make the lineup.

So that was where I used to see Soda Deason, and hear the name. Such a good name, with that unforgettable quality to it.

We visited a while. He told me about Rabbit Darnaby, about Rabbit bringing a big old catfish up out of the Paluxy that day, claiming it got struck by lightning. And folks gathered and crowded around, to see the only catfish in creation that was ever killed by lightning.

Then Deason talked about Rabbit's brother Lefty, who was a good ball player, and played a while pro in the minors, and Rabbit yearned to do the same. So every now and then he'd go to Abilene for a try-out in the West Texas—New Mexico League. In a few days here he'd come back home, and they'd ask him, "What happened?" And he'd say, "I never was able to find the ball park."

When I was leaving, Deason raised a hand sort of west and said, "Used to be some Hales lived out here above town." I said that must have been us, and went to look for the house.

Mrs. Bill Woodard lives in it now. She understood why I'd come and let me look around. For a good while I wasn't sure it was the right place. Been changed a lot. Been forty-five years since I saw it. I told Mrs. Woodard if I could find two certain things that ought to be in her yard, I'd know it was the house we used to live in.

First I went round to the backyard and looked in the grass and there, almost covered by St. Augustine, was a neat little concrete cap—the plug they put in the well where that wobbly old pitcher pump stood.

That house was in the country when I knew it. People would ask if we had running water and we'd say sure, it'll run out of that pump out back if you jack the handle four five times.

The other sign was a big cedar tree by the corner of the kitchen. I nailed a birdhouse in that cedar one time, and some wrens built in it, and raised. The tree is gone but I found the stump. So it's the right house.

I loved living in Glen Rose but I expect that old house, to my folks, represented a dark chapter of the Depression when there wasn't any money. For them, desperate times. Old place looks nice now. All painted and kept, with flowers and hanging baskets. That's good.

Last night after I slept a while in Amarillo, I drove on up across the Canadian River to Dalhart, where my Aunt Ruth Campbell lives in a retirement home.

She is my father's baby sister. She is ninety years old.

My father had four brothers and three sisters. Aunt Ruth Campbell is the youngest of those eight people, and the only one still living.

We needed to talk. And I needed to hear her laugh again. Aunt Ruth Campbell's laugh is a most special sound. It expresses a great deal more to me than a laugh ordinarily does.

I remember getting encouragement from that laugh, and hope. To me it said, "Times may be tough, but don't worry. We are here together, and we are all right, and there are things to enjoy and laugh about."

When I walked into the home at Dalhart, before I even saw her I heard that laugh, pealing along the hall to meet me. It was just as musical and beautiful as it ever was.

That sound came to me, in my early times, from so many places. From the front porch of a tenant farmhouse. From out of the pear orchard. From the cow lot. From the garden. From the end of a dining table draped in oilcloth. It is one of my favorite of all sounds.

Remember how all the animals loved her?

The wildest little pullet on the place would come pecking up and eat out of her hands. Those big fat Rhode Island Red hens would sing with her. Sure, sing *with* her.

Those old biddies would stand flatfooted in the chicken yard and stretch their necks and just s-i-i-i-n-g, and Aunt Ruth would be there among them, singing along, and sounding exactly the same way they did.

She'd wear that gray cat around her neck. Remember that cat?

She'd pick it up and baby-talk it and drape it around her neck before she went out to feed the chickens or gather the eggs. She'd put it on the way you'd wear a scarf, and that dern cat would lie up there, loose as a pound of liver, and ride as long as she'd let it.

You'd look out toward the barn and yonder would go Aunt Ruth, wearing that cat.

Did you ever have a relative you were especially glad to be kin to, and you didn't fully understand why? It took me forty years to understand why all of us felt that way about Aunt Ruth Campbell.

It was because she had class.

Living out there on that poor old farm. Punching sheets in a washpot with a bleached broomstick. Picking peas. Sweeping the front yard. Milking four old cows twice a day. Putting up peaches. And yet showing class.

Now that's a trick, to go out and feed chickens and wear a cat around your neck and still look classy.

One of the first to recognize this was Uncle John Campbell. He came out of Arkansas and saw her and married her. He was twenty years older than Aunt Ruth. I don't believe he ever got over the wonder of having her for a wife.

He'd be in that little old kitchen with her early in the morning. Sitting up next to the wood cookstove, waiting on daylight. Aunt Ruth moving around in there stirring up biscuits. He'd look at her and then he'd turn to you and shake his head and grin and he'd say, "Ain't she a purty thing?"

You ought to have seen her crank a Model T. Then dart around the front fender and slide over the top of that false front door on the driver's side and slip under the steering wheel, and all so smooth. Just smooth as milk.

And shoot? She could outshoot most of the men with that .22 target gun, and whip 'em at forty-two if they didn't watch out.

From Amarillo north to Dumas is fifty miles. Then it's another forty miles to where Aunt Ruth lives. So that makes 819 miles from my front door in Houston to hers in Dalhart.

But it was worth the trip just to hear her laugh again. I wish you could hear her laugh.

On warm summer nights like we're having now, I think of how my Uncle Billy Crockett would talk after he'd been sick so much and his mind was tired.

He was old as mountains then, and had lost his place as the

chief storyteller of the family. But he never realized he'd lost it. He would sit on the porch at night and try to spin his tales when they wouldn't quite spin. Often as not he would never get to the end of one, or much past the introduction, before he would wander off down some dim, near-forgotten path and off the main trail.

He'd clear his little skinny throat, and make his other preparatory noises, and he'd say, "Well, there's this about a buzzard."

Just as if everybody on the porch had been in a discussion about buzzards, and he had sat and let the others have their say, and now here he'd come to give the final word, and sum up. When the fact was, nobody present was on the subject of buzzards.

"The average person," he'd say, squeaky and high, "believes a buzzard goes around doing good, cleaning up the country and the roads, eating just what's died. Well, I've seen buzzards twenty-five and thirty in a bunch working around a cow having a calf, pecking the calf to death right where it hit the ground. A buzzard can be a vicious bird.

"The worst thing I ever saw buzzards do, I was working for the Cole Brothers out there. We were marking and branding on the Nance. Now the Nance . . ."

By "out there" he would mean on farther west where the big ranches were. He'd cowboyed on several of them when he was young. Went out there to homestead a place, and worked on ranches to get by. Lot of homesteaders would do that.

The Nance, that would be the name of a pasture, and he would stop to explain about that. And about the Murphy, and the Fitzhugh, and the West Buffalo, how they were pastures on one of those big ranches and named for families that once worked them, or for the kind of grass that grew on them.

No one on the porch was interested in hearing about the worst thing he ever saw a buzzard do, and it was good they weren't, because he would never get to it.

He would get off on cowboy stories, and tell about a fellow they called Curly and how he could drink a pint of whiskey without ever taking the chew of tobacco out of his jaw.

He would tell about another they called Slim that was double-jointed and could bend his elbow "backwards as quick as he could frontwards" and once on a bet he ate twenty-four Mexican peppers without taking a swallow of water.

His own mention of peppers would lead him off on a cure he knew for nest-robbing dogs that would slip in the henhouse and eat all the eggs. "Suck-egg dogs," he called them, with the greatest contempt, and the way you cured them, you took an egg out of the nest and made a little hole in one end. You drained out the yolk and the white and refilled the shell with hot sauce made out of Mexican chilies.

Then you put the eggs back in the nest and sat and waited for the dog to make another raid. When he did, and got ahold of that hot egg, he would do a lot of thinking before he ever again went anywhere close to a henhouse.

But talking about dogs (Uncle Billy would say) put him in mind of a fellow named Simpson, he thought it was, that raised coon hounds over in back of the Gibson place, and had all those big old boys that rode mules to school.

Talk about your cussing, that Simpson could cuss holes in the side of a house.

"Well, now wait," Uncle Billy would stop himself, and back up. "I'm thinking about the wrong man. Simpson never raised dogs. He had the mill at Gypsy Camp. They call it Turner Ferry now but when I was a boy they called it Gypsy Camp, on account of the Gypsies that camped there, and stole the youngest Turner girl that time."

Occasionally he would grab your attention, mentioning the theft of a child, or another interesting subject that made you want to hear more. But you wouldn't hear it because the idea of a child being stolen would get him onto "that skinny boy, with the big ears—what was his name?—that stole half a box of chalk at Liberty Hill School and the teacher called him a thief and he whipped the teacher right there in school, in front of all six grades. You talk about a fighter.

"But if you want fighters, the worst we ever had around here about fighting were those Wilson girls, those two oldest ones. Wasn't a man in this country could whip them both at once. One time I saw . . ."

One of the women on the porch would finally have to interrupt him. "Uncle Billy? Uncle Billy! Now you better come on to bed. You're gonna talk yourself down."

He would sit a minute, I suppose to get accustomed to his

own silence. Then he would let the women take his arms and help him inside.

Some day, I am hoping we will run across a bundle of my father's letters. They may be under a stack of clippings in a cardboard box, or stuck down in somebody's cedar chest. Or hidden away in the back of an old dresser drawer.

There's no way they could have been pitched into the trash, unless it was by accident. I still think we will find them.

They are all written on hotel stationery, from places like Lubbock and Wichita Falls. From Fort Stockton. Pampa. Monahans. Midland. Alpine. Amarillo. Borger. Big Spring. Mason. Pearsall.

Those were his last years of traveling and selling, just before the Great War grounded him forever with its tire and gasoline shortages.

He would write us how much gasoline cost at Pyote. What he paid for chicken and dumplings at McCamey, and whether they were any good. He would write us how the hotel clerk in Fredericksburg couldn't speak English. Things like that, so you could be with him wherever he was.

Once he wrote us from San Marcos and said the river was so clear there you could look straight down twelve feet and see catfish a yard long feeding on the bottom. I told about that at school.

I told a lot of things he wrote us. I told how he climbed the Caprock in a '27 Chevy without shifting into second gear. I hadn't seen the Caprock then and I pictured it as a steep mountain. I could see him gunning up the side of it, jumping ravines, raising dust clouds, scattering mountain goats.

When I finally saw the edge of the Caprock I was disappointed. Why, it had a two-lane paved road going up it.

One time he wrote a Serious Letter. To me personally. On my birthday, I think.

It was long. Oh, I mean ten or twelve pages of those skinny sheets of stationery from the Commercial Hotel in Lubbock. Written in green ink, in that graceful, even script of his. It was about Life. About what was Important, and what was Not Important.

I didn't much like that one. It missed me. Disappointed me. I didn't care anything then about Life. When he was in Lubbock he generally wrote about wrestling matches he went to. Or how the

Lubbock Hubbers came out against Albuquerque in a West Texas–
New Mexico League baseball game. So I can't quote you a line out
of the Serious Letter. The only one I ever got from him.

I would give so much, now, to have that letter.

He would write us about his little triumphs. To him they were
so big. And to us, as well. Triumphs like making a tough sale.

He would go into a store and the man who owned it would
meet him all sour-faced at the door and say, "Business is off and I
don't want to buy anything."

"That's all right," my father would say. "I didn't come to sell
you anything. Just came to visit. Did you have your operation
yet?"

He would then write an account of how that fellow, two
hours later, had given him an order for such-and-such an amount.
And all due to my father remembering from last October that the
fellow was talking about getting his gall bladder out.

Other times he would write about people he just got to know,
and cared about, and they didn't have anything to do with business.

They'd be families like the Claymores, lived out west of
Christoval there, and they had that boy that was sick all the time.
But they worked so hard on that old place, and put that younger
girl through school, and now they were all going into San Angelo
on the sixth of June to see her graduate.

I know we'll find the letters, somewhere.

Did you ever notice how fond people are of talking about first
times?

Not many days pass that you won't hear somebody talking
about the first raw oyster they ever ate. Or the first time they ever
saw television. Or rode in an airplane. Or drove a car.

Also *only* times. Things that happen to most people only
once. Getting married. Getting arrested. Getting snake-bit. Winning a lottery.

The atmosphere stays loaded with sentences that begin, "I remember the first time I . . ."

When I went back to the old hometown for the last high
school reunion, I heard a bunch of old birds in my class talking
about the first time they ever kissed a girl.

I am convinced no man ever forgets the first girl he ever

kissed, and most seem willing to give the details if anybody will listen.

Of course I am not talking about kissing sisters and cousins and the like. I mean a romantic kind of a kiss. One of my class-mates at that reunion confessed to us that the first girl he ever kissed was then present, and he pointed her out over at the punch bowl. She is the woman he is married to right now.

I'm not sure I would make that admission. It seems too like a weak record, but then we have no way of knowing whether he kissed other girls, before he married the first one. He didn't go into that.

She wasn't at that reunion but I remember so well the first girl I ever kissed. I could spell her name right, too. I won't do it here, though, because I doubt she would appreciate being advertised as a principal in that event.

She is fifty-five now. I saw her last at a funeral. After the ser-vice—at the curiously lighthearted gatherings that follow burials in country towns—I confessed to her she was the first.

She said she remembered the occasion and suspected where she stood in the order. And wondered, at the time, if I would ever attempt it again on any target. She was judging by the way I ran so fast, just afterward, and cleared three strands of barbed wire in the moonlight.

The first car I ever drove wasn't quite that big a thrill, but almost. It was a Willys Knight. I can't give you the model year. Early '30s, I guess. A hard car to drive because it had a shot clutch. All my father's cars were like that because he was a clutch rider. A common weakness among people who learned to drive in Model T's.

My first raw oyster was right here in Houston when I was twenty-six years old and that's a fact. Where I came from in West Texas an entire religion was built on the belief that you oughtn't to eat anything raw if it pretended to be meat. That included beef, pork, mutton, goat, fish, fowl, or anything that lived in a shell.

The custom out there was to cook meat until it no longer had any taste, and you could pick it up and break it with your fingers like soda crackers. So a raw oyster for me was a pretty high adventure.

My first airplane ride was over the Midwestern cornfields

near Wayne, Nebraska, in 1943, in a Piper Cub. I was supposed to be learning how to fly that machine. I never did, really, because it was such an amazement to me to be separated from the earth that way, after I had been bound to it so long. I wasn't able to hear what they were saying to me. Man, look at the sights down there. Yonder's a half-ton steer and he's not any bigger than a prairie dog. They ought to give you time to look, before they start trying to show you how to drive.

But that little Cub gave me what I suppose was the biggest thrill of my time. It came when they showed me how to practice a stall. You cut the power and put the nose up and then—that airplane fell. And fell. And fell. And fell. Until you could look up and see your heart and liver and lungs and other principal parts hanging in the clouds above.

It fell a hundred feet, I guess, instead of thousands. But since then, I have been through a war, and through thirty years of the newspaper business, and nothing has been as thrilling as that first stall in a Piper Cub.

Well, except for kissing that girl, in 1937.

-⟨ VI ⟩-

Cornbread, Beans, and Banana Pudding

Sometimes you will hear one of these old Texas parties with a lot of miles on him refer to a meal as "cornbread and beans." Doesn't make any difference whether it's steak, or chicken, or what, still he'll call it "cornbread and beans."

The reason for that is back in lean times a lot of those old gents made many a full meal out of beans and cornbread. Used to be a joke about what a balanced meal is—a spoonful of beans in the right hand, and a hunk of yellow cornbread in the left.

In those lean times they talk about, I used to travel in summer with my father when school was out and he was chugging around West Texas in an old wired-up Chevy. He was a traveling salesman and sold everything from magazine subscriptions to adding machines.

One night we stayed and ate supper with a couple out in the country, up close to Wichita Falls somewhere. That farm was a desperate place and it is a mystery to me yet why my father wanted to stay there.

But he was that way about staying with strangers. He would go up to an isolated country house that hadn't had a visitor, I don't expect, in weeks and weeks. He would sit on the porch, and visit, and tell jokes, and the people would end up saying, "Why don't yawl just spend the night?" He would say, "Why, we don't mind if we do." And we would stay.

Well, cornbread and beans is what we had for supper at the farm close to Wichita Falls that time. The woman put this big bowl of pinto beans in the middle of the table and brought out a platter of thick, hot, yellow cornbread and that was it.

She didn't make any mention of the lack of variety, she just set it out and said for us to eat and not hold back because she had another skillet of cornbread in the stove.

I was sitting directly across from the man. I didn't like to look at him but I couldn't help it. He was a big round-chested fellow with coarse hair all over his shoulders and his back. You could see it because the weather was hot and he ate in his suspender overalls without a shirt.

He had massive jaws, and a terrible beard. Not a cultivated set of whiskers but a beard he'd produced because he hadn't shaved in a week, and it had things caught in it here and there. Lint, I guess, or cobwebs, I don't know.

He had teeth on only one side. It's true, I can see his mouth yet, just exactly. When he opened up to spoon in beans it was plain he had a full lineup of teeth on the right side but none at all on the left, the first arrangement like that I've seen—and the last.

People in the country used to do that, go along all their lives without dental care, and live to be seventy-five and never once open their mouths in front of a dentist.

My father was a neat dresser, always, and at that farmhouse he came to the table with his white shirt buttoned at the collar and a necktie on and he sure struck a contrast, up against that old bird in the overalls. How strange, I thought, that we should be here in this place, eating beans with these people.

But my father seemed to enjoy it. He would brag on the cornbread until he'd have that farm woman snickering and chewing on her sleeve, and the man would say, "Well, it's just cornbread."

In those times they compensated for the lack of variety by eating a great lot of what they had. I didn't count how many plates of beans that old farmer ate and it's just as well because you'd have thought I was lying about it.

The way he'd do, he'd flood his plate with beans and a lot of the likker they swam in, and then he'd crumble cornbread all over the top, and mash everything into a sort of paste. Then he'd switch to a spoon to shovel with. Plate after plate, of mashed beans and cornbread that way.

There was a hunk of salt pork in the beans but it was never touched. My father used to have a story I wish I remembered, about salt pork in the pinto beans and how you could tell what

kind of fix a family was in by whether they ate the meat or saved it to cook with tomorrow's pot of beans.

When the beans were about gone, we changed over to syrup. It was gloomy-looking syrup, I remember that, dark and suspicious, served in the tin bucket it was poured into at the mill.

The man ate syrup with cornbread exactly the same way he ate beans, except in reverse—cornbread on the plate first, and then syrup spooned over.

Now that was not the first meal I'd ever made out of cornbread and beans, and it wasn't the last, but it was one I remember because of sitting across from that grizzly bear of a man and watching him.

Something to be said for cornbread and beans is that it is hard to fix them in such a way that they are inedible. Unless they are served half-cooked and rock hard, beans make at least reasonable fare. There is good cornbread and bad, but the worst I remember eating was not what I'd call vicious.

Did you ever go to somebody's house to eat, and have a special dish fixed in your honor, and it was bad? Oh, now that's torture.

The fellow at the head of the table passes you a plate of some kind of casserole, and he says, "Here, this is Mildred's specialty. I made her fix it just for you. Man, it's something."

And you take a bite, and it's just *dreadful*. There's an ingredient, or a combination of ingredients, that creates upheavals and outrages in you.

Now then, tell me how you're gonna handle that. There's not *any way* to handle it.

Before I'd suffer that kind of torment I'd ten times rather eat cornbread and beans again in that farmhouse near Wichita Falls.

Gene Lindquist at Webster has sent me a recipe for brains and eggs and it sure made me hungry to read it.

Been a mighty long time since I tied into a bait of eggs scrambled in calf brains. Back when I was wearing overalls way out in West Texas, in the dim and misty past, brains and eggs showed up on our table about once a month and the dish was considered a special treat.

We always ate it for supper. I hear people speak of brains and eggs now as a breakfast proposition but in my early times calf brains were too special to eat for breakfast.

A lot of citizens will wrinkle up their faces and announce that calf brains are not fit to eat, but that is just a matter of raising. I found out that brains were really delicious one night when I was extra hungry and they were the only thing on the table. That circumstance will cause a consumer to develop a taste for a wide variety of grub that doesn't seem appealing on first acquaintance. I have seen a tomcat learn to like cornbread under such conditions.

Seen children cultivate a liking for clabber that way, too.

In the early years of this column we conducted a sort of horseback survey of the customers to establish the public notion of what the most rural food in Texas is. We finally decided it was clabber.

It is now getting harder and harder to find a person in Houston who will admit to eating clabber, ever, and liking it. I have known guys who had such rural beginnings they'd confess they used to go a week at a time without anything for breakfast but turnip greens left over from the night before. Yet you couldn't get them to say they'd ever eaten clabber.

I have conducted experiments on clabber. I have gone into polite places, where people were sitting around crooking their little fingers and balancing cups and saucers on their knees and talking about operas, and I have made mention in such places of country grub like poke salad, and chitterlings, and pigs' feet, and even possum pie. But nothing will create a stonier silence than saying I once ate clabber practically every day, dipping it out of a crock with a teacup, and it was good.

Why this is true about clabber I do not know, but it is.

I think the greatest curiosity about food is that what's considered by some to be inedible is so often valued by others as a delicacy.

Take a raw oyster. In that dry West Texas country where I started out, an uncooked oyster to us was just what it appeared to be—not fit to eat. First time I saw anybody down one raw I classed him a savage who probably wouldn't mind eating off the same plate with dogs. My idea about oysters was that one ought to be fried to within an ounce of its life, and that it needed things poured all over it, so it didn't taste like anything at all except ketchup and greasy cornmeal.

Well, I promise you I have changed. I can now down as many oysters raw as a Cajun wrestler.

But out there in West Texas, a lot of my relatives still consider that an oyster needs the same preparation as a pound of liver before it's fit to eat. They'll sit and watch me gulp the things raw and shake their heads, and make mumbling sounds.

You know something that astonished me when I came to the coast country? That there were Houstonians who would drive all the way to Lafayette, Louisiana, to eat crawfish.

Crawdads! Oh, sure, I had eaten crawfish. As a sort of adventure we used to catch them out of stock tanks, and fry their tails in a skillet, and it was sporty eating. And not too bad, if you didn't mind the taste of mud. That's how crawfish tasted to me. Mainly like mud.

But that was before I went to Breaux Bridge over there in the Bayou Country and found out what crawfish are *supposed* to taste like. I would leave right now, to go there for crawfish bisque. Or etouffé. Or crawfish pie.

You know the best-tasting vegetable I've eaten lately? It was a dish of Brussels sprouts.

When I was growing up on homegrown produce, the word about Brussels sprouts had not reached our part of the country yet. As far as I know it had not reached there by the time I left home. I expect if my father heard me say I had eaten Brussels sprouts and liked them, he would consider I had abandoned the faith, and violated my allegiance to black-eyed peas and pinto beans.

On a night like this, when the air was still but snappy and the fire felt good, what we would do is eat.

The evening meal would begin at sundown and it wouldn't stop until time for bed. We would eat for four hours without stopping.

I am amazed, looking back now, that the entire family wasn't pig fat, but it wasn't. Not a one of us was fat. Most of us were so skinny we wouldn't throw a shadow at 5:00 P.M. Even those who were considered extra healthy, which were the ones nearest to fat, weren't anything but a trifle chubby.

Despite that we ate so long, every night.

Sweet stuff, too, and oily stuff, and starchy stuff. I can remember eating enough peanuts between supper and bedtime to put weight on a yearling bull. But it didn't put any on me.

It does now, though. The reason I am thinking of all this late-evening eating, I am sitting here stuffing myself with popcorn. I have had about a quart of it now and I've got room left. I expect I'll put down another pint, which will make the bathroom scale soar in the morning.

Tell me why it was, that in those early times people could eat so much and stay thin. Because they were more active? Worked harder? Maybe so.

On the farm, as soon as we got up from the supper table we went to the fireplace and began eating again. We would go to the crib and get a few ears of popcorn and shell them and pop the corn in a wire popper with a long handle.

In our bunch, popping corn at the fireplace was a man's job. The men never prepared food in the kitchen but at the fireplace they popped corn and took pride in shaking the popper in just such a way that all the kernels popped.

Sometimes we made popcorn balls, with syrup. Maybe honey if we had it, but mostly syrup, to make the corn kernels stick together. We never bought sweet stuff in town, but we bought the *makings* for sweet stuff.

Like cocoa, to make hot chocolate. Except I never heard it called hot chocolate until I went to town. We called it cocoa, a steaming cup of milk with cocoa cooked into it lightly in a stew pan.

At special times, like Christmas, maybe you would have a marshmallow to put in the cocoa. Make it creamier.

The girls would make fudge. I loved the house when the girls made fudge. I loved seeing them put a great hunk of Jersey butter into the candy pot and stir, and those yellowish streaks would blend with the chocolate and the aroma would make you grin. You couldn't keep from grinning.

Remember the way they'd talk about how to tell when the fudge was ready to come off the fire? It was tricky. It had to do with the sheen on the candy, the way the light from the lamp struck it. Boys didn't learn that. Girls did, the same as they learned how to sew and play jacks and hopscotch.

Then when they took the fudge off the stove, they stirred it forever. For half an hour or more, because if they didn't it wouldn't set up, as they said. I never understood that, why you would have to stir anything so long after it was already cooked.

When the fudge was ready to eat, we ate it. I mean we ate it all. Nothing was left over.

The making of after-supper treats was a fairly dependable indicator of economic times in a country household.

If you had fudge, things were pretty good. Because the cocoa was a sort of luxury and when cash was short you didn't find cocoa in the pantry. It was something you could do without.

When finances were limping along in the middle range, not real good but not too bad, there'd be sugar for making sweets but no cocoa for fudge. That's when the girls would make what they called buttermilk candy. It was all right but it wasn't a hint as good as fudge.

When things were *really* tough, that was when the girls made syrup candy. That meant even sugar was short and couldn't be used for foolishness, so they opened a bucket of syrup and made candy out of that.

Funny thing was, we always had plenty of nuts. Like pecans. Even in a short pecan crop year, if you wanted pecans all you had to do was crack and shell 'em, all you wanted.

Which is a little strange, seeing how much they cost now. Hoo boy. Not long ago I picked up a package of shelled pecans and when I got to the checkout stand in the supermarket I thought I had bought a dressed steer.

Peanuts, the same way. In our country we used peanuts to have fights with, the way we chunked chinaberries at each other. Every little old shirttail kid in the county went around with two overall pockets full of peanuts. What a kid like that used to carry in his pants pocket, shelled and salted and jarred, would sell now for $3.95.

Then dried fruit. I swear I don't know what's happened to make dried fruit so goldanged high-priced. Prunes, say. Why, prunes used to be poor folks' food. And dried apples, and apricots. We'd eat dried apricots after supper along with popcorn and parched peanuts and thought it was common.

And raisins? Other day I heard a mother fussing at a little child because he wouldn't eat the raisins he was supposed to get.

Listen, he's living in a strange time and doesn't know it. If he'd been born in 1920 he'd fight a kid twice his size for a handful of raisins.

Then graham crackers. You ever eat graham crackers now? One time in the deeps of Depression times we had some neighbors who were rich. The reason I knew they were, after supper you could go to their house and they'd be sitting around eating graham crackers and peanut butter.

They did the same as we did. They ate supper and then they continued eating until bedtime. Difference between them and us was that we ate popcorn and they had those graham crackers.

It's 11:30 A.M., so I am half an hour early for lunch on the Nash Ranch in Brazoria County. Of course it is called dinner here, in the country fashion. The evening meal is supper.

I have come, on invitation, to eat with the cowboys, see what Texas ranch fare is like now on an ordinary workday. The invitation was issued by Aunt Kate Hudgins, who is the cook and the high boss of the kitchen.

The custom is to drive around to the back of the big two-story ranch house, because no one lives in the house and a knock on the front door would never be heard. Aunt Kate will always be way back in the kitchen at 11:30.

The car is met by Jim Wilkes, a white-haired cowboy who has worked on the ranch most of his life. He meets all cars that come through the front gate, and greets visitors, and tells them the dogs won't bite but they will want to come up and smell. So I stand a while, and get smelled. Some of the dogs look as if they had rather I hadn't come.

Aunt Kate lets me in the back door. A long table is set in a plain plank-walled room off the kitchen. Go on in the house, she says, and sign the guest book in the living room. She is dishing up banana pudding into small bowls.

I sign the book, which has this quotation above the page in Old English letters: "Please thee to enter. Phyllis shall purvey some cooling draught to wash the dust away."

Aunt Kate—yes, she says it is all right to call her Aunt Kate— purveys a warming draught, not a cooling one. Coffee, in a big white cup, strong and black.

There are two cookstoves in the bright kitchen. I stand in the door and watch Aunt Kate pour a big pot of creamed-style corn into a serving bowl. "I've got to see whether my boys have come in yet," she says, and goes into the front bedroom to look out the window.

Sometimes she cooks for fifteen or twenty ranch hands, in busy seasons. But not today. She'll have only five. This is the slow time for ranch work.

This ranch was established by W. R. Nash, back in that other century. He had one daughter and no sons. Kitty Nash Groce was the daughter. She has been gone for years, but her personality is on this house. It was her home for so long. Around here she is called Miss Kitty, and spoken of as if she is still living. She had no children.

The Nash Ranch is administered by Baldwin Young, Miss Kitty's cousin. He and his wife come to the ranch frequently but they are not here today.

D. M. "Shorty" Kleine comes in the back door. He is the foreman. A husky, polite man. He has a permanent mark slanting across his forehead from all his years of wearing his hat at an angle that way. A lot of cowboys have that mark.

Aunt Kate is putting the bowls of banana pudding on the table first. It goes in the plates, just as if the cowboys will eat dessert before anything else.

Kleine and I stand by the table and wait for noon. He talks about work on the ranch. "We've had a bad January," he says, meaning the weather. Wet cold is so hard on cattle. The work now consists mostly of "hauling hay and grinding feed." And looking for a dry place to put it out.

Aunt Kate is carrying big bowls to the table now. The table is on a sort of enclosed back porch. Really austere. A Cardui calendar. Two towel racks. And what used to be a wash bench, I bet.

A wire snakes through a window and has a harness ring on the end of it. A bell pull. "Ring the bell," Aunt Kate says to Kleine. "You're not doing anything. Make yourself useful."

Kleine yanks on the ring and the old-fashioned dinner bell peals and presently here come the other four men who will eat. Jim Wilkes is one. Then Marvin Risinger. Kenneth Shaw. Tony Whatley. They are all quiet and polite.

Everybody has an assigned place. The foreman at the far end. As a guest I get a chair on the other end. The cowboys eat on benches along either side.

When everybody is seated, the little ritual begins. You pick the banana pudding up and set it aside, and bowls begin passing, going both ways. There is little conversation.

We have the corn, mashed potatoes, pinto beans, and a great bowl of smothered steak. It is meat raised here on the ranch. Everything is well seasoned and there is enough for fifteen men. There is iced tea in glasses that hold almost a quart. Hot biscuits and butter. Pickles and onions.

Jim Wilkes wants coffee instead of tea. Aunt Kate forgets his coffee for a long time. But he does not, I notice, ask her for it. Finally she remembers.

"She has rules," Kleine says, and grins. "One, you sit where she puts you, and you sit there every meal, in the same place. Two, you come to the table clean. (Clean as the morning's work permits, at least.) And you come dressed. You don't come without a shirt on. Then, if you want anything that's not on the table, just forget it, and eat without it."

I ask, what if she served a meal without meat? Wouldn't anybody ask where the meat was? Kleine says no.

The cowboys grin while Kleine tells about the two young men who worked on the ranch temporarily during hay season. They came to the table without shirts and with hay in their long hair and Aunt Kate chased them out the back door with a broom.

Aunt Kate does not eat with the hands. She stays in the kitchen. She has been cooking on this ranch since 1961. She left once and came back. Around West Columbia and East Columbia she is remembered as a cafe cook. Worked in a lot of cafes. She is a square-faced woman with sharp features. Despite her solid white hair, she moves in that smooth and efficient way that good waitresses and nurses move.

The custom is, when you get all you want, you pick the banana pudding up, where it has waited throughout the meal, and set it in your dirty plate and eat it. That saves Aunt Kate the trouble of stacking dishes when she cleans up.

When the men leave I hang around and visit with Aunt Kate.

"The way they got to calling me Aunt Kate, I worked in cafes, and I had all these nieces and nephews who'd come in. You can't kick a dog around West Columbia or East Columbia without you're kicking a niece or a nephew of mine. Well, they'd come in and call me Aunt Kate, and so everybody got to doing it."

She lives in East Columbia and drives fourteen miles to the big white house every morning. She plans her menus while she drives. Says she'd just as soon cook for twenty-five men as for five, that it's no more trouble. How does she know how much to prepare?

"I just think about what I'd eat, and then fix more, for a working man." Experience, is the way she does it. She started working at a railroad boarding house when she was fourteen. She's got to be up in her seventies now.

She talks about getting along with the cowboys. "We pick at each other but it doesn't mean anything. If they're cross and contrary, I don't pay them any attention and they do the same to me.

"But I give 'em plenty to eat. I give 'em a meat and three vegetables every day, and I tell 'em if they don't want potatoes they can eat beans. I'm not running a short-order house here."

It's time for me to move on. Aunt Kate is sweeping, polishing. She says it's not in her contract but she dusts the house, keeps it straight.

"I'm the only help they've got here," she says. "When I retire, and get where I can't work, I tell 'em I'm gonna get me a maid. Well, God pity her, because she's sure gonna have to jump."

On the way out I pass Kleine and the cowboys, and they have got a load of hay stuck in a flooded ditch. And it's turning colder. I can see that they won't have any trouble, this afternoon, burning up a meat and three vegetables and hot biscuits and butter and banana pudding.

Every year about this time I get a mysterious sort of emptiness inside me that nothing I eat will fill up. It may take me four or five days to recognize what the emptiness is crying out for.

Watermelon, is what it is.

I wasn't able to recognize the hankering this year until I visited a supermarket. I was moseying along among the produce, gasping at the price of first one thing and then another, when I came across a display of ready-cut watermelon.

You've seen that, I know. It's a fairly recent wrinkle in grocery merchandising. They cut a watermelon into halves or quarters and cover it with a plastic wrapping and sell it by the pound.

It's high-priced that way but I don't mind it. Because it won't take but about a fourth of a watermelon to satisfy my craving for the season. If I buy a whole one it probably will go mostly to waste, and take up too much room in the icebox.

So I go ahead, as I did this time, and pay nearly a buck for a quarter of a medium-sized melon, and try not to think how much I could have bought the entire melon for at a roadside stand somewhere.

The best thing I can say for buying ready-cut watermelon that way, you can see what you're getting.

All my life I have been associated with people who are supposed to know a great deal about watermelons. And I have yet to meet one who couldn't be fooled on the matter of whether a melon is ripe.

But I am interested in all the old ripeness tests, and I like to watch consumers buy watermelons. The way they shop tells something about their background.

An old country boy will always thump a melon. He will thump in three or four different places.

Then he may press it with the heel of his hand, to see if it has the proper amount of give.

Some will make a careful examination of the tail, where they claim to find several signs of maturity.

You know what the oldest of the old country boys will want to do? He'll want to plug that melon with his pocketknife. Which tells me that the ones with the most experience are saying that the only way to be certain a watermelon is ripe is to look inside it.

My father was a watermelon-plugging dude. When he stopped by the road to buy a melon he wouldn't make the first move toward his money until he was permitted to plug. He plugged deep, with a long-bladed pocketknife.

He didn't want the seller doing the plugging, he did it himself. Because some of those old roadside boys were shallow pluggers. They might take a plug that wasn't an inch deep. That wouldn't give you the vaguest clue to what the heart of the melon was like. It might be the color of a bedsheet, with no more taste than a green peach.

I was sitting out in the backyard polishing off my watermelon quarter the way I was taught, with a shaker of salt and a case knife, when the term watermelon feast came bulging up in my head.

Out on the T&P west of Fort Worth where I came from, we had a lot of watermelon feasts. I don't hear about watermelon feasts now.

When a little rain fell on that old sandy ground the farmers had so many watermelons the hogs couldn't eat 'em. So churches and service clubs and families and all manner of groups would have watermelon feasts. They'd ice down melons and keep cutting them until nobody could hold another chunk.

It's possible to eat too much watermelon. I did it at one or two of those feasts, and that may be why it doesn't take me long to catch up now on my watermelon eating.

But once a year I have to fill that gnawing emptiness, when my raising comes back on me that way.

The beginning of it was in Jasper. I had stopped at a grocery store there about three o'clock in the afternoon, looking for a pay telephone. Walking around in the store, I happened to spot a small jar of sandwich spread, and I bought it.

I hadn't tasted any sandwich spread of that kind in so many years. It's mayonnaise-looking stuff with little bits of pickle and I don't know what else mixed into it, so it looks speckled. Good cooks often look upon such a product with disdain and will not have it in their cupboards.

The reason I bought it is, sandwich spread of this kind is special in my personal eating history. The first time I saw any of it was in about 1933 or '34. My father brought a little jar of it home as a sort of curiosity. He was interested in new things on the market and liked to bring examples home to show us what was going on in the world of merchandising.

I thought the spread was beautiful in the jar, and tasted really splendid. We had it in the house, from time to time, as long as I lived at home. It never lasted long because we so often ate it not as a spread for sandwiches but as a special treat. We'd come home from school and if any of that green-speckled spread was in the pantry we would put it on bread or crackers and think we were getting a fine dessert.

Anyhow, there at Jasper I also bought a small package of soda crackers. In a roadside park south of town on Highway 96, I stopped and got out the knife I carry in my icebox and I spread the sandwich stuff on my crackers and ate every bit. I loved it, too.

Then I went on south. I had a few crackers left so down the road at Kirbyville I stopped again and bought me two bunches of fresh-pulled spring onions. I just felt a hankering for them. Eating the sandwich spread had made me hungry for things I used to eat and enjoy long ago. And at this season, those new green onions were always so grand.

They were the bulby kind, that have at the bottom of the green top a new onion maybe one-half to three-quarters of an inch in diameter. And so sweet and good. "These little green onions," we used to say, "are just sweet as sugar."

Well, of course any onion that was really sweet as sugar would not be any count at all, but that was the highest praise we could think of to heap on them.

Along with the green onions I got a nice big bunch of radishes, with the tops on, and a modest hunk of rat cheese. A few miles below Kirbyville there's a roadside park near the Farm Road 1004 intersection. I pulled in and poked around in the glove compartment and found a small picnic-type salt shaker I had thrown in there months ago. So I sat and watched the cars go by on the highway and ate those onions and that cheese and whittled the tails and the tops off the radishes and sprinkled salt on them and had a fine time.

I had intended to take one bunch of the onions home with me, because not all the stores in Houston have just exactly the kind that I love so well. But these were small bunches, not but four or five to the bunch, and by the time my crackers and cheese ran out I had eaten them both.

I hadn't gotten but a little way past Buna, coming on down toward Evadale, before I needed something to drink. Two bunches of green onions, even when they're gentle and fresh, can generate a great thirst. So at Kountze I stopped and bought some milk.

The store I picked didn't have milk in pints so I was obliged to buy a quart instead. Just next to the milk was a display of sand-wich meats. I happened to spot a package of sliced lunch meat with slivers of stuffed olive in it.

Do you know I hadn't eaten any of that stuff—didn't we call it olive loaf?—hadn't eaten any since 1939, the year I left home. The first I saw was when I got a job sacking potatoes at the grocery store and the butcher would hold up a big cylinder of that stuff and show the women how the olive was actually built into it that way. "Well I'll swan," they'd say.

For old times' sake I bought a little package of that lunch meat. Then of course I needed a loaf of bread. They ought to put up bread in packages with just two or four slices, for guys who want to stop in Kountze and make a sandwich.

I went on along the road, drinking my milk and nibbling on my sandwiches, through Saratoga and Moss Hill and Batson and Hardin. Time I got to Liberty I still had half the milk left so I bought a little box of those chocolate-covered cherries we used to love, to sort of finish off the milk with.

About seven o'clock I got home and for supper there was liver and onions, which is one of my favorite dishes. However, in this case for some reason I couldn't eat but a few bites.

Every Thanksgiving I think of old Tony. I see him clutching a tur-key leg, looking out across the tablecloth, chewing, grinning with a greasy mouth.

Something whispers to me that Tony is alive and still hungry and about 125 pounds overweight, although I have not seen or heard of him in more than thirty-five years.

He was one of a great procession of boarders we had in the house of my folks back in the old hometown. Tony was the great-est eater of them all.

Take the matter of the turkey leg. Tony is the only man I ever saw who would pick up the drumstick of a big Thanksgiving tur-key and clean it off quick and neat, just as you or I would eat the leg of a small frying chicken.

You think now, if you ever saw anybody do that—eat a whole turkey leg. I am talking about a bird that was meant to feed twenty-five or thirty people, not one of these little old ten-pound hens you find in supermarket freezers sometimes.

Also, when Tony was destroying those drumsticks, we were eating what country folks now call grasshopper turkeys. That meant birds that roamed the woods and fields, eating whatever they could find or catch.

I expect a mature turkey gobbler in 1935 had walked anyway five thousand miles by the time he lost his head to a Thanksgiving dinner, so his drumstick would consist mainly of tendon and gristle. I never did consider a turkey leg especially edible.

Yet here was old Tony, thinking it was a morsel. The other boarders looked on him kindly, when it came to turkey. While he was on drumsticks, it gave the others a chance at the white meat.

Tony had these peculiar eating habits that sometimes put him at a disadvantage, especially at festive meals such as Thanksgiving when the table offered so many morsels.

That is, he practiced the custom of eating one thing at a time. On Thanksgiving dressing, for instance, he would slop it into his plate until he had an Egyptian pyramid of the stuff. Then he'd take a spoon and he'd pat, and spread, and shape, and make depressions here and there, until his entire plate was covered.

Next he'd fill the depressions with giblet gravy, and for a while then he'd shovel in dressing and gravy, and nothing else. As I say, this was a disadvantage to him because while he was involved with dressing and gravy, other items such as sweet potatoes and rolls and cranberry jelly would be diminished by the other contestants.

Tony was aware of this weakness in his method, and that's why I can see him now, looking up from his plate, swinging his eyes over the table. He was gathering data, to make decisions on such questions as how much longer he could spend on dressing before all the English peas were gone.

I found Tony a fascinating study. He may be why I reached the age of seventeen weighing 119 pounds, from watching his style instead of fighting for my share of the potatoes.

He had a curious way of pouring liquids, such as milk, or syrup. He watched the container he was pouring from, instead of the one he was pouring into. I've seen him run his glass over, trying to get all the milk out of a pitcher. It's my belief he did that because of the feeling that if he didn't empty the pitcher, somebody other than himself would drink what he left, and this disturbed him.

Yet you mustn't imagine he was anything except just a big old good-natured bear of a person. He could throw out a left jab and snatch the last biscuit away from you, and still talk about a football score, or tell a bad joke he thought was great, and there wasn't a hint that he felt he was taking anything away from you.

He knew how to lose, in the same serene fashion. If he spent too long on dressing and gravy, and had to watch the sweet potatoes and marshmallows disappear before he got any, he shrugged and accepted, and didn't hold a grudge.

Tony was a big man, and strong as a low bridge. I hope this Thanksgiving he's eating where there's plenty of dressing.

I'm wanting to tell you about the adventures I've had at recording recipes. What I've learned is that the most experienced cooks are the worst in the world at telling you how to cook. Sometimes I think they don't even *know* how they cook. They just go in the kitchen and fix things. They don't pay any attention to how they're doing it, and the miracle is that they do it right.

They're like my sister playing the piano. Ever since she was tall enough to reach up and put her hands on the keys she could play the piano. You hum it and she plays it. But ask her how she does it and she goes blank. She doesn't know how she does it. It's the same way with good cooks.

A time came in my life maybe ten years ago when I thought I could live to be a hundred and thirty and never again get hungry for meat loaf. But I was wrong. Within the past six months I developed an awful craving for meat loaf so I called up a person I know who can cook meat loaf better than anybody else in this hemisphere and I asked her how to do it.

She told me and I made a meat loaf exactly the way she said. I won't say it was inedible because I found a dog across the street who worried it down. He didn't even thank me. I gave it to the dog because I didn't want that mess in my garbage.

The trouble with good cooks is, they can't give you precise directions. They'll tell you to put a "dab" of this or a "smidgen" of that and "a little" of something else, without having any notion of how much a dab or a smidgen or a little of something is. They can play the piano but they can't tell you how.

"You'll need to salt it," they'll say.

"How much salt?"

"Well, not too much."

Also, they never do anything the same way twice. I've had fine cooks tell me the secret to fixing good dishes is precision, measuring exactly, being careful to do everything just right. But the same cooks won't even have anything in their kitchens to measure how much a tablespoon is. They just fling stuff in and stir. If I do that I end up with a meat loaf that the dog may like.

On Wednesday I had a little visit with Opal Pearson here in Houston. She's one of the customers and she told me about her Uncle Luby Morrow who lived up at Longview, and how he used to cook chicken and dumplings.

Uncle Luby could do chicken and dumplings, oh, they were so fine, and Opal Pearson once asked him how he did it and here's how the conversation went:

"Take you about a three-pound chicken," Uncle Luby said, "and put it in a big pan. Cover it with water, put a good tight lid on, and let it simmer till the meat falls off the bone. Then you take some flour and a little salt . . ."

"How much flour?"

"Oh, for a chicken that size I'd say a GOOD cupful. Then put you in some shortening and mix it up real good and . . ."

"How much shortening?"

"Well, not as much as if you was making a pie crust."

"A tablespoon?"

"A BIG tablespoon. But don't use no baking powders. That's a mistake a lot of people make is putting baking powders in dumplins. Then you put you in an egg and some milk and work you up a good smooth dough . . ."

"How much milk?"

"Well, not as much as what you got egg."

"Half an eggshell full?"

"Yeah, the BIG half. Then you roll your dough out paper thin, cut it in strips, and drop it in your broth which is at a rollin' boil. Keep forkin' the dumplins down and separatin' them or they'll stick together. Let 'em boil at high speed . . ."

"About how long?"

"A right smart while. Then you turn your fire down to simmer, put the lid on tight, and don't let nobody take that lid off until them dumplins are done."

"How long do you cook them with the lid on?"

"Well, not quite as long as what you did with the lid off. And that's all there are to it."

Opal Pearson told me this recipe works only for those who know what a GOOD cupful and a BIG tablespoon are, and how long a right smart while is. Remember not to use no baking powders.

Recently I tried inventing a new sandwich, and I must say that I was really successful. Of course I have always had a natural talent for this sort of thing. I hope that doesn't sound boastful.

The first thing I did was to go to the bakery and buy a loaf of the highest quality, most expensive multi-whole-grain bread. I had sooner you didn't try to reproduce my sandwich if you are going to use that gummy white stuff that most consumers buy. I am talking about the kind of loaf that if you pick it up in the middle it will droop on both ends like a wet rope.

The bread I buy, you can put it in the bottom of the grocery sack and pile six cans of soup and a five-pound package of flour on top of it and when you take it out, the loaf won't even be mashed. Of course this kind of bread costs more than that other stuff they are calling bread. Fine champagne costs more than bad beer, too.

The only thing I went out and bought was bread. My feeling about inventing a sandwich is, you ought to do it mainly with materials found in the kitchen. Seems to me that is more in the tradition of the general sandwich field. I mean practically anybody, even a person without natural talent, could go to a delicatessen and spend $7.50 and get something to make a good-tasting sandwich. But where is the challenge in that?

In the back of the pantry, behind a large can of chili, I found some ham loaf. I suppose it is all right to call it ham loaf. It's the product that got famous in World War II, and had all those soldier jokes about it. I am not allowed to use brand names in the paper unless it is necessary to make the meaning clear. But you know what it is, I bet.

I opened the can of ham loaf and set it out on the cutting board and stood back and examined it a while, and thought what to do with it. (Did you ever see a sculptor look at an ordinary stone, visualizing the art he can make of it?)

After a false start or so, I decided to cut the loaf into super-thin slices. I experimented with several of those funny little cutting tools in the kitchen drawer and eventually decided on a cheese knife. It's the kind you draw, flat, across a hunk of cheese and it curls off a thin piece. Works like a wood plane.

Before I saw the way to cut it I wasted about a quarter of the loaf. Well, I ought not to say wasted. I gave it to the dog, who said it was good. This dog has a great interest in my cooking. Sits there and watches every move, and cooperates by eating my mistakes.

Next I took out a head of lettuce and selected half a dozen nice leaves, discarding a number of layers until I came to just the right ones. (The dog doesn't like lettuce. Too bad.) Then I washed the leaves and popped them into the freezer for a couple of minutes. That's the way to get your really good crisp lettuce leaves.

Then I spread an adequate but not generous amount of mayonnaise on the bottom slice of bread. I don't ever spread both slices at the same time when I'm inventing a sandwich, because by the time I get to the top I may be using something entirely different than I used on the bottom.

Another thing, please, if you make my sandwich, in the name of Julia Child and Ann Valentine and James Beard, don't spread salad dressing on instead of mayonnaise. It is a sin to do that, and you can go to hell for it.

Now I fitted a lettuce leaf over the bottom bread slice, trimming edges for neatness, and covered the leaf with a layer of thin-sliced meat. (Never let the mayonnaise touch the meat, in *any* sandwich.)

From this established base, I built in layers, a crisp lettuce leaf separating each. I thin-sliced a big radish, and arranged it into one layer. An excellent choice because it provided an inner crispness. Another layer was thin-sliced hard-boiled egg. Another was thin-sliced cheese.

I ended up with two layers of meat, and one each of radish, egg, and cheese. But the architecture and construction were so tight, so precise, that the completed sandwich didn't rise more than an inch and a half tall, and handled like power steering.

I named it the Layered Look. Serves one human and a black dog.

VII

Tales Passed Along

One of the more useful tools of writers, especially those who record the life and times and history of people, is the legend.

The very word—legend—don't you see it has a certain beauty? It tastes good on the tongue before it's spoken, and caresses the ear when it comes out, and wakes up the attention.

A legend is a curious animal. There is no saying exactly what one is. I've heard it defined in a rude way as a lie. But it's not. It's more an extension of the truth, a story that starts out to be factual but misses the mark and wanders about and enjoys itself.

I know historians who frown on legends. They look down on them, as if legends are crawling with germs which threaten to infect the record and distort it. Yet much of our history is well-seasoned with legend, and if that weren't so history wouldn't have any more flavor than battery water.

No one person can sit down and create a legend. It won't stand up. It's got to be launched from a pad of truth, sent out into the world, swapped, handed down, stored away for age, brought out and added to, and stored away again.

Some of the best-loved legends aren't ever offered up for public consumption. These are family legends, owned and operated by members of the clans they concern. They aren't always very good legends but they are treasured by those who have bred and fed them over generations.

Last week the postman brought a letter from an aunt who referred to something being "as big as Uncle Rhodie's bear." Well, Uncle Rhodie's bear is one of the principals in a legend that belongs to a raft of that aunt's kin. It is at least a fair example of a family legend.

It had its beginning long ago when this Uncle Rhodie was moving from Caldwell County out into West Texas. He was driving a pair of mules hitched to a wagon loaded with house-hold gear. He was alone, the weather was cold and wet, and Uncle Rhodie was keeping his spirits elevated with a quart of squirrel whiskey.

Out east of Menard he had crossed a creek bottom near the San Saba River when he heard a racket and turned around and there was a black bear, riding on his load along about midships. The load included the contents of the smokehouse and the cellar—hams, bacon, preserves, and the like—and the bear had hitched a ride and was back there digging into the stores.

I have no doubt at least that much of the story is fact, else it wouldn't have survived. The remainder of it may not have enough substance to hang a hat on, but then you understand it's no good just having a bear jump on a wagon and jump off again.

Uncle Rhodie, all full of whiskey courage, leveled down on the bear with his old Hawkins rifle. But he wasn't able to fire, seeing the bear had stationed himself just in front of a chiffonier which was once owned by Uncle Rhodie's mother-in-law in Mis-sissippi, and by which his wife set a great store. Any injury the bear might inflict on Uncle Rhodie would be nothing but a briar scratch against what his wife would do to him if he put a rifle slug through the mirror of that chiffonier.

So he was obliged to try dislodging the bear by swinging the rifle at him, and shouting insults reflecting on the character of bears as a general class of animal. The bear responded by walking up to the wagon seat and cuffing the rifle out of Uncle Rhodie's grip and insisting that Uncle Rhodie remove himself from the wagon and sprawl into the gravel of a dry wash.

All this activity did seem to disturb the mules, with the result that the citizens of Menard were, a few minutes later, treated to this marvelous sight: A wagon full of household wares, sailing through town, pulled by mules in a high lope, driven by a black bear holding a Hawkins rifle and a bottle of squirrel whiskey and eating a smoked ham.

One of the customers, who knows I enjoy observing the habits of small wild animals in our state, has written me an account of an extraordinary scene he recently witnessed with respect to raccoons.

All of us who are acquainted with them know that coons are capable of performing remarkable acts but I never heard of them doing anything like this before.

Customer said he was walking along the bank of the Neches River recently, west of Kirbyville, on the way to run some trotlines. Said he came to a little clearing and happened to spy, in the bright moonlight, a big old boar coon, must have weighed forty pounds.

Customer said he paused, and stood very still, and evidently the coon didn't see him at all. So he got a very close look at what transpired in the next few seconds.

In the middle of that little clearing was a low stump. Looked like a sweetgum, the customer said, but he couldn't be sure. About three feet from the stump, lying north and south, was a log. Evidently it was the log that belonged originally to the stump, but that is another unknown and anyhow it has no bearing on what was to happen.

While this customer watched, that old boar coon rummaged around in nature's litter there on the river bank, and came up with a stick about a foot long. Just a slim stick he could easily hold in one paw.

Well, that coon took that stick and hopped up on top of the stump, and shifted his paw down to the end of the stick, and rapped it, smartly, on the side of the stump. Right away, in answer to the signal, and to the astonishment of the observer, out of the brush hustled four more coons, a good deal smaller than the one on the stump.

The four new coons came and crowded up close together, shoulder to shoulder, along that log. They were facing the big coon on the stump. The big coon then stood on his hind legs, and raised his stick overhead, and brought it down just as if he was giving the signal to start, and that quartet of coons on the log then began singing, in perfect harmony, "By the Light of the Silvery Moon."

Well, when I got that far into the letter I did check the date on it, and sure enough it was written on the first of April.

Every now and then a customer will get sneaky that way with a letter, and have me all interested, and then spring the trap. Oh law no, I don't mind. I love it.

I remember a letter that came in back when I was at the peak of my interest in wild birds. My interest and enthusiasm surges and ebbs a lot, so that I might have a regular orgy of interest for a while in, say, trees, and from there I may go to country stores, then to bobcats, and on to old books, and then to beachcombers, and piano players, and nice old gals with silver hair who churn Jersey clabber and put up peach preserves, and so on and so forth. Anyhow, in that letter, the customer said she wanted to share the most exceptional experience she'd ever had in forty years of birdwatching.

Said her house is on a country road that has a ditch running along it, and in wet times it collects water. (I am reconstructing this the best I can from memory, as I don't have the letter now.) One morning she went down to the road to her mailbox and a January cold front had put a thin sheet of ice on the ditch water.

She happened to spot a jaybird who had discovered he could walk around on that ice. It tickled him to death that he could do it. He got to slipping, and sliding, and giggling, and whooping, and his racket began to draw additional birds. Here came more jaybirds, grackles, cardinals, a few finches, and even two woodpeckers, to join the game.

Then for an hour upward of fifty birds were there playing on that ice, taking headers and laughing at one another, having the most fun, some of 'em even getting flying starts and scooting along on their tail feathers for fifteen and twenty yards a clip.

Customer said she had time to run get her camera and she took up an entire roll of film of those ice-skating birds. But it was a cloudy day, and her pictures didn't come out.

When I was a shirttail kid, my father would tell the finest stories. But he didn't tell them often. When he did tell one I paid hard attention. I suppose that is why I am able to remember his stories so exactly now.

One of my favorites was about the time he was almost eaten alive by a panther that he ran across in Grandma Hale's pasture. He was only nine years old when that happened. That would have been about 1895.

When I was a boy (my father would say, telling the story), panthers roamed around here in this old timber. There were also bears, and wolves. When we would go into the pasture to hunt the horses or look for new calves, we were always afraid we would come across a bear or a wolf. But what we were most afraid of was a panther.

The reason was, if a panther got you he would eat you alive. Bears and wolves would go ahead and kill you and then eat you, but panthers would eat you alive, feet first.

Well, one time your Grandma sent me out to look for where one of her old turkey hens had hid her nest. I went across the hay field yonder, and into the timber the other side of the branch. Just when I was climbing the far bank of the branch, I looked up and I was staring into the face of a big old panther.

I suppose it weighed five hundred pounds. Its tail was twitching back and forth, the way they do just before they spring. That's why I didn't run. There's not any use in running from a panther if they want to catch you. They can jump thirty-five feet and land on your back.

Well, I got to noticing something funny then about the way that panther was doing. It was kind of licking at one of its front paws, and taking on, and making painful noises.

I looked close and saw it had a big mesquite thorn in its paw, stuck way in deep and festered and all. Well, I went on up to it and scratched it between the ears and it sort of purred, and I saw by that it wasn't going to bother me. So I took out my pliers and I pulled that thorn out of its paw.

(I would interrupt him, and ask how come he had pliers out there in the pasture. "Sometimes I carried pliers," he said. "Now do you want the story, or not?" So I would keep quiet.)

After I pulled the thorn out (he would go on), that old panther's paw felt so much better it stuck its neck out and gave me a big lick, right up the side of the face. Maybe you think *that* wasn't something, getting licked up the side of the face by a full-grown panther. Then it turned and limped into the timber and I came on back to the house. I never did find the turkey's nest.

Well, that night at supper I didn't tell about the panther because I figured nobody would believe me. I couldn't hardly believe it myself.

Two, three years later, one day about sundown me and Tom Guthrie and Holland Edwards were a-riding triple on Tom's fat old mare he rode to school sometimes. We were eleven, I guess, or twelve.

Holland was behind Tom and I was sitting last, sort of laid

back on that old mare's wide rump. It was about like being on the front porch. All of a sudden a big panther dropped down out of the trees into the middle of the road and that mare let out a scream and reared up and I came off over her tail and ended up sitting in the dirt. Tom and Holland hung on and I figured the last sight I would see on the earth would be those two on the mare, going down the road in a high lope.

Here came that panther, slipping on up to start eating me alive. Then I saw it stop, and raise its head, and sniff, and it walked on up then and gave me a big old lick up side the face, and went off and left me safe. The only thing it could be, it was the same panther that I had pulled the thorn out of its foot in our pasture two or three years before. (So that was the end of his story.)

After I got into school a way, I ran across the story that's in books about Androcles, the Roman slave who pulled a thorn from the foot of a lion in the wilderness. And years later, when Androcles was flung into an arena to be devoured, the lion that came forth to devour him would not do him harm. Instead it licked him on the face, because it was the lion whose foot Androcles had doctored in the wilderness.

I showed that story to my father, and asked him why the two stories were so much the same. He shrugged, and said the stories together give us a moral, which is that the world is full of very similar things.

Sometimes you have got to bow your neck and growl and keep on believing things that you enjoy believing, even when somebody is standing there showing you that what you are believing is wrong.

Only this past week I got my faith shaken up in one of my favorite stories about one of my favorite people, my Uncle Barney Hale. But I managed to hang onto my belief in the story, despite the fact that I was confronted with some stern evidence that it isn't true.

The story was first told to me by a poker-playing buddy of Uncle B's. I have treasured it for twenty years, and told it around to anybody I thought would listen to a poker story.

Uncle Barney was a good card player and sat in on a lot of poker here and there over the country. In fact he sat in on tons and tons of it.

In the story his buddy told me, they were out in San Diego on a trip to see what the West Coast looked like, and they had fallen short in the matter of spending money. So Uncle Barney had entered a stud game in the hope of earning a couple of honest bills.

In that game there was a big fellow who had a fat purse and wore a derby hat. I am able to see him exactly. In most stud games I have watched in my life, there was a big fellow with a fat purse, and even if he didn't have on headgear he'd be the sort who would wear a derby if he did.

In the stud game, at one point Uncle B had paired his first two cards and was hanging in there. In fact, about the only way he would ever stay in any stud hand for the third card was to pair on the first two.

On the last card, Derby Hat came up with a pair of jacks showing, and sat there looking as if he would swear by the Declaration of Independence that he had a third one in the hole. Uncle Barney had kings and probably the winning hand but he was beat. Because Derby Hat would bet the jacks too high and Uncle B wouldn't be able to call.

But something I always admired about Uncle B was that when he had to fold, he would figure out a way to fold in style.

All right, when the betting checked around to Derby Hat's jacks, he reached back and pulled that fat wallet out of his pants pocket and flipped it on the table, with half an inch of bills showing edgeways in the mouth of it.

Uncle B looked carefully at the wallet a minute, and then reached down and pulled off both his old shoes, and flipped one after the other on top of the wallet and said, "Well, if we're playing for leather, I will call you and raise."

Now that won't be the best poker story you ever heard, but it is my favorite because of Uncle B. I loved him something fierce and love the memory of him yet, and I enjoy seeing him pitch in his shoes and hearing him deliver the line.

Well, just this week I was roaming around in my copy of *The People's Almanac* and came across a section called "The Wit of Wilson Mizner." Mizner, according to the almanac, was a great wit, one of the funniest men in the country. He died in 1933. The almanac has an entire page of Mizner witticisms.

And here in the middle is a story about a fellow tossing his wallet onto a poker table, and another guy across the way pitching in his shoe and delivering the line about playing for leather.

I don't mind saying my spirit sank. My great old Uncle B poker story. Could it be? Was it really no more than an adaptation of a Wilson Mizner joke?

But I have now recovered. I am not going to let anything as harmless as an almanac stampede me into turning loose of my poker story. I intend to hang on.

Besides, for all I know, the source of Wilson Mizner's poker story might have been Uncle Barney himself, although he does not receive any credit in the almanac.

In my younger times I loved joke-telling sessions, when a bunch of folks got together and sat around for hours, taking turns at telling their funniest jokes.

An evening of pure joke-telling doesn't seem as much fun as it once was. However, there's a certain type of story that I especially enjoy and it almost always comes to the surface at any joke-telling session. I have learned to look for it.

It's a story told for the truth, and it may even be the truth, or at least partly, and it travels. What I mean, the place where it happened is always changing, and of course the teller of the story insists that it happened in his own hometown. Or that it happened to someone he personally knows.

A good clean example of a story of this kind is the one about why women cut the end off a ham before they cook it.

Generally this one will be told by a fairly new homemaker who is still learning about cookery. At a joke-telling session she will break in about the middle of the evening and say, "This isn't a joke but it was amusing to me. A personal experience." Then she will tell about the ham.

She was cooking her first ham, and had asked her mother how to go about it, and her mother advised her to cut off the end. She asked why cut off the end and her mother said well, that was the way *her* mother did it.

So they traced the practice back another generation to the grandmother and she said she cut off the end of the ham because that was the way *her* mother did it. But the grandmother solved the puzzle by saying, "I once asked my mother why *she* cut off the end of the ham and she said it was because the pan was too short."

I have heard famous cooks, including Julia Child, tell that story as having happened in their own families. During the holidays just past one of my customers wrote me a version of the same story out of her own family archives. I was delighted to get it.

I wouldn't suggest, not for bacon or beans, that anybody is fibbing. Because it is possible that with respect to cooking hams, the same set of circumstances existed in many different families.

My favorite tale of this kind is one I have come to think of as the what-have-I-done story. I have heard versions of it supposed to have happened in a dozen different towns. In Waxahachie, Ennis, Waco, Luling, and as far west as Midland.

When told properly by someone who will sit in a witness seat and swear he saw it happen, this is a really good yarn.

Consider the story as it happened at Waxahachie, according to the fellow I heard tell it.

A traveling company of Shakespearean-type players came to town. An English teacher in the local school promised an A in her grade book for any student who attended the performance. The football coach saw to it that half a dozen of his best linemen were there, because they needed the A's to stay eligible.

So you get the scene: Six big country-boy football players in the front row of the theater.

Okay, near the end of the performance, the female lead became ill and couldn't continue. In desperation the male star rushed out the rear of the theater and collared the first person he saw. She happened to be Flossie, the loose woman of the town.

Actor told her, "You want to make two dollars? Here, put on this costume and come on stage. All you have to do, when I pretend to stab you with this rubber dagger, fall to the floor just as I shout 'What have I done?'"

So here went Flossie, grinning on stage for her big moment. The play climaxed with the stabbing, and down went Flossie as the actor drew back in horror and cried, "What have I done?"

And a big tackle in the first row jumped up and yelled, "I'll tell you what you've done, you son of a bitch. You've killed the only whore in Waxahachie!"

Did that really happen in Waxahachie or wherever? I have no idea. I do think that, like all good stories that live and travel, it must have happened somewhere.

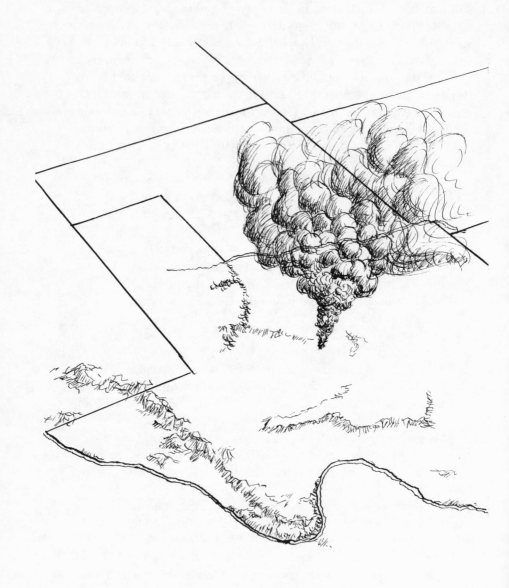

VIII

"Hey, Hemingway!"

We had gathered at the home of a friend, a small gang of us who can remember things that happened half a century ago. We got to talking about events in our early lives that we considered good and exciting.

One gent told about saving his money when he was ten and paying a dollar for a donkey. A woman told of her mother taking her all the way to Corpus Christi in 1931 from Menard, to see the ocean. Somebody else told about his grandfather raising a Tom Watson watermelon that weighed ninety-six pounds.

When it came my turn to get the floor I told about our house catching fire and burning in 1928. It did not burn all the way down, as we used to say, or all the way up, but the top half of it burned, all the roof and the attic, and that was by far the best thing that had happened in my life up to that time. Nothing happened to top it until my father bought me a bicycle when I was a senior in high school.

The house burning gave me something to talk and write about at school practically until I got that bicycle. When the assignment would be, "Write a theme about a memorable event in your life," I would always write about the house burning. I bet I wrote two dozen themes on that fire.

I would begin by setting the scene, and tracing the fire all the way back to the coal mines of Palo Pinto and Erath counties. Because in those times a great many homes in West Texas were heated by coal stoves, and the stovepipes often were fitted into flues set in beaverboard ceilings.

I would then explain the significance of that, from the viewpoint of fires getting started. Because I needed a lot of words, in themes. They would tell you to write three pages, or five, or even twenty if it was a term theme. Stovepipes disappearing into flues set in beaverboard ceilings was a subject good for four or five paragraphs.

I would tell how I was the one who discovered that the house was afire. I think it was my sister instead but I certainly did not intend to make her the heroine of one of my own themes. My policy was, let her write her own themes if she wanted to be a heroine.

At 5:30 A.M., as I would write, I awoke and turned on a light and right away I knew something was wrong. Because the coal stove was red hot. My father had built too big a fire in it and had gone on out to milk the cow and it was pretty near melting the metal of the stove. The glowing redness was climbing way up the stovepipe and into the flue and the fibrous beaverboard was scorching brown and smoke was pouring out of the seams in the ceiling and I judged from all these signs that something was burning.

"Fire! Fire!" I shouted. "Everybody out! The house is on fire!" Actually it was my sister who shouted the warning that way but I took credit for it in the themes because she was only a girl and had no business being important.

I then rushed into the kitchen and rescued my mother. I would say in the themes, "The kitchen was so full of smoke I could barely see her standing at the stove, fixing breakfast."

That was true about the smoke. But it was not smoke from the fire in the attic. It was from the kerosene stove that my mother cooked on. Her kitchen was smoky every morning but with the fire going in the attic I thought the kitchen smoke made a pretty good line in the themes.

"We stood outside in the bitter cold while the firemen scaled the walls and chopped holes in the roof." I loved to write about the chopping of the holes that way. I ought to have made it singular, since only one hole was chopped, and in the first few themes the one hole satisfied me.

But as I learned more and more about writing themes, I was able to see four, six, and finally a dozen firefighters scaling those walls, and chopping holes everywhere, and it made ever so much better a story. I could tell from my grades. I could progress from C's and B-minuses right up to A's merely by increasing the height of the flames and the density of the smoke and adding two or three onto the total number of firefighters injured in fighting the fire, which I finally stopped calling a fire. I renamed it a holocaust.

By the time I got that bicycle in 1939, my memory of that fire had improved so much that I could look back and recall that it had destroyed not just the top half of the house but the entire structure, plus the shed where we kept the cow, and a neighbor's barn. And yet even today the members of my own family recall this as an ordinary event, and are unable to see what an important fire it was.

One evening last week I was invited to a meeting of a writers' club. I had never before attended such a meeting and I liked it pretty well.

After the program we were standing around visiting and somebody asked me what I liked best of everything I had read the past year.

I didn't give an honest answer to that. The reason I didn't, I supposed the person who asked the question had reference to books. So I thought of a book title and gave it as an answer.

But I wish now I had given the first answer that stirred in my head when I heard the question. What I have read the past year that I liked the best was not in a book. Nor a newspaper or a magazine.

It was in a letter from Raymond Hicks out at Bandera. And it was only one sentence.

I am not able to quote the sentence exactly because I can't locate the letter. I expect it is buried somewhere in the confusion around this desk. It mentioned a girls' basketball team from one of those little towns out west of Bandera. Utopia, I think, or Tarpley.

The sentence said that the team was coming home late at night from playing an out-of-town game and up close to Seco Pass a mountain lion ran across the road in front of the school bus.

That's all there was. The writer didn't add any detail, or explain the significance of the event. He didn't need to. Which is what I like about the sentence. It said so much so quick.

A hundred years ago, it was an event worth talking about and writing letters about when a mountain lion, in any part of this state, crossed the path of travelers that way. The fact that it can still happen says a great deal about that lovely broken country out there beyond Bandera.

The sentence also says a lot about the values of the person who wrote it. Oh, it says so much about many things.

Just once in a great while one of the customers will write me a sentence, or a brief paragraph, of that quality and I love to get one. I have learned to watch for them. They pop up in unexpected places. Sometimes they'll be buried in the middle of a long and involved letter and sometimes they'll be tacked onto the end, as a sort of postscript. So you have to read everything, to make sure you don't miss one of those little gems.

My father, long ago when he was away from home on his traveling salesman job, used to put in a short jewel like that sometimes. I don't have the letters now but I remember the kind of thing he would write. Something like this:

"When I was in Wichita Falls I went by to see Robert and Louise Holland. They have six children, four girls and two boys, and run a big two-story secondhand furniture store. They live in the upstairs part and all work in the store. Every summer they close it up for a month and go camping in New Mexico."

That's all he would write about that family, and he would never mention them again. And we had never heard a word about them before.

But because of his one paragraph, we would care a little while about that family, and we would be able to see them. We could see that big store, with the curtains upstairs where the living quarters were. We could see those children and the parents working together in the business. We could see the sign that they put on the door when they closed up in the summer: "Gone camping. Be back September 1."

My father liked large and close families, is why he thought it worthwhile to write us about the Hollands. It said a great deal to us about them that they worked side by side all year long in that store and then stuck together to go camping every August. It also appealed to my father that anybody could be free of the bother of business for an entire month every year. It was a luxury he never knew himself.

Or he would write little one-sentence accounts of the minor adventures he had while traveling. Maybe he'd say, "When I was driving yesterday from Lubbock to Post I switched off my motor at the top of the Caprock and put it in neutral and coasted four and one-half miles before I came to a stop."

As far as I know he never saw any mountain lions in his travels but if he had, I believe he would have written about it much the same way that Raymond Hicks did.

Of course I am altogether different, myself. If a mountain lion ever runs across the road in front of me, I will probably write about it for a week.

While watching TV I saw E. L. Doctorow, the writer, sitting as a guest on Dick Cavett's talk show and one thing they discussed was the color of paper Doctorow writes on. He writes on white. *Cheap* white, he said.

Cavett is a plenty intelligent citizen, but he indicated the color of paper a writer uses is of interest to him. The habits of people who write stories for a living seem to be of interest to a great many readers, even intelligent ones.

Personally I have always been more interested in the habits of carpenters and bartenders and hardware clerks and nice motherly women who make blackberry cobblers in linoleum-floored kitchens.

But hardware clerks seldom get on national talk shows. If one does it's because he has written a book, and then he talks about his writing habits and not his hardware store habits.

He will tell the host, "I write between five and seven o'clock in the morning at the kitchen table in my pajamas, working with lead pencils on a yellow legal pad, with the dog at my feet and a copy of Philpot's *Synonyms* beside me."

I suppose then, as those words go broadcasting around the nation at the speed of light, thousands of aspiring writers take them unto their hearts and do likewise. Go out, I mean, and buy legal pads, and a copy of Philpot's, and for all I know, a dog. Figuring, I suppose, that if a hardware clerk can write a bestseller equipped like that, so can anybody.

The fact is that some people who already make their living by writing will change their work habits to fit those of another writer who is earning more money.

I was once guilty of this myself, but I have the defense that I became guilty of it on the orders of a respected physician.

Back in the 1960s I went wobbling into that doctor's office with a contrary knee joint. It had quit bending the way it ought to, which made walking awkward, and it kept me awake nights by throbbing a lot, so I loaded it up and took it to this doctor.

He decided the trouble was that I sat in a peculiar way when I worked, causing the nerves in my knee to knot and kink sort of garden-hose style.

"Why don't you write standing up?" he said. "Did you know that Ernest Hemingway wrote standing up?"

I didn't know that. I didn't know, either, before I went to him that this doctor was a Hemingway buff of the highest order. He could quote passages not only from *The Old Man and the Sea* and *For Whom the Bell Tolls* but also from *Green Hills of Africa* and *The Torrents of Spring* and other titles I didn't know were Hemingway's.

He talked to me about Hemingway a lot more than he ever did about my knee (while I sat there paying for the lecture). The conclusion of his discourse was that I ought to write in a standing posture.

"I believe it'll help that knee," he said.

Today I believe he meant, in his heart, that it would help my prose. That it would make my stuff sound like his hero.

Well, I wasn't worried about sounding like Hemingway but I was interested in improving my knee, so I stood erect to work. I stayed up five years.

Got me an old chest of drawers and pushed it up close to the desk and put the typewriter on it. Adjusted the machine for height by sticking Volume 23 of the encyclopedia underneath. And for the next five years every sentence I wrote was produced in a standing position.

I got used to standing and stayed up even after my knee quit hurting and I had forgotten why I stood up in the first place. In addition to the stuff I wrote for a living, I wrote a novel standing there at that chest of drawers.

The novel didn't sell, but it got me invited to a couple of these writers' workshops, where people who want to write books come and ask questions of those who already have. The thing I could say about that book that most interested the audience was that it was written standing up, off the top of a chest of drawers. Everybody seemed to like that. It gave the book distinction over the thousands of others written that year from a sitting position.

That novel's greatest fan was the doctor, who evidently felt he had made the story possible by standing me up. He bought ten copies, and gave them around to friends, and said the style reminded him a little of Hemingway. He is the only critic who was able to see that.

We were at the neighborhood icehouse, sitting beneath the tree in the back. The outside tables have been wiped off, and the one that had the rickety leg all last summer has been nailed firm. There has even been the promise of paint.

One of the benches is homemade. It is like benches I have known at dining tables covered with oilcloth. Country families used to put such benches against the wall and all the children crowded along the bench to eat. Its surface became smooth and shiny from the sliding of all those skinny little buttocks encased loosely in blue overalls.

The man who sat across from me at the icehouse, I think of his name as T-Shirt. When March comes, no matter how nippy, this gent shows up at the icehouse in a T-shirt on his top and he never seems cold. I always expect him to have a package of cigarettes folded in the sleeve of the shirt, the way that apartment house super on TV does.

Yes, sometimes I give them my own names at the icehouse. One reason is that many give no names at all, and almost never full ones. Like the woman Flora, that I have mentioned here before. She sat at the end, always at the end. She is simply Flora, and no more.

She called out. "Hey, Hemingway!"

Hemingway is not a name I have given anybody at the icehouse. It is what Flora and the other regular customers call a tall young man with dark curly hair. He wears jeans far too short for his legs and he is called Hemingway because he writes stories.

The icehouse regulars are not at all certain what Hemingway wrote but they know Hemingway is the name of a writer. What they do know is what's on television. Know all the situation comedies and the characters and the families and the ratings and what nights they come on and when. They know that.

"Hey, Hemingway! Hemingway?" Flora still calling. "Come on out here and sit, and give us your story again." Then to me. "Hemingway read us his story last Saturday in here."

T-Shirt grunted. "Ain't much of a story, you ask me."

Hemingway came grinning to the table but said no, he didn't want to talk about the story again.

"Well, I liked it," Flora said. "Are you gonna have it printed somewhere?"

Hemingway explained to her it's not a matter of *having* it printed, that he had sent it off, submitted it to a magazine, and it would be rejected or accepted.

"Well, I think you ought to have it printed," Flora said. "Come on, tell it."

Hemingway said no again and Flora said, "Well, just tell what it's *about*. This feller here's a newspaper reporter (nodding at me) and he'd want to hear about it."

Flora, I am fairly sure, believes I am a sportswriter. The others who notice my presence at all believe the same. They hear I work for a newspaper and they cannot imagine any reason a person would work for a newspaper except to be a sportswriter.

"It ain't about much of anything, you ask me," T-Shirt was saying, about Hemingway's story.

"Sure it is," Flora said. "It's about this young fellow on the beach at Galveston, see, and he's walking along, and he's thinking about this girl, that's left him. He's carryin' the old torch, you know? It's a love story. Well, he . . ."

Hemingway couldn't stand that. The only thing worse than summarizing one of your own stories in public is having somebody else summarize it. He said:

"Well, no, it's not really a love story. And it wasn't really Galveston. It could be any beach anywhere. The guy is walking the beach and sort of reviewing his life. He's looking out over the ocean and thinking what people would say about his life, if it ended right there. There's a girl he thinks about, but it's not a love story. He thinks of a thing he did to his brother one time, a sort of bad thing, and about his folks, and his dog, and the undertow, and the bottom of the ocean, and whether there's a second chance, whether you would get to come back and try again. It's just a guy thinking about things."

"It ain't got any action," T-Shirt said.

"That's true," Hemingway agreed. "It hasn't got any action. It's a story about death. It's about the contemplation of suicide."

Another snort from T-Shirt. "Well, you got to have action."

Flora patted Hemingway on the forearm. "Well, don't worry, honey. Maybe you can put some in it."

We went in, because it was cold. Every spring they rush the season a little, and fix up the tables in back when it's still too cool to sit outside at night.

Now then, I think I have found the secret at last.

So I have gone out and bought myself a special dictionary containing the key words in twenty-six different languages. The way it works, say I want to know what the word *sister* is in other tongues. Well, I look up *sister* in this dictionary and there she is, translated on one page into twenty-five languages. So in a matter of seconds I can see that sister in Italian is *sorella*, in Russian it is *sestra*, in Swahili it is *dada*, and so on along the line. I've even got sister in Esperanto, *frat'ino*.

This dictionary is going to help me make a lot of money, and here's how. For years and years now, I have been trying to write a book that will sell millions of copies and make me so rich I can quit the newspaper business and sit on the front porch and wave at cars. But I have had no luck at it.

Just in recent times, though, I have noticed some important clues. I have studied a large stack of books that were highly successful and they all have something in common. Which is, that the authors all throw in, here and there, a few foreign words to prove that they know something the reader does not.

These foreign words are always in italics and the purpose of them is to keep the reader mixed up about what the writer is saying. That, I think, is the path to success—to prevent the reader from understanding what is going on.

Here is the simplest sort of example:

"Nora rose early. She felt well, so refreshed after a restful night. She bathed, dressed, and breakfasted. Then, before leaving the apartment, she had a thought. Today, she told herself, I will wear my blue *kapelusz*."

Doesn't that have a special touch? It could have been written by one of your really famous authors. Of course, I know exactly what *kapelusz* means, but I will certainly not tell you. You are not supposed to know. This is the way the real pros do it. I ought to have seen it before now.

Listen to this now. This is me writing. You might think it is a rich author with a beard but it is only me:

"In his Tokyo hotel room, John was nervous. He couldn't shake the feeling that something was there near him, in the room. Hark! A rustling sound. There it is again! Was it coming from— yes! from the closet. He drew his .38, stepped silently to the closet door, and threw it open. He gasped. There, staring him in the face, was a huge *nezumi*!"

Hey, this is fun. No wonder the professionals write such long books. They are only entertaining themselves, and making all that money in addition.

Let's try another one. A dining scene, say. I have always just hated scenes in which a character orders food in a foreign restaurant. But now I think I am going to like it since I have learned the way to write such scenes myself. Here we go:

"By the time the boat docked at Helsinki, Nora was famished. She had not eaten since early that morning. She went directly to a restaurant. She began with *keitto* and then ordered the *paisettu kala*, which was served with Russian *garchitsa* and of course the local *sieni* which Nora thought was especially fine. For dessert she ate a huge *rauha*."

This gives me such a feeling of power. To think that I know everything Nora ate in that restaurant, while you are very likely still in the dark about it. I expect you are also wondering whether Nora wore her blue *kapelusz*. Well, I don't mind telling you that she did not. She wore her red one.

Let's see now, let's try this:

"Juan's line of vision was partially obstructed by the heavy *fronda* and the tall *cizanas*. He pushed his *costal* to his back and snaked through the *cizanas* to the brink of the *penasco*. Now he could see, and he had been right. They were at a great distance but they were, indeed, *pepinos*. Hundreds of them. He remembered them from the *komkommer* fields in Holland. Carefully he made his way back through the *brasada* to give his report. '*Que pepinos!*' he muttered. 'I have never seen such big ones!'"

If you have figured out what Juan was seeing from the ledge, then I have failed. Next time I will make it harder, and have him up there looking for *groselleros*, or something like that.

Let's have a scene from a detective story. The best whodunits now have lots of foreign intrigue and that means plenty of foreign words in the stories to keep you uninformed:

"In Ben Adhem's quarters, John paced, hands locked behind him. He was making no progress. Every lead took him to a brick wall. The answer, he told himself now, was of course the *kaftor*. The loose ends, he knew, would not come together until he found that *kaftor*. The sunken ship, the dead woman at the fountain, the missing jewels, the answer to these mysteries, the answer to everything, was hidden with that *kaftor*."

This is the most fun I've had all year. I see now why those famous writers grin so much. They can even make mistakes and nobody knows it. I made at least one today. Back there in Helsinki when Nora was dining, I had her eating a large parachute for dessert. I bet you didn't even catch it.

Not so long ago I attended what they call a panel discussion.

In a panel discussion, three or four people sit before a crowd. The panelists are supposed to know things that the members of the audience are interested in. The audience asks questions, and the panel members answer. Well, you have seen panels, I guess.

The reason I went to this particular panel discussion, the members of the panel are all in the same general dodge that I am. That is, they write things for a living. Stories for magazines. Pieces for the paper. Novels, and other kinds of books.

The discussion got onto the matter of reward, and each member of the panel tried to describe the greatest reward that comes to him or her, from doing this writing.

One woman told a little story that interested me a lot. She had written a book, and soon after it came out she was riding on an airplane. Along came a fellow and sat down beside her and opened a book and began reading. The author was pleased to see that it was her own book.

For more than two hours, she studied that guy while he read her book. It was plain he was into that story mighty deep.

He did not want a cocktail when the waitress came to take orders. He did not want a pillow. He did not look out the window, or go to the bathroom, or make conversation.

He just kept his beak stuck in that book.

At last the writer of it couldn't hold her silence any longer. She said to the fellow, "Excuse me, would you mind telling me what you think of that book you're reading?"

He answered, "Why, it's just fantastic. It's a marvelous book. I can't stop reading, and yet I don't want it to end, either. It's the most engrossing story I've ever read."

Naturally the author was pleased. She said, "I am glad to hear you say that, because you are reading my book. I wrote it."

Then it was the reader's turn to be pleased, finding out that he was sitting there beside the author of the best book he'd ever read. The two became friends before the airplane landed, and they exchanged letters later on, and Christmas cards, and that, according to the woman on the panel, was her greatest reward as a writer—getting to know her readers, and hearing them express the pleasure they get from reading what she writes.

From what I have heard, this woman also makes a pile of money writing books, and it seems to me that is worth at least a mention as a part of the reward, but never mind. I liked the airplane story all right.

A thing like that has never happened to me, not in more than thirty years of writing for a living, and I don't think it ever will. I will now tell you why, if you care to hear.

In 1957, almost exactly one year after I began filling this space in your morning paper, I was riding a bus from Houston to Edna. I have not ridden the bus much in my work, but that time I did, going to Edna for a reason I now forget. Edna is down there on U.S. 59, right in between Ganado and El Toro.

When the bus stopped at Rosenberg, a fellow got on and sat down beside me, and he was reading the paper. It was this very journal, and what is more he was reading on the page where one of my own pieces appeared. (I suppose you see the resemblance between this incident and the one involving the author on the airplane.)

He stayed a long time on that one page, and it was evident to me that he was reading my stuff. Now and then he would rub his chin, and chuckle, and it was so good for me to watch. At that time I had it in my plans to become a syndicated columnist and be famous everywhere, not just in Ganado and El Toro. I could tell from this fellow's reaction that I was off to a good beginning.

At last, the same as the author on the plane, I couldn't keep quiet any longer so I said, "Pardon me, sir, do you ever read this fellow here?" I tapped the paper at the place where my byline was and he looked and said, "No, why?"

At that time I was carrying about forty pounds of air pressure and that remark took at least twenty of them out of me. But I plowed ahead and said, "Well, sometimes he gets some pretty good stuff in there."

"Is that right?" said the fellow. "Let me see." And he read my piece, which I thought was so beautiful. He seemed to read it twice, and said at last, "Well, maybe he is just having a bad day."

Since that happened I have never had the spine to go up to any of the customers and ask them what they think of something I have written.

From this swivel chair where I sit when I write most of this stuff, I spend a good deal of my time looking out the window into the backyard.

I have managed to cultivate a deep interest in everything out there, dead or alive, that I can see. The least important backyard event can take place, and I am pleased to let it divert my attention a while, and keep me from doing what I am supposed to be doing.

A small green worm can come measuring his way up a stalk in the flowerbed (as one is doing at this minute). Do you think I won't notice him? Listen, I *welcome* that worm. Because he provides me something to stop and look at other than this keyboard, or the awful empty whiteness of the next page that I must fill.

All the time I have been writing sentences for a living, which is something like thirty years, I have been this way—on a constant search for reasons to stop writing and do something I like better. I can't remember ever producing a sentence that I didn't stop and look around in the middle of it for an excuse not to finish.

(A squirrel has come off the roof and is having an argument with a jaybird over whose turn it is at the feeder. I wonder if that feeder needs filling. I will go out and look, in a minute.)

It's a popular notion that writing sentences this way is great fun. It's not, though, no matter how many times you hear people say it is. The reward, or the punishment, comes later. If there's going to be any fun it'll come afterward, never during.

You would think it might bother me, to have half-finished sentences sitting around here. But it doesn't, not the slightest particle.

Sure, it would bother me *never* to finish a half-completed one, because that would mean missing the deadline and that's not thinkable. Without the deadline I might go years without finishing a sentence, but I am not sure about that, as I haven't ever not had a deadline.

(The calico cat is out yonder in the grass now, sneaking up on the dove that has come to eat the grain I tossed on the patio. The grass needs mowing and the cat likes it that way. She can hunker down in it and the dove will walk right into her whiskers before it sees her. Wow! A close call, that time. Doves are so dumb.)

Half-finished things other than my own sentences do bother me. A half-painted door does. An undropped shoe upstairs does. A melody interrupted and left on a hanging note will send me up the wallpaper, and I have to get something done about it right away, even if I have to sing it myself to a stopping place.

(Two doves are out there fighting now, on the patio. I've found that doves, the symbol of peace since Bible times, are mighty ill-tempered. Hey, wait a minute. They may be mating, instead of fighting. Can't really say. Make a note to think about that. It seems significant, and important, that in animal-watching it's hard to tell, with so many species, whether they are doing battle or making love. So that maybe it's close to the same thing, and not the opposite as we think. Look at cats. Birds. Snakes. Humans?)

But if they would delay the deadline for me, shoot, I could walk away from one of my unfinished sentences and never look back at it. I could even go off and leave an infinitive half split, and drive to Canada and live all summer in the woods and never worry a second that I'd left anything undone. In fact, I would get a wicked satisfaction and a malicious pleasure from having left the condemned thing half-finished and gotten away with it.

(The mulberry tree by the front porch is fixing to have ripe berries. I can't see it from here and I haven't looked at it in a month. But I can tell the berries are almost ripe because a big squeaking bunch of cedar waxwings comes by here twice a day, to check that tree. They don't stay because the berries aren't ready, but pretty soon when the berries reach the right stage a great many waxwings will come swooping in here on that tree and they'll have about a seven-day mulberry orgy.)

My friend Mel called and said could I come on by, that he had another plot ready for me. He meant a plot for a mystery novel. He thinks up at least one a month, and writes it down and saves it for me.

I do not want any mystery story plots but that doesn't discourage Mel. He is convinced we're at the brink of becoming rich and famous by collaborating on a mystery. He has developed what he calls The Formula. He writes it with capital letters that way.

The Formula states that Mel thinks up the plots and I write the stories. He would like to write them himself, and he has tried, but he can't find a publisher with enough sense to publish them. So he struck the idea of collaboration. He says I am weak on plots anyhow, but he admits I am able to compose a fair sentence on one of my better days. He points out also that I seem to be acquainted with a publisher or two. Therefore we should be able to go a long way together on these mysteries.

When he called I told him I was tied up and couldn't come. Then he said, "Christina is making ice cream." I asked what kind and he said, "Fresh peach." So of course I went. There was no choice. Christina's homemade fresh peach ice cream is a blessed event. It occurs only once a year and not being there when it happens is something like missing Christmas.

We sat in the kitchen at the breakfast table. Mel talked from the notes he had made on his yellow pad. "I call this one *The Case of the Crooked Cowboy*. It's about this cowboy who works on a ranch and he has a secret way of making money and it's illegal. Crime on the range. How does it sound?"

Promising, I told him. It didn't sound promising, but Christina was at the drainboard taking the top off the freezer. It was no time to get into an argument about mystery stories that will never be written.

"This needs to be a spare story," Mel said. He has picked up these writing terms, I think, from book reviews. "Keep it taut. No more than fifty thousand words, and only four principal characters. Now then, I think . . ."

She was lifting the dasher out. The creamy soft peachy goodness clung to the dasher's ribs and little wooden flippers.

". . . and we have the cowboy, of course, and the ranch foreman, and the deputy sheriff." Mel was giving me his characters. "Finally the ranch owner, who's a beautiful widow thirty-eight years of age . . ."

She always waits for exactly the right peaches. They're a special variety. She knows this produce guy, and when the peaches come in and they're at the proper ripeness he calls and she drives all the way out there for the peaches to make this ice cream once a year.

". . . because they begin to notice the cowboy is living higher than he ought to be on fifty dollars a week and room and board. He buys a new pickup with double wheels in back and a color TV and orders handmade boots out of San Antonio and . . ."

She was spooning out the first dish, which was for me because I was a guest. It was not quite as large as I'd hoped.

". . . this deputy goes sneaking around and he discovers the cowboy's secret. It's a thirty-acre patch of marijuana in a creek bottom. Deputy hides out, to see who the cowboy is selling to and how he gets the stuff off the ranch . . ."

The first few bites were pure glory. I bet if angels in heaven ordered off the mortal menu they would all ask for Christina's fresh peach ice cream.

Mel was carrying on. "The deputy disappears. The feds come in, to work the dope case, and they find one of the deputy's boots so they suspect foul play. But they can't find his body, and they can't figure out how the dope is leaving the ranch . . ."

Christina asked if I'd like another bowl. It was like asking a mule if he'd like more corn.

". . . finally the beautiful thirty-eight-year-old widow figures out that the cowboy is hiding his marijuana inside these big round bales of hay that you see in pastures now. On the pretense of selling hay to neighbors, he was hauling that dope off the ranch before the very eyes of the feds, and that's how he disposed of the deputy's body, too. Hauled it off inside one of those hay bales. Well, what do you think of it?"

I said I thought it was the finest in all my experience. I was talking about Christina's ice cream but Mel thought I meant his plot, and I went on out and didn't bother to correct the impression.

-{ IX }-

"This here's a paper man . . ."

Last Tuesday afternoon my friend Mel called me and wanted to know if I could slip off from work about 3:30 and ride up to Montgomery with him to look at a pony he is thinking of buying for his granddaughter.

Well, I don't care anything about looking at ponies and besides, as I told Mel, it was Thursday and I can never go anywhere on Thursday without lots of preparation, as Thursday is one of my bad days on the typewriter.

"What do you mean it's Thursday?" Mel scoffed. "It's not but Tuesday, man. You certainly make a fine representative of the press. How do you expect the public to have any respect for you as a newspaper reporter if you don't even know what day of the week it is?"

I tried to explain to Mel that I am not a newspaper reporter but a columnist, and he ought to learn the difference between the two. Because one day if he makes the mistake of looking a real newspaper reporter in the eye and calling him a columnist he might get a punch in the snoot.

A newspaper reporter is a person who goes out and covers riots, and earthquakes, and elections, and other important events that must be written about immediately. What a newspaper reporter writes may get printed just a couple of hours after it is written.

But now a columnist, as I told Mel, is altogether a different proposition. What a columnist writes may not show up in the paper for two days, or three, or maybe even a week, depending on what kind of deadlines he is saddled with.

Deadlines, to a columnist, are the most important things in this life. Some columnists will say that other matters are more important but they don't really mean it.

"What does that have to do with you not knowing the difference between Tuesday and Thursday?" Mel asked.

It has *everything* to do with it, I told him. *Your* Tuesday, and the one everybody else observes, is my deadline for Thursday. Therefore Tuesday has *become* Thursday to me. Just as it is also Sunday.

"Also Sunday?" Mel asked. "How can Tuesday be both Thursday and Sunday?"

Because, I said, Tuesday is my Sunday deadline as well as my Thursday one. When Tuesday comes I say to myself, well, it's Thursday and Sunday today.

"How about Wednesday?" Mel asked.

Wednesday is Friday, I told him.

"Because Wednesday is your Friday deadline, is that right?"

Right. It's all very simple and I never have understood why anybody finds it strange. Thursday, for example, is Monday and Tuesday, just as Tuesday is Thursday and Sunday.

"By that," Mel said, "I suppose you mean that your deadline for Monday and Tuesday comes on Thursday. Why is that?"

I told him I don't know why. A columnist is allowed to question almost anything except deadlines. They are simply assigned to him, given to him, the way God gave Moses the Ten Commandments on the mountain that time, and they are not to be disputed. You just take them and live by them.

Maybe you think it is bad to violate one of the Commandments, but at least you may get forgiven for that. To miss a deadline is unforgiveable. You can never, never be forgiven, as long as you live, for missing a deadline.

"How about Monday? You haven't mentioned Monday."

I said Monday is Wednesday. I mean to me it actually *is* Wednesday. If somebody says, "Come on Wednesday," I am obliged to think, "Go on Monday."

"How about Friday, Saturday, and Sunday?" Mel said.

Those are non-days, I said. They are not in my personal week and I don't observe them, because I have no deadlines that fall on them and they are therefore insignificant. I use such non-days for activities of secondary consequence, such as conducting interviews and traveling about and taking pictures and having the typewriter repaired.

"If I wait till Friday, then," Mel asked, "will you go with me to Montgomery?"

Of course I had to ask whether he meant his Friday or mine. Because if he meant mine he was talking about Wednesday, when I couldn't go.

The deadline has caught me, of all the strange places, at the office.

Since I don't stay around here much I don't even have a chair of my own to sit in, but I don't mind that because I can sit at Marge Crumbaker's desk. Which is where I am now.

Marge is practically never in the newsroom except in the mornings, and I don't show up until after 1:00 P.M., so she lets me share her post this way. And doesn't even complain about my habits, except when I commit little felonies such as going off and leaving her typewriter running, or putting her black felt-tip pens in my pocket by mistake.

Marge's desk has its good and bad points as a place to work. One bad thing is that her phone rings all the time. Another is that the desk is at the entrance to the newsroom, and when the tour groups of visitors file through, as they do frequently, you get stared at, and studied, and commented on a lot, and that can make you feel like a resident at the primate house.

This may be why they have furnished Marge with a tree to hide behind. Very few workers in this vineyard get trees by their desks, and Marge is one, and so when I am here I get a tree sort of by default. It is eight feet tall and grows in a great bucket and is called a schefflera.

I would feel more at ease with a sweet gum or a post oak, or even a mesquite or a yaupon, but it is Marge's desk and I say if she wants schefflera then give her schefflera.

She keeps a neat desk, I will say that for Marge. In fact I can look around this newsroom and see a large percentage of neat-kept desks, which is in opposition to the tradition that reporters are forever surrounded by rubble.

I have to say that I am upholding the tradition, at home where my own desk is. It looks like the collection point for a scrap paper drive, and no reporter would care to share it with me this way. It has an unhealthy appearance somehow. Also explosive, or anyway flammable, as if it shouldn't be approached by anyone bearing open flames.

The desks of some workers are just that way, and as far as I know nothing can be done about it. Every few months I do try. I straighten up, and put things into stacks, and throw away about 60 percent of the volume, and I feel so fine about it.

Then two days later, it is all back. I feel somebody is *sending* it back, but I have never caught them in the act.

We have got some marvelous workers in this newsroom. When they leave here to go wherever they go, their desks are absolutely slick. Nothing left. Not a paperclip, even. How is that possible?

Do you mean to tell me that everything they need to work with will go in a drawer or a filing cabinet? Don't they ever end up with things that refuse to be put away? Don't they ever come in with walking canes whittled out of driftwood, or three or four ears of yellow corn, or five-gallon lard buckets that are bound to be good for something when cleaned up and painted?

Things like that come home with me, whether I want them or not. I have got a red beer barrel, empty, that I am not sure I should keep but until I decide, I am stuck with it. You tell me where to file a red beer barrel, I wish you would.

I have got a ten-gallon milk can as well, the kind that dairy farmers used to put their milk in until the truck came to pick it up. Such cans are no longer used, except for such purposes as holding walking sticks whittled out of driftwood by nice old gents who live on beaches. Do you expect me to pitch a perfectly good ten-gallon milk can into the trash, just because it can't be hidden in a filing cabinet?

The newspaper desks that I have loved the most over the years were those of the old-timey country editors. Desks piled up to the editor's eye level with papers, and goodness knows what else.

In this newsroom we have only one desk that is in the same league with an old country editor's. It belongs to C. W. Skipper, the television editor. If you ever come through here on one of the tours, get the guide to point it out. Pretty soon that desk will need sideboards. It's just beautiful. I think they ought to give Skipper a tree.

A few miles south of Hearne on Highway 6 there's a sweeping curve where I always slow down and think about Ed Lee.

Tell you the truth, I sort of look for him. Not seriously, because there's no chance whatever that I will see him again in that same place. Still, I enjoy thinking that one of these times I will make the curve and there old Ed will be, pedaling along on his bike.

And we could have a reunion, and talk about all the things he has seen on the road since 1956.

I was going up that way just last week, and when I came to Ed's curve it hit me that, almost to the day, it's been twenty-three years since I saw him.

One of the main reasons I keep remembering Ed, he was the first stranger I talked to when I began this job. And Ed encouraged me, when I needed encouragement.

For about a year I had been talking to my masters here at the paper, hoping to convince them that stuff like this would work, and be worthwhile. My position was that if they just gave me a little gas money and let me roam around, I could talk to bums under bridges and nice old ladies sitting on front porches and whittlers on courthouse lawns and they would have interesting things to say that people would want to read about.

When finally the boss said okay, go ahead, I began having doubts about my own idea that I had been talking up so long. Maybe it wouldn't work. Why would strangers want to talk to a guy with a pencil and a notebook, and tell private things?

Well, Ed Lee was the very first one.

He was coming south, on the way to the Valley, and running late. Generally by Christmas, before the bad winter storms, he'd already be down around Weslaco on the Rio Bravo. I can't remember now why he was delayed. Something about his bike, seems like. A gear gone bad, and he had to order it.

It was one of those narrow-tired bikes that weren't common then. We called 'em English bicycles, or racers, with all those different speeds and the brake grips on the handlebars.

The first look at him said he wasn't local. He had the road written all over him. His bedroll strapped on so neat, and the little box back there where his tools rode. Such a small, spare man. His thin face was almost calloused from those thousands of miles in the wind. Bet he didn't weigh 115.

I flagged him down to find out where he'd been and where he was going, to see if he would talk. Boy, did he ever talk. For hours, in a sort of high-pitched, tight-mouthed manner that's common to people who face the wind a lot and travel dusty trails.

We ended up fitting his bike in the back of my car and he rode with me and I turned around and got him a little closer to the Rio Grande.

He talked about life on the move. He'd been on that bicycle for years, migrating in winter to our Valley or to Florida. Then moving on out again about April, following spring up through the country.

He'd even go up into Canada. Go west sometimes, and pedal up the side of a mountain and top the Divide.

He'd sleep in parks or along the side of the road. But if he got caught by the weather, he didn't mind coughing up the money for a bed.

He wasn't any bum. He was a knife and scissors man. Had his stones and things in that little toolbox, and in towns he'd go house to house and sharpen all your knives and scissors for whatever you could pay. Maybe thirty-five cents.

Or for a meal, maybe. Or a sweater you didn't want any longer. Or even a place to sleep on the back porch or in the garage. People knew about knife and scissors men then, and were glad to see them coming.

I don't think I've seen one since Ed Lee in '56. I wonder what kind of reception a guy like that would get now, punching doorbells and asking women if they want their scissors sharpened.

Since Ed, I've talked to dozens of rovers, who stay on the go all their lives. I've never heard one say exactly why he picked that life. I don't think they know. It's just in them to keep moving. The old itching foot.

The thing I liked best that Ed Lee said, he said after all his miles he had found more good in the world than bad, that most of his days he pedaled with a glad heart.

Before he rode away he said he'd send me a card from the Valley. I've learned they'll all say that. They never do it. Ed might have thought about it, though, if he ever passed along Highway 6 again and came to the sweeping curve.

In a job like this, it helps if you don't mind doing duties that would seem odd and even embarrassing to the average worker.

I personally don't mind odd assignments at all, as long as they don't involve heavy lifting or cause pain. I can't stand much pain.

About a week ago I carried out a curious little assignment up in Angelina County. The ten o'clock news was about to come on the radio, and if the weather wasn't freezing it didn't have far to go.

I drove out and parked under the Texas 7 bridge on the Neches River about eighteen miles west of Lufkin. I put on my heavy jacket, and pulled my toboggan cap over my ears, and stood by the car and honked the horn. And honked some more. And listened. And honked. And listened.

The reason I did that, I was instructed to. One of the customers gave me that assignment. He said if the conditions were right, that wolves in the river bottom would answer my honk, and come to it. The longer I honked, the closer they would come, until they would get right up close to the car.

The idea was to see how long I would be willing to stand there and keep honking.

Probably he was talking about coyotes instead of wolves. I doubt there are many full-blood wolves, if any, in that part of East Texas. But people in those woods often refer to coyotes and wild dogs and crossbreds as wolves.

Standing under a bridge in freezing weather and honking at coyotes at ten o'clock is not the oddest customer assignment I ever had. I have done plenty of things odder, and a lot of them I have never told you about.

It's just that I am a sucker for jobs that the customers think up. Of course I am not obliged to go and do whatever the customers say, but I often can't resist, especially if there seems to be an element of harmless mystery involved.

Maybe a letter will say, "Next time you pass through Onion Switch, take the first dirt road east of the church, go through the second cattle guard on the right, drive five hundred yards west and stop under the big sycamore. Park heading due south, and see what you see."

A letter like that doesn't promise that I will see anything at all worth looking at. But still I will go and look because maybe I will see something I haven't seen before.

The first little mystery assignment of that sort I had was shortly after the column began in 1956. Somebody wrote and said drive down the west bank of the San Bernard River, stop at the little island just upstream from the river's mouth, and keep quiet, and listen for the fiddle music.

Of course there's a story that goes with that music, but the letter didn't say so. It just said listen. I went down there three or four times. Finally I got the story from Charlie Ducroz, who lived on the bank of the San Bernard and heard the music many times.

Story is that back in pioneer times, a settler and his wife were paddling up the Bernard in a little bateau. At The Narrows, there where the island is, the boat got sideways of the current and swamped and the couple drowned. The man was a fiddler, on his way to a wedding.

Some still insist that on calm nights you can stand on the bank of the river and hear fiddle music there. Fiddler's Island, they call the place.

Ducroz told me he had heard the music at the island, and also several miles back upstream, near his home. Said it did sound a little like a fiddle. But sometimes more like a hum, a buzz, and it acted strange.

It would move, he said. It would hum and zoom just over-head, and then zip off across the river, and then come back. Ducroz said you could scare it off, temporarily, by hitting the side of your boat with a paddle. No, he didn't have any idea what caused the noise.

I went down there to The Narrows at night, at high noon, at sundown, all times of the day. Never did hear anything. And I haven't even met anybody lately who's heard the music in recent years.

I also went to that Highway 7 bridge on the Neches more than once, to see if I could honk up the coyotes. Oh, I've heard coyotes, lots of times, and wolves too. But I can't get one to sing to me under that bridge. The other night I stayed until my feet felt frozen.

If there *is* a coyote living near that bridge, he showed good sense by not coming outdoors on a night like that.

If I last long enough, and finally get done everything else I want to do, I intend to write a book about the adventures I've had running around in the woods and over the prairies, representing a big-city newspaper.

I am talking about the adventures that I haven't put in the paper. You might think I have told everything already but I haven't. Not anywhere near it.

Why, I could write one entire chapter in that book about going up to country houses where mean dogs live. One day I may tell you about the time in San Jacinto County that a large mean dog refused to let me get back in my own car, after I had got out of it and gone through a gate. I am just not ready to tell that one, though. It sounds too much like a lie.

Another time I may tell about how I came close to getting put in jail in Matamoros because I was confused about the meaning of a certain Spanish idiom, and said something to a Mexican policeman that I didn't know I was saying. Trying to use the native tongue in a foreign country can be risky. It may be two or three more years before I am ready to tell about that one.

Why, only this summer I was thrown out of a small restaurant on Surfside Beach when I wasn't doing anything but just sitting there eating bacon and eggs. I do not yet know why the fellow threw me out. I really didn't much mind it as I was practically through eating already, but the reason for the throwing out is still a curiosity to me. I have been afraid to go back in there and ask.

Also in that book I could print the interviews I've conducted and never did put in the paper, and tell why they weren't used. Been a few of those.

I wouldn't mind, right now, giving you a small sample of one chapter that will go in the book if I ever write it. The chapter will deal with going way, way back in the wilderness, and trying to convince the person I went to see that I have come on a legitimate mission.

People who live way, way back in wildernesses don't very often see the representative of a big-city newspaper. When they do see one, they figure he is there for only one reason, and that is to sell them a subscription.

I will give you the beginning, at least, of such an encounter.

Imagine that I have driven to the end of pavement, and bounced along six or eight miles of dirt road, and stopped at a locked gate, and walked on in half a mile to a house, and here is a gent in suspender overalls and no shirt. He does not look friendly and neither does his big old dog.

I ask if I can speak to him a minute.

"What about?" he demands.

I tell him I work for the morning newspaper in Houston and—and before I can finish he says, "I don't want no paper."

"I'm not selling anything, I'm . . ."

"I get one paper already and I got no time to read it. And it's too dern high. How much your paper cost?"

"I don't sell the paper. I write stories for it."

It will be necessary to repeat at least three times that I don't sell the paper. When finally he accepts that I write stories instead, we get into the area of what *kind* of stories.

"You write about huntin' and fishin'?"

There is an established pattern here. I have learned to relax and let it happen, instead of trying to explain what kind of stories I write. First he will guess that I write about hunting and fishing. Next he will try sports—football and baseball games. Then he will think of car wrecks and bank robberies and things like that. Then he will give up, and at last I can tell him why I came:

"I heard in town you still work your farm here with an ox team. I'd like to see the team work, and write a story about it."

Then we will have a long, long discussion about why I want to put anything in the paper about him and his team of oxen. He will point out that one of the oxen is old and doesn't work very good and he is going to buy a secondhand tractor next spring. It will take about ten minutes to convince him that I have really come all the way out there to write in a big-city newspaper about him plowing a field with those old steers of his.

This kind of stuff never gets into the paper, and some of it is fairly interesting. I always enjoy the part about the payment. Before we go look at the ox team he will ask how much it's going to cost to get a story in that paper about his steers.

It may surprise him a little that it doesn't cost anything at all. And it may also set him to thinking again about why it is that I

want to write about his steers then, if I'm not going to charge for doing it. It will strike him that maybe I will pay *him*, instead of him paying me.

You understand all this goes on while we are standing out in the yard. I am still not entirely certain he won't sic the dog on me when I explain that no, I won't pay him anything for showing me the ox team.

We get it settled, finally, that no money is going to change hands and he may let me come sit on the porch and make the dog go under the house. He will ask about the camera I'm carrying and when I tell him I want to take a picture of him with the ox team, we have the trouble about him changing clothes.

He'll want to go in and put on a white shirt, and change those old shoes. Sometimes it takes a lot of argument to keep him from getting dressed up. He will not see any sense in having his picture taken unless he is wearing the best clothes he owns, even if in the picture he is plowing behind an ox team.

Oh, a lot of other little things happen that you never read about. There is the exchange we have, for instance, about whether I know Joe Biggs. We are in the same business, Joe Biggs and I, and the ox team man insists I ought to know him.

"He's Old Man Jim Biggses boy. You come right by his place on the way out from town. Has that big tin barn?"

I say I don't remember meeting a Joe Biggs.

"Well, he's been aworkin' for that paper a long time."

I ask what department he's in and it turns out he's a printer and works for the Beaumont *Enterprise*, or maybe the Victoria *Advocate*.

You understand that even after all this discussion, still I may not get to see the ox team work. My man may just suddenly decide he doesn't want to fool with it, so I will take my little notebook and my picture box and walk on out.

Before I go I may get to see the fellow's wife. Her curiosity will finally make her come out on the porch. I will not be introduced to her but I will be pointed out, as a sort of novelty that has come down the road.

"This here's a paper man, Maude. Works for a paper in Houston."

I always listen close to see if she will say it:

"Well, we don't need no more papers. Hadn't got time to read the one we get now."

Fly Balls and End Runs

Eagles rip Raiders. Tigers maul Cards. Cats take Hornets.

If you are a sports fan at all you will recognize that those short sentences are written in the style of headlines on football stories. A good many such heads show up every week in this and other newspapers during football season.

For a long time I have been fascinated by the verbs used by the guys who write heads on football stories, especially in editions that carry accounts of dozens and dozens of games. That's when the head writers get a strong test.

Going back up there to the beginning, what those heads mean of course is that the Eagles beat the Raiders, the Tigers beat the Cards, and the Cats beat the Hornets.

Even assuming that the verb *beat* could be fitted into every game-story head, the folks on the copy desk wouldn't want to use it all the time because then every head would sound the same.

So they look for substitutes, punchy verbs that will go into tight places. And this is how all those football teams, instead of just getting beaten, are ripped, and clipped, and sunk, and flogged. Also toppled, tumbled, blitzed, and stomped.

I have never discussed this with anybody who makes a living writing sports heads, but I am able to see that it is not any cinch job to think up all those verbs. They must fit not only the headline space but also describe what one team did to the other.

For instance, to say that the Buffaloes mauled the Gobblers might fit your character count exactly, but you can't say that if the score was something like 21-20. Because that is just not a mauling.

It is more like an edging. Buffaloes edge Gobblers. Or a nipping. Buffaloes nip Gobblers.

But it can't be a ripping. Before it's all right to say in a headline that the Buffaloes ripped the Gobblers, the Buffaloes need to win by anyway four touchdowns, maybe 27-0.

Even 27-0 is not a mauling. A mauling, from what I've seen in the sports section, is from 50-0 on up, the same as a burying. Cards bury Trojans.

A stomping—Eagles stomp Raiders—is a lopsided victory, yes, but it's not as bad as a mauling. Stompings stack up roughly beside bruisings, poundings, punishings, and lashings. Also routings and smotherings. Bucs smother Ducks.

In games that end with ordinary scores neither lopsided nor close (21-12, 14-7, 16-10), headline writers consider that the losers have merely been whipped, sunk, handled, floored, topped, or clipped. I notice some sports desks class a victory such as 21-12 to be a clobbering. But most, the *Post*'s included, hesitate to say anybody has been clobbered until they lose by more than three touchdowns.

So to be clobbered is pretty much the same as getting trampled, bombed, torpedoed, flogged, or thrashed.

You see very few good punchy verbs that go well in headlines over upset stories, in which the loser was supposed to have won. Shock, is one. Panthers shock Colts. Other times, when the underdog wins, the favorite is said in headlines to have been surprised or stung. Or stunned, which is a good one. Bobcats stun Gators.

It is plain that this search for fresh verbs in sports headlines is constant and desperate. Sometimes, in special situations created by the nicknames of teams, the headline writer finds relief in words like scalp, hook, strike, lasso. Redskins scalp Patriots. Steers hook Celtics. Rattlers strike Bulldogs. Cowboys lasso Mustangs.

Occasionally the headline writer can elevate his spirit by producing a little pun. No matter how weak a pun it is, it will be considered a marvel if it fits into a head. One appeared on page one of the *Post*'s sports section just last Saturday, after Galveston's Ball High won a big game. Headline was: Ball rolls over Dulles.

Which reminds me of the most memorable sports head ever to appear in this newspaper, at least in my time. There was a big league baseball player named Julio, and he pronounced it the

Spanish way with the J taking the sound of an H. He once knocked a home run to win a game and the headline was: Julio jits jomer.

Headline writers everywhere have hard jobs, and we should all be kind to them.

"Did you ever make a touchdown?"

That was my friend, Mel, asking me that. It was Friday night and we were passing a high school stadium. The lights were blazing and we could hear the horns tooting and the bass drum thumping and we could hear the buzz of the crowd. Football season had got going again, in the heavy heat of that September night.

I had to tell Mel no, I never had made a touchdown if he meant in a real football game, with lights and bands and crowds. I asked him if *he* had ever made one, because I figured that was the reason he brought the subject up to begin with.

He smiled his dreamy little smile of nostalgia and said, "It's the greatest thrill a young kid can have, making a touchdown in a big high school football game."

But answer the question: Had he ever made one?

"In my junior year," he said, ignoring me, "I weighed 143 pounds in pads. I was an end, and I spent all my time on the bench. A second stringer.

"I played behind a big old limber-jointed boy by the name of Foster. Spider Foster. He was about six two and weighed maybe 160 and he could sure snag passes. So by the time the season was about half gone, I hadn't played much more than five minutes.

"That was a source of embarrassment and frustration for me because I was in love that season with Flora Kessler. She had long brown hair and was in the pep squad. She wouldn't have much to do with me. I figured if I could just distinguish myself one time in a football game, Flora might go to the show with me on Saturday night." He paused a minute to reflect.

I tried to push him along. Come on, now, tell me about making the touchdown.

But he was going to have the story his own way. "When you see all those substitutes sitting on the bench in clean uniforms and never playing, what you may not know is that they have seen plenty of action during the week, in practice.

"We didn't have much of a running game that year, and so the coach was always afraid Spider Foster would get banged up in practice and be on the sick list Friday when he was needed for catching passes.

"So all week long, in scrimmage, I would substitute for Spider on defense especially, and get run over forty times, while Spider sat safe on the bench and waited for offense.

"The coach would take me aside now and then, and talk to me about how we all had to pay the price and wait for a chance, in football or in life. Remember, he'd say, you're taking all these bumps for the team. And I would nod, and say under my breath, no, coach, I am doing it for Flora Kessler."

Get to the point, I said. Tell about the thrill of making the touchdown.

"All right, we're playing Dunlap, one of our big rivals. It's the last quarter. They have a dropkicker that year to do field goals and we're behind 10-6 when Spider gets a helmet in his stomach and loses all his wind for about ten minutes. They carry him off.

"The coach calls me to him and puts his arm around me. I remember his face is the color of ashes. He says to me, 'Go in and tell Billy to run 52-B. And you listen to me, Melvin. If you ever caught a pass in your life, *you better catch one now!*'

"So it's my big chance. That 52-B is a go-for-broke pass play. It starts out perfect. I fake the block on the defensive halfback and get behind him and cut toward the outside. I look back over my right shoulder and here comes Billy's pass, spiraling beautifully."

And you dropped it, right?

"Why no, I gather it in. And I'm free. Speeding down the sideline, flying on to victory, knowing my Mom and Dad and my sisters and Flora Kessler are watching, and it is more than I can bear and I step on my own foot and fall down on the four-yard line and we lose 10-6. The coach wouldn't speak to me for almost a year, and neither would Flora Kessler.

"That was thirty-five years ago," Mel said, with his sad grin, "and I have not gotten over it yet."

Somewhere I suppose boys are still playing scrub baseball on vacant lots but I haven't seen it in a long time.

Scrub is the same game as workup baseball. I never heard the term workup until I was grown. To my bunch it was always scrub.

To start a game you could stand in the middle of a vacant lot and yell "Scrub One!" Then from across the street would come an answering shout, "Scrub Two!" and so on up to twenty or more. Your number indicated where you played. That is, the fellow who yelled Scrub One was first at bat, while the number twelve guy was out in the field somewhere.

Those vacant-lot scrub games inspired a good many special rules. Like five fouls and you're out. That rule was aimed at those old boys with good bat control who tried to stay in town all the time. Staying in town meant being at bat. They'd stay by standing up there and knocking forty fouls in a row on purpose. So they got legislated against.

Sometimes when the game was short of players you would get called out for knocking the ball to right field. Because if any field was going to be minus a defensive player, it would be right. Few fly balls were hit to right so nobody wanted to play there. In team play, you always stuck your weakest fielder in right.

Today, in professional ball, right field is played by high-paid, hard-charging guys with bullet arms, and the weak fielder will be over in left. But it was just the opposite in our old vacant-lot games.

But about playing scrub, what I loved about that game was that it offered a great personal challenge, a chance for individual victory against huge odds. And you could achieve the victory by playing it smart. You didn't have to be tough, or even a very good baseball player. But you had to study, to observe.

Sometimes you could go out and find yourself a really big scrub game. Maybe there'd be twenty-five guys milling around in the outfield hoping to catch a fly ball because the one who snagged it got to move directly on to bat.

All right, you'd have only three men in town doing all the hitting so it didn't take long to study them. Notice one steps in the bucket. Means he's apt to pull a fly ball down the left-field line. Another crouches, sort of like Pete Rose does now, and holds his bat level with the ground when he's waiting on the pitch. So play him in short left-center to hit a line drive. Third batter's got that little dip in his swing, like Mickey Mantle and most of all those long-ball hitters, and he looks strong, and his stance is slightly closed, so play him straightaway in deep center.

Then when it works, when you've played the hitter right, you can pretty nearly see your name on the ball when it leaves the bat. A high, deep fly, way over everybody's head but yours. You're standing back there waiting and you could catch it in your hip kick, it's that easy.

So then you go trotting toward home plate, weaving through the crowd, and they're saying, "Why, you lucky dawg!" But you know it's not luck. It's something you did because you knew what they didn't know, because they hadn't studied. It was a splendid experience, and mighty satisfying.

Couple of the customers have gigged me a little for suggesting that intramural sports some day may replace the sports competition we have now between institutions.

All right, that'll be a long time coming, but I do challenge the position, common among sports fans, that you aren't having real competition if you don't get on an airplane and fly half across the country to play a bunch of strangers. It just ain't so.

The fiercest and most exciting and satisfying sports competition I ever saw or took part in were games played on vacant lots and bald prairies and city streets and corn-patch turn-rows.

I can't remember defeats more bitter or victories any sweeter than we used to taste on a city park softball field here in Houston in the late 1940s. Every weekend the *Post* would get up a team to play the *Chronicle*. You think it didn't make any difference who won? Hoo boy.

The late Harry Johnson, *Post* city editor in those days, was the manager of our team. If the *Chronicle* beat us on Sunday, Harry survived it with very little grace.

In all the years he ran the city desk he said an ugly word to me only once, and that didn't have anything to do with putting out the paper. It came on Sunday, when I was running between second and third and got my feet tangled up and fell down and was tagged out, and the *Chronicle* won the game. You'd have thought Harry had lost the seventh game in the World Series.

But what I love most about intramural or sandlot games is that they can provide beautiful moments for individuals who really need such moments, and can't get them any other way.

I think about a pudgy kid named Carl something, from my days in school out at Lubbock.

He was a history major and wore thick glasses and corduroy pants and thick-soled canvas shoes. He couldn't run from here to the bathroom, and he had the coordination of a bale of hay. But he was always hanging out around the softball fields where the intramural games were played.

Nearly every student enrolled played in that league. You wanted to play, you got nine other guys and you played. You'd find a piccolo player out of the band on shortstop, and a fullback off the varsity football team on third. It was a fine setup. I mean there was no fooling around. Everybody played to win. We celebrated when we did, and we grieved when we didn't. I believed in that, and I do still. There's not anything wrong with wanting to win.

One afternoon our team came up a man short, and we had to recruit that Carl something to fill in. He was forever around, hoping he'd be asked. We put him in right field because that's where you always put your weakest fielder. You didn't have as many left-handed pull hitters then as you do now, and the right fielder could sleep a lot.

We stayed lucky. Nothing but a few lazy grounders went out to Carl, and he managed to lay down in front of 'em and hike back to the infield with the ball. The only damage he did was striking out all the time.

Then in the last inning, he became a hero. He caught a fly ball, and it wrapped up the game for us. If he'd missed it, two runs would have scored and we would have lost.

You have to understand it was an impossible catch, for the reason that this guy did not know how to catch. He couldn't have caught a fly ball if you'd given him a shrimp net and four major league outfielders to hold it.

But this one he caught. I still think he was running from it, trying to escape. It hit his fist some way, and careened along the inside of his arm, and bounced off his head and shoulder, and shot up straight, and he grabbed it, I expect to keep it from hitting his glasses.

So he was a hero, and we mobbed him. The piccolo player whammed him between the shoulder blades, and so did the fullback from the varsity, and we lifted him over our heads, and the girls passing by stopped to see who it was, and I would not take a silver dollar for the memory of that old boy's eyes, glistening in triumph behind those thick glasses.

I feel certain that from that day, life for him was better.

This is the season of the year that you see them, sitting with their pretty wives and young children in short-order cafes around 10:30 or 11:00 o'clock at night.

There'll be two of them at least, maybe three, and they're wearing softball uniforms that are red and white. Or blue and white. Or green and white. Across their backs are big letters that read "OK Tire Service" or "Quality Cleaners" or "Ken's Radiator Shop."

They have just played a softball game and now they have come to the cafe to talk about it and to be seen in their uniforms. One in the bunch has been careful not to brush away all the red dirt-stain on the outside of his left pant leg. Because the stain shows that, even at thirty-four and with ten years' service at the plant and a kid in the fourth grade, he still goes into second base hard, and on his back.

That's the thing you notice about them, that they aren't boys any longer. They look broad-shouldered and healthy but the gray is showing now in their thick sideburns and the Pearl and the Lone Star and the gravy are showing around their necks, and hanging over their belt buckles a little.

I listen to them sometimes.

"Ain't no way we can win a ball game with ol' Red on third. Hell, he can't even throw across the infield."

And other reasons like that, to explain why they don't win. Winning a game played under dim lights in a city park is still almighty important to these guys.

That fellow Red, that they talk about? The one who can't throw across the infield? You know why he's playing third on the team? I know why. I don't know Red but I know why just the same.

Because he has been playing third base for a softball team sponsored by Ken's Radiator Shop or Quality Cleaners or OK Tire Service ever since he was twenty-one. He is now forty-six and he won't quit.

He imagines he is just as good as he ever was. He has announced he intends to play till he's fifty, and his best friend is the manager, so there is small hope of getting him off third base.

The young ones, the thirty-four-year-olds that still go into second base in a cloud of red dirt, they just have to accept ol' Red, and carry him. Because there is nobody harder to unseat than a forty-six-year-old third baseman on a city-league softball team. Unless it is a seventy-two-year-old soprano in the church choir.

The reason his teammates put up with ol' Red is that they will put up with practically anything to keep the opportunity to play, to do something athletic before an audience.

No, wait, do you think I am putting them down? Why no. Listen, I was once a thirty-four-year-old softball player myself. How do you think I know all this?

The way a guy gets hooked, early in his life he experiences at least one exquisite moment of glory as an athlete in a spectator sport. Any kind of sport, just so a few people are there watching.

Say he's a high school boy of seventeen. He is a third-string bench warmer. The season is over and he hasn't even lettered yet.

Then one nippy Friday night in October, at 9:25, within a space of twenty seconds, his life changes. It happens when he is sent in with a tricky play in a desperate try to save the game. And it works, and he speeds eighty-two yards down the sideline and scores.

Now that is a mighty intoxicating experience, strong stuff for a seventeen-year-old boy to handle. Because for days afterward, he will be treated by half the folks in his community as if he has delivered the universe from the very fires of Satan.

It is the greatest thing that ever happened to him up to that time, and perhaps the greatest that ever will.

So you can go to a city park in summer, and find guys playing softball at thirty-four, or even forty-six, and you can depend on this: That in the past they have known, to one degree or another, the same experience that seventeen-year-old boy had.

And they are out there still searching, hoping to recapture the vaguest suggestion of that beautiful old feeling. They will tell you they keep playing for the exercise, or something like that, but I know the real reason.

All right, all right, I admit it. I didn't know a month ago whether the Houston Rockets played ice hockey or soccer, and I didn't care.

I thought Del Harris was a pro golfer. I thought Moses Malone was a Baptist preacher up in Nacogdoches County. I thought The Whopper was a hamburger with double meat.

But I have got 'em all straight now. Overnight I was converted, and suddenly I'm a stompin', shoutin', born-again Houston Rocket fan. I hate the Celtics, and I think the referees are bums, and I believe Gene Peterson is the best play-by-play radio announcer on the planet.

Gene Peterson? You don't know who Gene Peterson is?

I didn't either until one night last month. I was rolling along toward home, just doing the old double nickel and spinning the radio dial to keep awake, and this fellow came on spouting some kind of a foreign language.

What he was saying was past my understanding, but I got fascinated by his style. A sort of rapid chant. Was he an auctioneer, selling tobacco in Swahili? An electronic evangelist, speaking in tongues?

I put my good ear close to the speaker, and now and then I could catch a word, and then a phrase, and within fifty miles I was understanding about half of what was coming out and I could tell this guy was describing a basketball game.

The game was being played between Los Angeles and Houston, and Houston won. Toward the end this announcer got so excited I thought he would pop a blood vessel. He would shout. Then he would chant a while in the most astonishing machine-gun way about the action. Then he'd erupt into a yell. And a moan. He'd fuss at the officials. Criticize the players. You could tell he wanted to cuss, or needed to. I sort of got to liking it. I don't mean to say I understood it all. But I did seem to hear that Houston was involved, with Los Angeles, in the playoffs of the National Basketball Association.

That sounded suspicious to me. I asked a sportswriter friend if it was true. He said, "Yes, but don't get worked up about it. They'd have to beat the Lakers two out of three games. Ain't no way they're gonna do that."

They did, though. I listened to Peterson's broadcasts, and I got so I could understand nearly everything he was saying.

The Rockets then had to beat San Antonio four out of seven. I didn't even know San Antonio *had* a pro basketball team. But it does, and a mean one, too. Time Houston finished off San Antonio, I wasn't only a Rocket fan but a Peterson one as well.

I never heard a guy who could get so much said, so fast, about action. In that way he reminds me of Kern Tips, the greatest football play-by-play announcer who ever sat behind a microphone. Tips could tell you on the radio more about a football play than you could see sitting on the fifty.

Some who were supposed to know the inside stuff about sports broadcasting used to say Tips would describe things about a football play that didn't actually happen. I don't know if Peterson is doing that or not. How would I know? Why would I care? This is show biz, man. The guy is entertaining me.

No, I don't know him. Never met him. Probably never will. I don't go the same places as people in that work. Sort of like Gene Elston, though. Somebody asked me the other day if I know Gene Elston, who calls the Astro games, and I said, "Sure, yeah."

Afterward it hit me that I'd answered wrong. I never have met Elston. But I've ridden so many thousands of miles with him, listening to him tell me about ball games, it didn't seem natural to say I don't know him.

After the Rockets had plowed on and beat Kansas City four games—incredible!—old Gene Peterson was my buddy. We were in this thing together, pal. A month ago I didn't even *like* pro basketball, and look at me now. Ain't nothin' like winnin', hey Gene?

By the time you read this, the second game of the championship series with Boston will have been played and the Rockets will be two games down, or tied. If it's two games down, don't worry. You wait'll we get those Boston dudes down here.

After that TV network finally decided to put the Rockets on a live broadcast, I turned the volume down and stuck with Peterson on the radio. The TV announcers were against us. At least Peterson is on my side.

You think I want objectivity? Are you serious? Man, I want *flagrant favoritism*. I want to know how they're robbing us. I'm new at this game and need help.

When Larry Bird travels and the refs don't call it, I need to be told. I want to know about it when those big dudes double-team Malone under the basket and pretty near flatten him and it's not called. Peterson tells me all that stuff. When Rick Robey plays dirty, Peterson tells that too. Right on the radio Tuesday night he said, "Rick Robey is a dirty player."

Hot dawg! Now that's *tellin' 'em*! Man, I haven't had so much fun out of a game since we played tin-can shinny on the streets of Fort Worth back in 1932.

Any time I am in Texas City and have a spare hour, I like to drive out to the end of the Texas City Dike and observe the fishermen.

I can't think of a better place to study fishermen at close range. You will find certain piers and jetties and stretches of river bank where fishermen will be more concentrated. But the Dike is five miles long and has a paved road running along its middle. You can poke along and watch the anglers on ten uninterrupted miles of fishing space, and never get out of your car.

The Dike isn't shown on most highway maps. On a detailed map of the Texas City area, it shows as one of the most extraordinary features of the state's coast—a five-mile finger of land pointing straight out into Galveston Bay.

You might ask why it is worthwhile to observe fishermen. I think it's a constructive activity for anybody who is interested in understanding, so far as it's possible, the nature and the behavior of human creatures.

Fishing as it is done now, as a sport, is one of the most mysterious of all the amusements indulged in by humankind. That is my view of it. I simply don't understand why so many millions are so nutty about fishing. Even back when I was fishing several times a month myself, still I didn't understand entirely why I was doing it.

Fishing, as recreation and amusement, has some severe shortcomings. One is, most of the time a fisherman is fishing, the chances are good that nothing whatever will be happening. Furthermore, while nothing is happening the fisherman will most likely be experiencing some kind of physical discomfort. Now isn't that right?

There on the Texas City Dike I spoke to a couple and wondered how long they had been there. They said since noon. The time then was 7:00 P.M. They had reeled in a little string of what looked like croakers to me. Time those fish were cleaned they might have been enough to flavor a quart of soup. I'm not certain.

That pair had brought along almost nothing for creature comfort, and had been sitting seven solid hours on the Dike's granite riprap. I don't know why they weren't paralyzed.

Yes, it's true, I have done the same, or its equal. I used to fish with a bunch of guys up at Huntsville. We were bad about rushing the season every spring. We'd go up to Rayburn early in March, and spend the night in a motel, and get out on the lake in weather cold enough to shock polar bears. We'd tie up and sit out there and the spray would put ice in our very whiskers. We'd cuss ourselves for being out there, and say, yes, but since we're here we might as well stay, and we'd stay. I'm not sure why.

It wasn't because we might hook something that would look good hanging on the wall, or something we could take home and eat. Of all the millions who fish, mighty few are meat fishermen, or trophy fishermen either.

I have some little theories, about why they go out and seem to sit there waiting for something to happen.

Maybe they are searching, not fishing. Searching to experience again a special time, or year, or day, or even a moment that was rich and good and that happened to involve the outdoors, and being off and away, and being in tune with the land and the water, and being with somebody they loved.

The best time I spent fishing was with my kids. I loved to put them in the boat and let one of them run it and I would sit up in front and when the motor was shut down, I'd be a human troll motor. Paddle them, quietly, to likely places. Swing the boat so a cast could be made up into a still pool. I loved doing that.

They thought it was strange. Why do you want to paddle for us all the time? Don't you want to fish? Had you rather paddle than fish?

But I knew something they didn't—that in a short time, such a very short time, they would be gone, and gone forever, and I would never have them again, not in that special way that I had them all to myself in that little boat, and I was right, I never have. You can never paddle for them again, not really, after they leave.

But that's only why going fishing was special to me, personally. Probably all of us who go have our special mysterious reasons. I am convinced the reasons have little to do with catching fish.

If you get down around Texas City, drive out on the Dike and study the fishermen and see what you think.

──⊰{ XI }⊱──

Natural Wonders

It's a devout hope of mine that before I quit, I will get to see a whooping crane take off from his winter home down on the Aransas National Wildlife Refuge and head back to Canada.

Anybody who has seen it seems to have trouble hiding the excitement in his voice. It must be one of the grand things left to see in nature.

Just a few days ago I stood on the bow of a boat in Aransas Bay and watched three whoopers stalking around in that shallow water and I thought maybe this was the time, that finally I would get to see that dramatic departure.

They didn't fly, as it turned out, but they might have. The time is getting near, and there was a strong warm south wind, the kind they like to leave on.

They go into a climbing turn when they take off. And circle, pumping those great black-tipped wings that may span seven feet, and they keep circling until they find a wind layer they like. Maybe 3,500 feet, maybe higher, before they head north.

By the time you read this, probably some of the seventy whoopers that wintered on the government refuge down at Austwell will be flapping up the middle of the country toward Canada.

The boat I was on belongs to Pat and Carl Krueger, who took a little bunch of us up the Intracoastal Canal from Rockport to see if we could get some whooping crane pictures. We saw seven of the cranes but couldn't get close enough for good picture-taking. Not with my camera, anyway. You need zoom lenses and all kinds of fancy business for good wildlife photography.

Once we watched three of the cranes feed quite a while within I guess 150 yards of the boat. We couldn't get any closer because the water was too shallow. But those great birds paid us almost no attention. Somehow, a whooping crane being such a rare bird, you expect that he'll be spooky and distrustful of boats and noises.

Later on I talked by phone to the manager of the Aransas Wildlife Refuge, E. F. Johnson. He said the cranes are tolerant of boats because there's so much traffic on the Intracoastal Waterway, which runs along the east side of the refuge's Blackjack Peninsula. If you get out of a boat, Johnson said, that's when they take off. I don't see how you'd do any good getting out of a boat, though, in that marsh. Probably sink up to your billfold in mud.

Johnson said even when you approach the cranes in a shallow-draft boat they're most likely just to walk away from you, rather than fly. Thousands and thousands of visitors to the refuge see the cranes, but not many get to see a whooper in flight. I've been on the refuge half a dozen times and once went along on the airplane ride and helped make the head count on the cranes. But I've never seen one fly, or heard one trumpet.

One of the cranes we saw the other day had a red leg. I found out from Johnson the red leg was a band, placed on several baby birds in the nests up in Canada. Interesting thing about that to me was knowing we were seeing a bird a year old, or less, and there he was standing out there probably four feet tall. Adult whoopers get as tall as five feet. Which means a lot of humans in this world could stand and look almost eye to eye with this crane. Now that's a lot of bird.

The thing I liked the best about going to the refuge again was seeing brown pelicans. On the way home from trying to take whooping crane pictures, we had a fine show put on for us by a little flight of brown pelicans.

The thing about that is, it's something you didn't see on the Texas coast just a few years ago. Because these funny old birds were gone from our beaches and bays and inlets, gone entirely. Now they are coming back.

What got me interested in brown pelicans was that they disappeared. It was a little scary. It may be the natural order of events on this planet for species to become extinct, the way the dinosaurs did, but for a creature as common in our environment as a pelican to drop so quickly out of sight, man, we had to be doing something awful wrong. For the Texas coast not to have a brown pelican was like a Texas farm not having a mockingbird or a Texas ranch not having a cottontail rabbit.

Five years ago, Johnson told me the other day, you couldn't find a brown pelican in Texas. Not one.

Poison got the blame for that. DDT, specifically. DDT is banned by law now. Whether or not that's the reason I don't know but the pelicans are returning. Seventeen nesting pair have been counted in Mesquite Bay, across the Intracoastal from Blackjack Peninsula. Johnson says the pelican count has gone now to 113 birds for the Texas coast.

The best thing about the brown pelican is that he will let you get closer to him than a whooping crane will, and at times he likes to fly around boats at low altitude. I have a suspicion he is observing the wildlife on board. Keeping an eye on us, maybe, to see what we will think of to do to him next.

In the rocky, broken terrain of the Texas Hill Country and the Edwards Plateau, a good many caves occur. Some are summer dwelling places for multitudes of bats.

I got to visit a dandy bat cave recently while camping on the James River, near where that short stream feeds into the Llano southwest of Mason. The cave is on private property.

The time to go to a bat cave, if you wish to see any bats without going inside, is late afternoon, around sunset. Probably they'll begin flying out before the sun is gone entirely.

Once you get within about a hundred yards of it, the opening to this particular cave is not hard to find. Just follow your nose. The odor is pretty unpleasant. I have stayed half an hour around things that smelled worse, but not lately.

Evidently the odor comes off the guano, although I have read that some kinds of bats give off a musty odor and an expert can identify the species by that smell.

I went to the cave with a couple of companions. We took a vote and decided that in thirty minutes we watched at least a million bats fly out of that big hole in the ground. I don't know why we picked a million. But I think if you had been with us you'd not have argued that the figure was too high.

The main opening to the cave is something like fifteen feet high and twenty-five feet wide—a big hole in the side of a solid rock hill. When we arrived the bats had not begun to come out but they were getting organized.

They were already in flight, inside the cave. We stood near the entrance and watched them flying past the opening, thousands and thousands, making their high-pitched squeaks. I am talking about a river of flying creatures, probably eight feet deep and at least that wide, in the tightest possible formation, moving in one direction inside that cave. Which suggests that the cave has a circular interior, enabling the bats to make 360 degrees while they are warming up for the evening fly-out.

When they began to emerge, the stream of creatures seemed smaller, as if it adjusted its size to accommodate a curious flight pattern followed at departure. The stream came from the center of the opening, then veered right, and flew a tight, ascending circle. When the circle was complete, the stream took off down a little ravine. Every bat flew the same heading.

Evidently this corkscrew maneuver enables the bats to gain just enough altitude to clear the tops of mesquite and blackbrush growing at the head of the ravine. Once in a while a bat would hit the brush, and hang on a limb a few seconds, then flap free and rejoin the flight. We stood close but the bats seemed not to notice us. Individuals at the edge of the stream would fly within six inches of our heads, but none ever touched us.

A bat may be expert at avoiding obstacles in flight, but it is not the best-flying creature in nature by a long way. It flies a fluttery, erratic path. But the fact that it flies at all makes it unique. This is our only flying mammal. We have gliders—such as the flying squirrels—but among mammals only the bat is capable of true flight.

We visited the cave on a warm evening. Watching the flight, I became aware of a pleasant cool breeze. It had an unnatural quality, like the gentle puff off an air conditioner. Until one of the friends with me remarked on it, I hadn't realized that the breeze was coming off those tens of thousands of fluttering bat wings.

The mouth of the cave faces, I believe, almost due north. The bats departed on a northeast heading, went into a shallow climb, divided into bunches of several hundred each (maybe several thousand each), and kept on that northeast course until they looked like swarms of bees to us, and then faded from sight.

Later on, surely they dispersed to flit around all night and feed on insects. But they kept in bunches until they were a long way from the cave. Why?

Why indeed. Dozens of other questions arise about these remarkable little flying animals. What a marvel of organization they represent. Consider the departure from that cave. Imagine the result if every bat decided to come out of there when it pleased, and not wait in line, and the devil with the system. Why, half the colony would be killed in the stampede.

Maybe even more extraordinary than the departure is that the bats regroup and return, early the next morning, in a similar orderly way.

Texas has bats, and then it has bats. William B. Davis's *Mammals of Texas* describes two dozen species known in this state. I am guessing, from the book, that what we saw out there in Mason County is the guano bat, *Tadarida mexicana*, but I'm not sure. The book says that not all bats feed exclusively on insects. Some eat fruit and nectar. Some eat fish.

Just at sunset we saw a neat thing. A big hawk dived into those dispersing bats, and briefly scattered a small segment of the flight. The bird didn't seem really interested in catching a bat. It simply broke through for an instant, the way a chesty boy will charge through an organized game being played by smaller children, to show his contempt.

I shot up an entire roll of film, but that late in the day I didn't get a picture of one thing you'd recognize as a bat in flight.

About the middle of the afternoon I was sitting in a fishing camp out on the James River near Mason, watching a whitetail doe and trying to figure out what was special about her.

I have kept company with deer for a lot of years but this one seemed unique somehow. She had come splashing downstream, loping through the shallows where the bottom is rock and the water a few inches deep.

She came out of the river just opposite our camp and picked her way, with ease and dignity, up a ledged bluff. That bluff rises I suppose 150 feet. You don't walk up it, you climb. I have gone up it, sliding and grunting and grabbing, working from rock to rock and ledge to ledge, generating miniature avalanches, demonstrating to nature what clumsiness is.

And here was the doe, moving up with so little effort, in fluid leaps and curvy turns and it was just beautiful. Then it struck me why the doe seemed extraordinary: I had never before seen a deer climb.

All the deer I have known and fed and watched were in fairly flat territory. The Coast Prairie. The Brush Country. The Post Oak Belt. Not many rocky bluffs there.

At the top of the climb the doe stood a moment on her hind legs and made an arch of her slender self and went over a low barbed-wire fence and into the brush. It wasn't a leap, it was a slither or something. I don't know what it was but it put her over the fence. Her forelegs were almost touching the ground again before her back feet lifted.

I tried to visualize a better picture of what physical grace is, than that deer moving up the bluff. I could not. I've watched goats make that climb, but against the whitetail they're flat awkward. Maybe a mountain lion would best the deer for beauty of movement. I'd give a considerable sum to see a cougar go up that bluff.

Late in the day a couple of us climbed it and went on upstream to the top of a little mountain. It was like looking almost straight down on camp from a twelve-story building. The site was much prettier than it was the night before, when I came near freezing in the wind, sleeping on the ground.

One of our compadres was on the river fly-fishing. The sun was low and the light would catch his line and make it golden.

We went down the mountain on the far side and walked a quarter of a mile up a narrow canyon, with steep rocky walls and elms and sycamores and oaks beside pools of water, clear and cold.

We walked up on a big hog-nosed skunk turning over rocks, looking for whatever hog-nosed skunks eat. Bugs, I think. The skunk looked at us with what I thought was mild curiosity and seemed to find nothing of interest and went on back to hunting. The hog-nose is the one with the wide white stripe that runs from the top of the head to the end of the tail. Instead of several stripes and spots like our other kinds have.

At a bend in the canyon we got into a flock of wild turkeys. Hunters talk about how tough turkeys are to get a shot at. Evidently these knew we weren't hunting. They kept their distance but didn't really go anywhere. They were getting ready to roost.

We sat on the canyon floor and watched a dozen hens work their way up the side of a cliff on the way to roost. They moved with a kind of flutter-hop. A short jump, aided by a quick wing flap. Sometimes just one wing.

Something new for me was being close to a wild turkey when it explodes out of a tree. An adult bird coming off the roost, just over your head, makes an extraordinary racket. The wing action necessary to propel that heavy body is so great, you think you've flushed a helicopter from the top of an elm tree.

But maybe better: The next morning after breakfast that flock of turkeys flew over us. They came down the river in perfectly spaced formation and banked at the camp and turned into the sun and gave us a few of their notes. I'd never seen a flock of wild turkeys in flight and it was worth the trip.

We had several flights of sandhill cranes, too, sending down that exotic call they make. I wish somebody would invent a musical instrument that sounds like a sandhill crane. I bet the sound would be a credit to any symphony orchestra.

Anyhow, that's why you go.

Earlier this week we dwelled a minute on that question. Why will people go forth into the wilderness in winter and sleep on the ground in bitter wind and eat scrambled eggs mixed with sand and ashes and tremble with general discomfort? They don't go to hunt. Not even to fish, though they take tackle.

What they go for is the stuff I've mentioned here. The quick pieces of artwork nature produces, for those who'll buy a ticket. Like a sunset turning a flyline gold, and whitetail deer giving lessons in grace.

Other stuff, too. The campfire things, like two guys coming to visit from a ranch nearby, and singing Mexican songs in the smoke, and telling a few benevolent lies.

Then the after-reward, that may be best of all. When you get home—which I am now—your bed is so sweet again. Do you have trouble sleeping these nights? Here's what you do. Take a sleeping bag and go out on a cold night and bed down on a river bank, on rocky ground. Stay two nights, and when you get back you won't have any trouble sleeping.

It is ten o'clock on a hot still morning and I am here by the window, listening to the locusts sing in the backyard. Must be a dozen of them in the big hackberry. They have been singing since before seven.

This is the insect that entomologists call the cicada and most

Texans call the locust. A true locust is a grasshopper but I have a dictionary that says it's all right to say a cicada is a locust. The accepted names of a few bugs endorse this usage. The seventeen-year locust and the thirteen-year locust, for example, are both cicadas.

Whatever you call him, the cicada's song is the sound of deep summer. When I hear it I think of slow, hot afternoons long ago, when I didn't have to do anything except just exactly what I wanted to do. So I love that locust sound.

Another reason I am in sympathy with the cicada is that he has something in common with you and me. Which is, that in order to fulfill the purpose of his life, he must constantly expose himself to enemies who are eager to do him harm.

The cicada exposes himself by making that whirring noise that carries so far. He is obliged to make it in order to attract a female cicada, so he can mate with her and produce more cicadas. This is his assignment, his reason for being.

But as he makes that racket, he draws not only female cicadas but a regular platoon of enemies.

Birds, being the foremost. Just yesterday morning at about this same time I sat right here and watched a big jaybird fetch a cicada out of the hackberry and sit on the mimosa limb and make dinner out of the poor thing while it was still buzzing.

If the cicada had kept quiet, maybe he would still be among us. But of course he is unable to keep quiet.

He has another interesting enemy called a cicada-killer. This is a large solitary wasp which slips up and zaps him and carries him off to its den. This wasp had rather eat cicadas than any other kind of wasp food.

I am not able to find in bug books that the cicada's call attracts wasps, but I expect it does. It draws female cicadas so why not wasps?

This summer I have even seen a calico cat catch and eat a cicada. So this insect's enemies range up into furry things with four feet.

They include small boys. A while ago I looked in Walter Linsenmaier's fine book *Insects of the World* and Linsenmaier says "it is next to impossible to catch" a cicada. Maybe Texas cicadas are sluggish but I never did find them that tough to catch. After I read that line I went out and tried to catch one and failed, I admit. But then I am not as quick as I once was. Used to catch 'em fairly easy.

Back yonder before small boys thought they needed toys that cost $17.50 apiece, they used to make playthings out of cicadas. You can tie a piece of thread just behind the cicada's broad head and let him loose and he will use those strong wings to fly around on the end of your thread. It's like you've got a trained insect.

Then you can stick one in your shirt pocket, such as in school when everybody is supposed to keep quiet, and give him a light tap with your finger once in a while and he will buzz. It's sure impressive to your friends, having a pet bug in your shirt pocket that will answer your tap that way.

When my children were little I showed them these cicada tricks and this may have impressed them more than anything else I have ever done, as long as they have known me.

Of course there are some who will argue that it is unkind to treat a cicada that way, tying him up and sticking him in shirt pockets. And I expect the cicada would agree.

But isn't it true that you and I and the cicada are kinfolks in this way: That if we're going to accomplish anything of much consequence, we've got to make a racket, and be seen, and take risks.

Say a cicada set out just to enjoy life, and avoid birds and wasps and calico cats and schoolboys. So he spends all his time hiding behind leaves, sitting on a limb and drinking sap, which is the most pleasure of all to a cicada, and he never makes a sound. All right, he might live to be a very old insect.

But he's not going to keep quiet. Because then he would be a bug without a purpose, and that's the awfullest thing of all.

By reading the mail I've found out that a good many people practice the hobby of putting words into the mouths of birds. They'll listen, you know, to owls and killdeers and crows and try to figure out what these birds are saying.

I didn't imagine so many people were interested in this kind of thing. Maybe it's all a part of the Great Discovery of Nature which has taken place in just the last few years. People are always discovering what's been there in front of them all the time.

Well, back a few weeks ago, I made what I consider to be a significant observation about the mockingbird and I thought I should pass it on.

You may not know the racket our state bird makes has always caused a lot of argument, even among bird experts. They argue about whether he really mocks the calls of other birds, and sometimes they have discussions about what words are coming out of his throat.

Even a bird expert of such standing as the late Roy Bedichek once devoted two chapters to the mockingbird in his book, *Adventures With A Texas Naturalist.* In one of those chapters he dwelled a while on what the bird is saying.

I don't have a copy of that book before me now but I remember Bedichek was once told by a bird-listener that the mocker is always shouting, "Thief! Thief! Thief! Police! Police! Trouble-trouble-trouble-trouble-trouble!" I'm not certain those are in the right order.

There were other words, too, but those are all I remember.

Bedichek didn't seem satisfied with them. Said he could fit the words only fairly well into the mockingbird's song.

I never have been able to fit them in at all, anywhere. Not those words or any others that observers have credited this bird with saying.

But I've always tried. I was trying on the Fourth of July, listening to a mockingbird that's lately taken over a telephone pole and a post oak tree not far from this typewriter. And suddenly it hit me, why it is so many people have trouble deciding what the mockingbird is saying.

Our everlasting gringo superiority has misled us to assume that this bird is talking English. When all the time he is yelling everything in Spanish. It's a fact. I can prove it.

To begin with, you have got to know why a mockingbird sings. The reason is, he is looking for a mate. Even in the depths of summer when he yells from the top of a telephone pole he is between wives and wanting another. I learned this from reading Bedichek.

You will have to admit then that it makes sense to guess that the mocker, if he's saying anything at all, is calling the names of females. This guess got me on the right track. It then led to the solution of the mystery when it hit me that every name the bird called was a Spanish one. So here is what he's yelling:

"Chica-Chica-Chica-Chica-Chica-Chica! . . . Dolores! . . . Dolores! . . . Maria-Maria-Maria-Maria-Maria-Maria! . . . Rosalia! . . . Rosalia! . . ."

Over and over that way, calling one lady bird after another, as if he is not really particular which one accepts his invitation as long as she's got a Latin name.

The mockingbird, as far as I've been able to establish, is not capable of expressing a complicated thought in Spanish. True, my own Spanish is almost a felony offense so the bird may indeed be saying more than I can catch. But chiefly I believe he deals in single words and short phrases.

"Venga!" he shouts. "Venga-venga-venga! Adelante! Adelante! Cuando? Cuando? Cuando? Aqui! Aqui! Aqui! Si-si-si-si-si-si!"

The phrasing, the rhythm, the accent of this bird is so purely Spanish that I'm astonished anybody ever dreamed he spoke English.

This particular one I've been hearing is fond of spouting certain phrases that I haven't been able to connect up with a mockingbird courtship. He'll say, just as plain:

"Como se llama . . . Estados Unidas, Estados Unidas . . . mas-o-menos, mas-o-menos, mas-o-menos . . ."

Ignoring the repetition, the literal translation would be "What is your name?" And then, "United States." And finally, "more or less." Which makes no sense, so I think that bird merely likes the sound of those words and throws them in just to show off.

Hey, aren't you up? It's seven o'clock in the morning and I am sitting under a cedar tree on the South Fork of the Guadalupe River a few miles west of Kerrville.

The past two nights I have slept here, or at least a little way upstream where a friend has a sort of river retreat. I have been here before. Sometimes the friend lets me bunk at this Hill Country place of his, long enough to clear my sinuses and blow the exhaust of Houston out of my lungs and my head.

I love this spot. When I first arrive and my resistance is low I actually lust after it in my heart. If I had about $300,000 in my pants pocket I would try to buy it. I doubt it could be had for less, and it might take more.

The improvements here are not fancy but a good deal of ground goes with this place, including a considerable amount of the river bank. You go to pricing river bank out here and you'll think they are talking about street frontage on Westheimer.

Another feature of this little jewel is a small mountain. (I make the place sound like it's for sale, which it is not.) Well, not an entire mountain but a part of one. All the mountain a man would ever need.

I am looking up at it now. Before I leave this afternoon I will climb it again. It is maybe two hundred feet from base to top. (All right, then, call it a hill.) About two-thirds of the way up there's a rocky ledge where you can stand and watch sunsets and listen to your heart sing.

The mountain is covered with limestone and thin, black, loose soil and cedar and scatterings of Texas oak and feather-top blue-stem. And whitetail deer and coons and wrens and pretty little striped snakes that don't even scare you. A really nice mountain. Everybody around here calls it a mountain.

If they made me choose between the mountain and the river I would suffer such a torment, deciding.

I can see the river from my place under this cedar. From here the water looks green but it is so clear and cool. When you stand on its rocky bottom you can see bream nosing around your ankles in four feet of water.

Small white, sudsy-looking spots about an inch in diameter are floating downstream. They resemble detergent spots from somebody's wash. The owner here says oh horrors no, he has been on this place more than forty years and the foam spots have always been the same. They are produced by the rapids and the low waterfall at the foot of his back steps.

From here the rapids and the waterfall sound like a heavy, steady rain falling on roofs and trees and rocks. A pleasant sound to go to sleep by. You just let it drift you off, to wherever pleasant sound goes.

Above the small falls the water is shallow and swift and what you do is find a handhold so you won't be swept away and you lie on the rock bottom and that fast water tumbles and swirls around you and it's like a whirlpool bath. Gets the knots and kinks out of your muscles and seems to lubricate your joints.

In another three weeks, lying in those rapids won't be so comfortable. Water will already be too cold.

Winters here can be plenty snappy and summers really hot. Yet I don't know of a place in Texas where the climate, year round, is any better than right here under this Guadalupe cedar in the Hill Country.

Yesterday at 2:00 P.M. I sat here and the fellow on the radio in Kerrville talked about temperatures in the nineties. Still, I was comfortable. The skimpy shade of this old cedar combined with a breeze sliding down off the mountain made my spot here as pleasant as an air-conditioned room. But the nights are best, because of the sky. In Houston the lights and the smog won't let us really see the sky.

Last night I stood out in the clearing a long time and got reacquainted with the Milky Way. Hadn't seen that heavenly streak in so long.

But I don't mean to say this place doesn't have disadvantages. The main one is, once you have been here a couple of days, you have to pick up and leave.

"You know I haven't ever seen what you'd call a real mountain?" he said. "Except in pictures."

He was sitting in a highway cafe, watching a TV set. Nobody else was there but me and a combination waitress-cashier who stood at the front window looking out at the rain. There was a cowboy movie on the television and it was showing some mountain scenery and I guess that's what caused the fellow to make the remark.

"Well, me neither," the waitress said. "So you're not by yourself."

I paid my coffee check and left and rejoined the traffic stream and wondered whether it was important to that stranger, to see what you'd call a real mountain. To some people it is, and to some it isn't, to see things they haven't seen before.

Texas in the main is a flat state and I guess we've got thousands of citizens who never have seen mountains. You'd think from the traffic in the summer that everybody is traveling, seeing mountains and seas and rivers and forests, but everybody isn't. Some are born and grow up and live and die in Texas and never go see a mountain, which is their own business. Maybe they don't want to.

For a flatland person, meeting up with a real mountain the first time is an emotional experience. It stirs his insides. It's the same as seeing his first ocean, or his first locomotive, or his first giraffe.

In West Texas, where I grew up, any promontory taller than a mesquite passed for a mountain and was so called in the local tongue. But what we labeled a mountain wasn't anything but a prairie dog mound compared to the real article.

I was beyond voting age before I ever saw a mountain. Crossed the Rockies on a troop train, the worst kind of way to see the country. I didn't even pay those mountains any attention.

Then later on I rode over the Alps in Europe dozens of times, at altitudes up to 27,000 feet. But the Alps were cold and unfriendly and I didn't like them. Besides, an airplane at that height isn't any better for looking at mountains than a troop train is.

Sure, we've got some dandy mountains out west of the Pecos here in our state, and I love every one of them. The sun setting on the walls of the Chisos may be the grandest sight in Texas, but our domestic mountains out there don't exactly awe me.

No, I never did meet a mountain, and recognize it for what it was, until I went way down into Mexico the first time.

I was driving down the east side of the country, all alone, on real estate as flat as between Odessa and Midland. Clouds were thick and low and so I wasn't looking up, just watching the burros by the side of the road and waving at little children.

Suddenly the clouds broke and the mist disappeared ahead of me and I glanced up at the sky and it wasn't there. In place of the sky was this solid, dark, blue-green wall, rising straight up by the side of me.

I pulled over and twisted my neck and peered up through the windshield and couldn't see the top of it, anywhere. It seemed to bulge out, and hang over me. I got out and for the next half hour I just stood rubbernecking, knowing for the first time the magnitude and the strength and significance of a real mountain.

Well, yes, they'd told me I'd be running into that Sierra Madre Oriental range, but I thought maybe I'd see the thing a mile or two before I got to it. Instead the clouds had curtained it off, and I went round a curve and there it was, in the middle of the road. I stayed around a long time, feeling the power of that mountain and shooting my camera up the side of it. All the while, cars and trucks and donkeys and Mexicans went parading right on by, paying no attention, not even noticing that I'd just got through discovering a mountain big as the entire state of Illinois.

I didn't tell anybody for years how that mountain affected me. I wish now I'd told the fellow in the cafe about it—the one who said he never had seen what you'd call a real mountain, except in pictures.

~❈ XII ❈~

Bad Signs

One evening this past week I drove downtown to meet a bus at the Greyhound Station. I guessed wrong on how thick the traffic would be and got there way early. So I parked on La Branch near where it crosses Texas Avenue and walked awhile.

Over to Crawford and past the old Union Station. North across Prairie to Preston and back to La Branch. The George Hotel. The Star of Hope Mission—"Welcome. Jesus Saves." West on Texas as far as Christ Church Cathedral.

There is a period of comparative quiet that comes to downtown when the sun sets. Traffic has thinned and the pace of events slows. A time of waiting for the night.

Stillness, in a place that has so recently seen all that activity. Men in work clothes stand almost motionless on the streets. In front of the bus station. At the hotels. On the walk at the mission, where the evening meal will soon be served. Even those who move walk slowly. The hurrying is done for the day.

But there is an exception. A young woman, maybe a secretary out of one of those office buildings back toward Main. Had to stay late, I suppose. She clutches her purse with both hands and hurries to her car. Yonder goes another woman being escorted into a parking lot by a policeman, or maybe a security guard dressed similar to a policeman.

I don't feel entirely comfortable myself, walking in this neighborhood. There was a time I sure did, though. In fact, my first two or three years in Houston, one of my favorite walks was along Texas Avenue from Union Station to the Rice Hotel.

When I first went to work for the morning paper, I would often get sent to do interviews or cover meetings at the Rice. The Rice was where everything happened. If a big shot came to town, he would stay at the Rice. This was before the Shamrock was built. I am talking about '47, '48.

It I had time, I liked to park near Union Station and walk along Texas to the hotel. What a fine, big-city street. The Ben Milam. The William Penn. Grand names for hotels.

Before I moved to town from up on the Brazos, when I would visit Houston I liked to stay at the William Penn. The Rice was a little too fancy for my purse. It pleased me to tell people I was staying at the William Penn. Uptown, you bet.

I used to hang out in the cavernous lobby of the Union Station when I had no business there. I just wanted to hear the music. It came out of a dignified black man who would stand in the middle of that great lobby singing about the trains. Not calling. Singing. Singing the train names and the places they'd go and the towns they were coming from. So beautiful. With all the interest there is now in folk things, I hope somewhere somebody has that man on a tape. I would dearly love to hear it.

Something else I'd love: Right now, if a genie rose up over me and said I could have anything to drink I want, I would tell it to conjure me a cup of Rice Hotel coffee, the way it was in 1948. I am cutting at a cup of coffee right now that I made myself, and I would have considered it pretty good if I hadn't thought about Rice Hotel coffee.

One reason I didn't mind going to all those meetings at the Rice, you could sit there and drink the world's finest cup. The Ben Milam had good coffee too. The coffee at both places had a railroad dining-car quality. Thick and hot and giving off such lovely aromas.

It saddens me a bit that I can no longer feel at ease walking along that street I once admired.

I went back and sat in the car and had a while longer to wait. A man came and leaned on a parking meter near me. He had the look that makes us nervous about walking in certain parts of downtown Houston at night.

The derelict look, I mean. He stayed there at the meter a good long while and I got to study him. It occurred to me that he might come to the car and try to panhandle me, but I soon changed my mind. I decided he wasn't even aware of me or my car.

He didn't need money for a bottle. He already had a bottle.

He took it from beneath his arm. It was in a brown paper sack. He drank from it without showing what the bottle contained.

He didn't seem drunk to me. He looked—well, forsaken. But not drunk because he was steady as a tombstone. After he had drunk and put the bottle back under his arm, he stood holding onto the meter for several minutes and I could not see him move an inch.

I have watched the men at the Star of Hope do that, when they're out on the walk waiting for the meal. Say you have five guys. Each one will take a parking meter and hold onto it lightly and stand still for minutes and minutes. Lined up that way, they make a study in stillness. I have considered whether it would make an interesting photo or painting, but I suppose not because it would look contrived, as if you had instructed five men each to take a parking meter and hold on and be still.

The fellow with the bottle wore a blue denim cap dark with soil, its bill curved into a horseshoe shape from being grabbed and pulled. He had on a black coat, a coat that originally came with a suit. Dirty khaki pants. A pretty good pair of shoes, though.

While I studied, he put a hand in the inside pocket of the coat and brought out a folded brown paper. He unfolded it slowly and took out of the folds a white slip, another piece of paper, and studied it.

Then he looked up, not at me, but into the street. He showed this rugged, well-traveled, Johnny Cash-type of face. Not old but just tired and dark. So many of the men on the street in that neighborhood have such dark faces and it's not a racial thing. Makes you wonder if it's a darkness that has come out of their experience.

While he was looking up from the slip of paper, staring into the street, I got to see his face, a good long look, and the eyes were sunken way back into the face, so white back in there, and they didn't seem to belong to the face. They were like eyes that belonged to another person, trapped inside this fellow holding onto the parking meter with his little slip of paper. I could see forty tragedies in that face.

Suddenly I was taken over by an awful hankering to talk to that man. To hear his story. To know about the piece of paper and what it meant. To learn about the eyes trapped inside him.

But he didn't want to talk. When I got out and spoke he

seemed to notice me for the first time and he said, "No, no," and walked off, fairly fast. South on La Branch, and left on Capitol. Not toward the mission.

This neighborhood, where I used to feel so fine walking on the street, will change again. It has gone way down from when I first knew it. Soon it will come back. The tall buildings are moving toward it from the west and south. I will say in another fifteen years it will be a new part of town again.

Living in a big city drags me down at times, but it's not the big things that do me in. It's the combined weight of a lot of minor pains.

Such as having to stand in five or six different lines in one day. I hate that. Stand in line at the bank. At the post office. At the parking lot. At almost every store.

Listen, I stood in line half of eternity just to pay for a pair of socks. Along comes somebody I know and asks what I'm doing and I have to say I'm in line to pay for socks.

That hurts me. I think of everything I *could* be doing. Floating down creeks. Climbing mountains. Watching sunsets. Eating home-made ice cream.

What am I doing instead? Standing in line to pay for a pair of bleeping socks.

They're always telling me not to fight it, to relax and let things happen and don't bother so much.

I'm tired of hearing that. I think a person has a right to be impatient. Take a place like a supermarket. Don't you agree that the express checkout line, at least, ought to move, move, move? Of course it ought to, all the time. But it does not.

All right, I stop at a grocery store to pick up a carton of milk. That's all I want, okay? One carton of milk.

Very few customers in the store. Only two checkout clerks are in business. One is express. Nine items or less. That's me, with one carton of milk.

So I get in the express line and study the enemy. The enemy is made up of everybody in line ahead of me. Only three strong.

Which sounds thin but you never can tell. You learn to watch. All right, look at the big guy now being checked. Notice his basket. He has got anyhow fourteen items, and isn't allowed but nine.

He's supposed to be at register four, behind that woman with a week's groceries.

This guy is the very kind of persimmon that keeps the system from working. Keeps lines moving slow. I'd bet you six pounds of ground round his fourteen items won't go through on a routine checkout. He'll produce a snag, you watch.

All right, there it is. He has picked up a jar of ripe olives that doesn't have a price on it. Our little checker calls to Brenda on register four to ask the price on ripe olives.

As far as I know every supermarket in creation has a checker named Brenda who knows all the prices. But on this day, just because I am there waiting to pay for half a gallon of milk, Brenda is stumped. Ripe olives? She does not know.

So we stand, and wait, while a stock boy is summoned to run down the price, over yonder the other side of the store a block away. The line lengthens.

Next up to bat, behind the ripe-olive guy, is a woman with a very large purse. She has made the limit—only six items—but that big purse makes me nervous. Depend on this: Big purses are a bad sign when you're in a hurry.

She is already off to a poor start. She holds the purse with both hands until her six items are checked and totaled. Now she opens the purse, so deliberately, and lifts out her checkbook.

She fills out her stub, first. She even does the subtraction to get a new balance. Then she makes out the check as if she is drawing a picture. Tears the check out, blows on the ink, shuts the purse. Asks the checker if it is cold enough to suit her.

Then starts the purse-opening ritual once more, as soon as the checker asks for her driver's license. I want so bad to tell her if she is going to enter that purse again, look for a major credit card while she is in there because the checker will want one of those, too.

Just behind the big-purse woman, and just ahead of me, is a woman with a baby. Her purse is also pretty big. When I notice that, I make a bold decision. I leave the line and change over to Brenda at register four because she is now sacking up that woman with a week's groceries.

You know what she does before I can get there? Yes. She

switches off her light, snaps a chain across the chute and shuts down. And I must go back to express where I have lost my place and end up number six in line. Three big purses are ahead of me and I'll be lucky to get out before my milk sours.

That kind of thing gets really heavy on my spirit.

My father has been gone for about twenty years. Sometimes I find myself wondering what he would think of the world now, and how he would get along in it. Not so good, I am afraid.

He had certain strict notions of how people ought to look and act in public. Some of them I considered unreasonable, especially when I was the one obliged to conform to them. But I see that today he would be miserable about so many things.

He was a salesman, all his life, sometimes a traveling one and sometimes a clerk in department stores. His idea was that customers who were even vaguely interested in buying what he had to sell should be treated almost like royalty. He thought they should not be required to take a step or lift a hand or do anything that would make it harder for them to spend their money for what he was selling.

I thought about this when I was writing checks for the monthly bills the other night, and trying to follow the instructions sent out with these condemned computerized invoices. It has become common for the company sending out these bills to instruct the customer to write his account number on his check. The implication is that if he doesn't, he may not be credited with the money he is sending in.

One firm I do business with has assigned me a fourteen-digit account number. Groups of zeros show up in the number here and there, and every month I have to count them to be certain I am not writing a triple set of the things where a quadruple set ought to go. I always get mad when I write that number. But I keep writing it because I am afraid that if I don't, my money will be credited to the account of somebody named Leo Haley or Leonard Hall. I produce little fantasies in which I call up the manager and complain to him that I didn't get credit for the check I sent last month, and he says, "Well, that is just tough, buddy, because you wrote only three zeros in your account number when there should have been four, so now Leo Haley has got your money and you will never see it again."

I think about my father because the idea of a customer having to write out a fourteen-digit account number, in order to be credited with money he is paying to a company, that would have been intolerable to him. He just would not have done it.

There are so many other more significant grievances a consumer could have, I suppose it is wasteful to complain about writing fourteen-digit account numbers on checks. And I wouldn't mind it so much if anybody at the *company* was writing out fourteen-digit account numbers. But nobody is, not a one of the whole gang.

Look, all I want is for the company to share the burden. I don't want to be the only one keeping records so that the firm can make money off me. I ask for just one eighteen-year-old clerk in that place to sit on a stool and copy down all those digits the way I am doing now. Why must I do the firm's work alone?

But do you know what they say, around that office? I am able to see and hear everything there. They say, "Don't worry about that Hale. He will keep right on copying digits because he is afraid not to. We have got him in an awful press. Let's change his account number, and add a few digits. Hit him with a couple of additional zeros, and some of those strange numerals that resemble capital L's, and maybe two or three 7's that look like question marks."

At other times I shudder to imagine what a scene my father would make now, say, in restaurants. Listen, I have seen that man get up and walk out of a greasy spoon cafe because he wasn't served the sixty-five-cent plate lunch as fast as he thought it ought to be served. Or because the gravy on the potatoes was cold.

I have hidden behind newspapers in drugstores while he lectured the soda fountain manager about how rotten the coffee tasted, and how the pot needed to be washed, and how the cleaning boy should not be allowed to sweep around a table where customers were drinking.

Do you see what a misery it would be for him now, to go out in public? More than that, I expect he would get invited to take his business somewhere else.

When he was on duty in the various stores where he worked, you would think he was the owner of them. (He never did own much of anything, though, not even a house.) He didn't want a customer to walk in the front door without being spoken to and welcomed instantly.

If he was way in the back, waiting on somebody else, and a person came in the store traveling in the mousiest, quietest manner, he would know it. He would see that person, and call out that if the customer would make himself at home, somebody would be there to wait on him in just a few seconds.

He had some kind of radar that enabled him to tell when a customer had come in, even if he wasn't able to see. I have been with him while he was back behind the shoe shelves, entirely out of sight, and suddenly he would drop the broom or whatever he was doing and go hustling up front, yelling hello and how-are-you and what-can-I-do-for-you. When I hadn't heard a sound.

So that was his style. I felt it was extravagant but that he had a right to it. The only thing was, he expected when he went out to spend his own money that he ought to be treated the same way. Even in those times, when merchants needed a buck so bad, he didn't get what he wanted in the way of service and courtesy.

In these times—well, I think it is good that he missed them.

People are so jumpy now, and suspicious of strangers. I'm sure they are wise to be that way but it's sad to me, that all this crime has made it impossible to trust those we don't know.

This fear of strangers is so intense now that I no longer like to stop at a house and ask directions.

Recently I was up in Panorama Village, looking for a house I couldn't locate. I saw a woman out on her driveway, and I pulled into it to ask if she knew the street I needed.

The second I turned in, I was sorry I did it. Because I frightened her. She rushed in the garage and into the back door and, I'm certain, locked it. I stood there on the drive a while and tried to look harmless and finally she cracked the door to speak to me, and found my street for me, too.

So people still want to help one another. But it's so much harder to do now, because of the thieves and the drunks and the robbers and burglars and dope addicts and rapists and other brands of weird parties.

Once in a while a person who lives in the heart of Houston

will ride along with me on a short trip to the country. If he hasn't been out of the city in a long time, he'll imagine that just as quick as you get into the country, this distrust of strangers stops.

But it sure doesn't.

I have to grin at some of these country folks I talk to. They'll say they wouldn't want to live in Houston where all that crime is, that they like to be out there where folks can still trust one another.

And what have they got tied at their front step? A ninety-pound guard dog that would lay open the preacher himself if he came around while nobody was home.

Some farm women will no longer come out to answer the call of a stranger at the front gate. I know this is true because I see them go in the house when I turn in off the main road.

Of course you have still got a good many of these intrepid country women with loaded shotguns over the fireplace and they are not afraid of the devil in a red suit. The problem there is that I am afraid of *them*.

I have called at country houses where men and women both were home, and nobody would come out. But I got the feeling this was not so much a matter of being afraid, as not wanting to be bothered by a flock of dumb questions.

Whatever the reason, going up to a country house, at night especially, is a much more sensitive proposition now than it was even ten years ago.

But listen, if you want to know what it feels like to get looked upon with suspicion, do this:

Go into a little country town where the bank has been robbed in the last six months. Then around 2:00 P.M., or somewhere near closing time, walk in there to get change, or to ask directions. Don't go directly to the first window. Pause a second at the door, and look all about, as if you are interested in counting the number of folks present.

Hoo wee. You will feel the tingle of the stares. Because some of these little banks don't see many strangers.

In the city, I notice people using particular care and caution in what they consider to be risky situations. Around parking lots and public buildings at night, for example.

Up until about a year and a half ago I hadn't used what you could call a big-city post office in a long time, and I have always considered a post office to be at least as safe a place as a church, and maybe safer.

Now I often stop at a large post office at night, sometimes late, and I notice people being on their guard. I have learned that if I go in that big lobby and a lone woman is in there, she will leave, immediately.

And sometimes I notice them sitting in the car in the parking lot, waiting for me to come out and drive away. So they can go back in, I suppose. I understand why they do this, yes, but still it makes me feel odd, or something.

I guess all of us have had the experience of scaring a member of the family in our own home.

My friend Mel says when he stays home all day, he must go about the house singing. Else his wife Christina will forget he's there, and if he walks in on her without advance racket, she will yell and jump pretty near onto the drainboard.

He says when he comes home from the office he announces himself at the door, and calls out that he is not in the mood to rob or rape anybody. Mel often exaggerates, but I am not sure how much he's exaggerating on this.

This week I had an invitation from a bunch of hikers to walk back in the woods about ten miles, and spend the night, and walk back out again. I turned it down.

No, I haven't lost my sense of adventure altogether. In fact, I would enjoy walking two days in the woods. It's that spending the night that bothered me. I've developed an unbreakable habit of doing my sleeping in a bed.

In my dim and misty past I slept plenty of nights in places other than beds. Front porches. Haylofts. River banks. Benches in railroad depots. And lots and lots of chairs that weren't meant to be slept in.

But that was when I had more elastic than now. You could bend me in those times, almost any old direction, and I would pop back into a close copy of how I was before.

Not any longer. You bend me in the wrong way now and I *stay* bent. And my recollection of sleeping on the ground is that you often wake up bent backwards.

The hikers said, "Don't worry about that. We will provide you with a comfortable sleeping bag."

Yes, but I will be required to carry that thing on my back, isn't that true? Here is my theory on carrying beds: Anything light enough that I can carry it all day in the woods is just not capable of making as thick a bed as I will need by sundown.

Way back yonder when my kids were small, and I was doing all those peculiar things fathers do, I went into the wilderness one time and slept in a bag that way.

I didn't much like it, because things got into the bag with me. Things with lots and lots of legs, and things equipped to bite and sting. Things that wanted me for a host, and came home hidden in my clothes.

I had known all these creatures before, in my early years in the country, and felt I had graduated from them. It didn't seem smart for me to go out into the woods and lie down on the ground and invite them back. I feel that way even yet. I say it is somebody else's turn to sleep on the ground.

I did have a weak spell a few years ago when I decided I could get along sleeping not in a bed but a vehicle. That's when I bought that halfbreed truck I used to mention. I put a low-slung camper on the back of it, and bought me a little mattress. It was going to be my way of staying out of these expensive motels when I traveled about.

The question I asked myself was: Why should I pay all that money just to sleep, when I could stretch out in the back of that truck?

I found out the answer soon enough. The truck was too cold in the winter. Too hot in the summer. The mattress was too thin. The ceiling on the camper was so low it was like crawling into a sleeping bag.

So I gave the mattress to the dog and went back to motels.

Since I got this little station wagon I'm traveling in now, I have tried to sleep in it only one time. Notice I said *tried*.

I had meant to spend the night in Hallettsville but I got in there too late, and not a motel room was left in town. I drove on toward Victoria, but before I got there I was so blamed sleepy I had to stop in a roadside park. By then it was after midnight so I said, well, I'll just lie down in the back of this machine and make a night of it.

But you know I couldn't do it? Couldn't go to sleep. That surprised me a little. I have taken naps beside the road in this state so many times, and felt perfectly safe. But my attitude about that has changed now. I no longer feel at ease.

In that roadside park there on U.S. 77 north of Victoria, two cars rolled in behind me just about the time I stretched out. I expect the people in them were trying to catch a nap, the same as I was. But when I shut my eyes, I would hear muffled voices, and footsteps on the gravel, and I would feel the need to raise up and look around, to make sure nothing threatening was going on.

Nothing was that I could see, but I never was able to feel safe in that place, and finally drove on. It makes me sad to know that we have all become afraid of one another that way.

I wish I knew what the people in the other cars thought when I drove off. Probably they were glad to see me leave, and felt safer afterward.

It's true. I think now I'd rather sleep in the woods with the bugs, than in a car along a public road.

There are times when the system just doesn't work. I am talking about the system by which we trade our services and cooperate to make everything function and to get along in the world together.

A few of my pessimistic associates insist that the system is slowly breaking down and one day won't work at all and we will have chaos. I am not ready to believe that. The malfunctions in the system come in spurts, it seems to me, and most of them are minor and some are ridiculous and even funny.

I have been having trouble with the system now for about a week. It is only 8:30 A.M. now and twice already this morning I have run into malfunctions.

It happens I am on the road right now, in a motel as usual. This morning I went to the coffee shop and ordered two eggs soft-poached, which is one of my favorite ways to have eggs. They came out hard rubber. I could have bounced them like tennis balls, and that destroys the reason for poaching eggs to begin with. If you want eggs to bounce you can hard-boil them.

Well, that is a minor malfunction in the system, true, but

don't you see when they run in streaks this way they add up and they wound the human spirit.

In the motel where I stayed night before last, I was not able to work. I mean I couldn't use this typewriter, which is electric, unless I moved the bed and the heavy chest of drawers and rearranged the entire room.

Why? Because one end of the electrical outlet at the desk-dressing table, the only reasonable place to type, was on the blink. If I plugged in the typewriter I couldn't use the lamp. If I plugged in the lamp I couldn't use the typewriter. And I couldn't use the typewriter without light.

I could do you a fairly thick book about the weird little things that happen in motels. Most of them are due to malfunctions in the system.

The other night I was sitting in a motel room chair reading and I became aware that an occasional drop of water was hitting me on the head. The blinking ceiling was leaking. Turned out to be condensation from a cooling unit in the room above. Another little malfunction in the system.

This current streak of malfunctions began at a post office I went into. It had no stamps. Let me say that to you again: *The post office had no stamps*. How are you going to have any confidence in the system when you can't buy stamps at a post office?

I bought a new pair of pants and they had to be altered. Pick up your pants, they said, on Wednesday. Okay. On Wednesday I was leaving town and on the way out I went by the store and picked up my pants and bought a new belt to go with them. Belt cost $12.50.

That evening I was going to do an interview and wear my new pants. I thought, the way things have been going with the system, those blamed pants will have been cut off four inches too short. Or they will not be the ones I bought. They will turn out to be red-, white-, and blue-striped.

But no, they were the right pants, and they fit all right. Ah, maybe the system is getting straightened out and back on track. So I put on my new $12.50 belt and the buckle broke. The metal part of it just came apart. Separated into two unholy integrated parts. It would take a factory-trained state-licensed blacksmith to put them together again.

Then somebody came along and flipped a cigarette and it landed on the hood of my little creamy-colored station wagon. It stayed there, and burned itself out in the still night, and burned away an inch-long spot of my hood paint. Made me feel bad. It's a violation of the system to toss lighted cigarettes onto the hoods of creamy-colored station wagons.

The system doesn't always damage me when it gets out of whack in those little ways. Sometimes it just confounds me.

It gave me a new experience on this very trip. I pulled into a gas station. A full-service station, as the oil companies like to call them. Meaning it had no self-serve island.

Well, nobody was working there. The place was wide open but nobody was there. A radio was playing by the cash register. I looked in the wash bay and the grease rack and around the back and in the restroom. Nobody.

I needed gas and got tired waiting so I pumped it myself. Washed my windshield and checked my hood and put in some battery water.

Still nobody came so I filled out a gas ticket and ran my card through the machine and signed it and left the carbon on the cash register and drove on off. How strange the world is when the system's not working.

⁓⧘ XIII ⧙⁓

Blessed Events

A while ago I began writing a report on something I wasn't able to get very interested in, so I have put it aside and changed subjects. I am in the home of a friend, Saturday morning at ten o'clock, and I am about to have a visitor.

Actually I have already had the visitor, for a few seconds. She came in and looked around and scurried out again, and is now studying me with one eye, half her face hidden behind a partly open door.

She has light brown curly hair and great dark eyes and there is just a suggestion of olive in her perfect skin. The first time I saw her she had no hair at all and she was the color of ripe strawberries from top to bottom. She was a week old then. That was four years ago.

I believe this is the fourth time I've seen her. She became beautiful before she was six months old and is growing more so daily.

I have never heard this child speak a word. I have seen her pull her mother's ear close and whisper things, but I don't know the sound of her voice. Her mother assures me she talks, that she can talk the straw off a broom when she wants to. But if company comes, she shuts down and stays quiet.

I am unable to find a fault in that. I have known so many small children who begin producing thunderous noises the minute their parents have callers. It has always been hard for me to find anything to admire in loud children.

But then of course that is merely a personal preference. You meet people who seem to enjoy every racket that's associated with a child, as if all noises that kids make deserve to be celebrated.

Let me tell you something nice about this little girl, watching me now with that one eye. She likes me. There is no explaining it but she does. Her mother says it's true and her father does as well.

Yet I have never given her a reason. I mean I have not brought her gifts, not one. Never done her a favor. Never even spoken to her except to say hello, and then she didn't answer me.

Still, she likes me. I confess it pleases me. I would be an awful bum not to enjoy being liked by such a pretty little person.

Her mother would scold her for being here now, staring at me. I was given this room to work in for a while, and they told her not to bother me but in her silent way she came to visit, and her parents are in another part of the house and don't know about it.

She has come into the room now, keeping quiet as cotton. She has a little car, a toy, and she scoots it along on the carpet and pretends to be absorbed in her playing. But now and then she looks up at me and almost smiles.

If she sees me watching her she looks away, back down at the toy, but every time she moves she comes a little closer.

Oh, I don't expect her to talk to me, or sit on my knee the way so many little children do. That is simply not her style. Her manner suggests that she is glad to be near, and that for some reason I am an interesting old gaffer, sitting here making click-click-click noises on a black machine. But don't go trying to make talk with her, or she'll leave.

So I have not made a sound except for typing, and she has allowed herself to come stand here by my chair, and watch. Her hands are clasped behind her, as if she is saying that she won't touch anything, that she only wants to see.

I like that. Most children this age have got to get their mitts into everything and mess it up.

I have held out a hand to her now. She looks at it several seconds and finally decides it is all right and she touches my palm with one finger. So I take that little finger and guide it along the keyboard, so that she produces a row of letters:
A B C D E F G H I J K L M N O P Q R S T U V W X Y Z
Oh, I wish you could see the delight that came to her face when she saw that her own hand was causing those marks to appear on the paper. She suddenly laughed, a sort of musical giggle that ran several notes up the scale, and she went out. This is a really nice little child.

This past week I discovered an interesting thing about little babies.

I was in the home of a young couple for a brief visit, and I rode with them to the grocery store. They both went in and asked me to stay in the car with the baby.

This child is around seven months of age, I think they said. As a general rule I do not care to be minding babies in supermarket parking lots. But this little party didn't seem due to make trouble, as it was buckled into one of these car-seat concerns such as young parents put their offspring in when they go driving around town.

Then too, its mama and papa would be gone only long enough to spend a hundred dollars or so on groceries, which in these times means maybe half an hour or even less.

Some days I get accused by the customers of not liking children in any form. Which is not true. I don't much mind staying with them in cars, if they behave. It's just that I don't enjoy bobbing them up and down on my knee, like grandparents do, and hugging them up, and telling them how smart and beautiful they are.

Small babies as a broad class are too moist and slobbery to suit me.

I know, long ago somebody put up with my own slobberiness. But I later put up with it in two of my own, so I figure I paid that debt and am ahead of the game by one slobbery child.

Anyhow, I was there in the car with this baby, and I will say it's not a bad specimen. It comes up short in the matter of hair, and is shy most of its teeth, and has a pretty serious bay window. But I saw a smart light in its eye. Furthermore, it wasn't crying or dribbling, and that makes points with me. I can deal with babies as long as they don't cry or dribble.

I figured it wouldn't hurt to say a couple of words to it, just to keep it company. There wasn't anybody else to talk to anyhow so I said, "Well, little buddy, what's happening?"

It considered the question, I could tell. It took its fist out of its mouth and made a couple of bubbles and answered as follows: "Churblah."

I begged its pardon. And it gave the same answer. "Churblah."

When I heard that sound, I felt a tiny nudge from deep in the record of my own times. I had heard it before, I felt. Heard it come out of one of my own dependents almost thirty years ago.

Don't you agree that's interesting? That two little babies, unrelated, members of separate generations, would produce this same sound?

While I was dwelling on that, my little buddy put its wet fist to its nose and made the sound again. "Churblah."

Listen, maybe this is a word being made. Or two words, or a significant phrase.

I made a quick test. I grabbed one of its tiny toes. It looked down, and wiggled its foot, and looked up at me, and back down, and it said, "Skoo." Maybe an L-sound was in there. More like "skloo."

Then I punched it gently in the stomach. (I'm telling you this kid has got a pot problem. Are they feeding it on pizza and long-necks?) It giggled wetly when I poked it in the belly. And it said, "Shillups."

Then I went back up and put my finger on its nose. Would it say "churblah"? It did.

I felt a key might have turned in a rusty lock. Could this kid be talking a language? One that adult humans don't know about?

I touched its toe again. "Skoo." (I couldn't detect the L-sound the second time.) I poked its stomach. "Shillups." Back to its nose. "Churblah." I went over the territory three more times. Twice it wasn't consistent, and identified its skoo as its shillups and its shillups as its churblah. But then it's young, and entitled to errors.

Don't you agree it's possible that tiny humans could have their own tongue that we don't recognize? We credit the young of many species in nature with all manner of precocious business. Being able to run, swim, fly, sing, the second they're born. Yet here are miniature humans, supposed to be at the top of the evolutionary scale, and we presume them to be entirely without talent or understanding until they're three or four years old.

They might be speaking a language that's more efficient, even more beautiful, than the one we'll force them to learn. We'll scold them, at a tender time in their lives, and make them quit saying skoo when they mean toe, and to please us and to avoid scolding they'll abandon their tongue and take ours.

Wouldn't it be interesting to set ten little babies apart from adult influence in the matter of speech? And see what language they would end up using? Did you ever notice two babies holding to the rail of their respective playpens, firing back and forth at one another with what we said was infantile gibberish? They might have been speaking The Language.

In the time it took for its parents to spend a hundred dollars in that supermarket, I isolated ten sounds made by their offspring. I can't call them words. They might be entire thoughts, and much more than single words.

Churblah. Skoo. Shillups. Flige. Bifish. Goosh. Skittly. Shilla. Gleg. Moofa.

Really now, who knows? Maybe "churblah goosh" would properly be written "cheib la hoos" and mean "My nose needs blowing," which in the case of my companion in the car, it did.

But that small citizen is all right. I would be smarter if I understood all that goes on inside that little noodle.

On this Mother's Day, a great many women will not receive flowers, or pretty-wrapped gifts, or long-distance phone calls for the reason that they have never given birth to any babies. But among these childless women you will find some of the best mothers that ever wrapped a sore toe.

The first such mother I remember was named Flora Mae and she is probably still with us somewhere. If she is I expect a baby is sitting on her lap this very minute.

She was a neighbor of ours long ago. Flora was the eldest of four or five girls in that family and she raised her little sisters as if they were her own children. The father of that bunch died early and their mama went to work and Flora kept the babies.

I can see her walking home from the grocery store when she was around seventeen, I suppose. They had a big old wobbly baby buggy. Flora would be wearing a pink cotton dress. In the buggy she'd have a toddler or two, riding with the turnip greens and the canned goods. A couple of older ones would be marching along beside, and a tiny one would be in the crook of Flora's arm.

We used to look out when she passed and say, "Flora's got an extra one today." Meaning she'd have a neighbor's youngster, or a little cousin from across town. That seemed curious to me, that the very person who had the most children to take care of always ended up with extras. The mother of one child almost never took on a second one that wasn't naturally hers. But a woman with five or six was apt to feed seven or eight on a given day, and keep in a good humor about it, too, as if a couple of more didn't matter when she already had a houseful.

My folks kept up with Flora long after we moved away from that place. When my son was born in 1949, Flora sent him a little long-tailed nightgown thing. At that time she was taking care of some of the babies of those younger sisters we used to see her wagging around when *they* were babies. She was pushing forty then and had never married and as far as I know she never had a baby of her own.

Isn't that an irony for you, that Flora will go on the record books as a non-mother, when she loved and cared for many more babies than most mothers ever did?

Some childless women seem never to get enough of mothering. I remember a woman I'll call Pearl, which may not be right. But it was an old-fashioned name like that. She ran a little restaurant on the beach at Santa Monica back in the '40s when I was out there.

She collected young people the way hobbyists collect shells or stamps. She would love them and feed them and loan them money and worry about them and cry and laugh with them. Some nights, after hours, twenty or thirty of us would be gathered around Pearl in the back of that little restaurant, staying close to her because we hadn't been home in a long time and we were lonesome for our own mothers. We were too old to admit it but it was true.

The kind of thing she would do, she'd go to the variety store and buy up a bunch of inexpensive greeting cards about two weeks before Mother's Day. She'd put 'em in a basket in the back room where we all hung out and she'd have a little notice posted reminding everybody when Mother's Day was. So if a guy had forgotten, he could address one of those cards and get it in the mail at the last hour so his mother would get something from him on that special day.

She'd do that for us and yet I can't remember, the one Mother's Day that I was out there, that we did anything for her. There she was being a mother to us all and we didn't have sense enough to give her even one of her own greeting cards on Mother's Day. We ought to have given her a banquet.

I could list half a dozen or more childless women who ran rooming houses or boarding houses or dormitories where I stayed and who were fine mothers, without anybody ever to call them by that sacred title.

Old Mrs. G. Bless her heart. She operated a roachy sort of hotel where you rented rooms by the week. I stayed with her one summer. You talk about charity, that woman conducted a home for the destitute. She'd let you run six weeks late on the rent if she thought you were a decent sort.

Some guys took advantage of her and never did pay. I might owe her a couple of bucks myself, still. I hope not.

She was a great round woman who wore tenty dresses and felt houseshoes and rolled her own smokes and played chess by mail. She read detective stories and hummed hymns along the halls. When she talked you thought of the noise a concrete mixer makes. She could scare off a burglar by roaring at him.

But she was a fine childless mother. Called everybody "honey bunch." She'd say to a guy, "You're lookin' kindly gaunt, honey bunch. You have anything for supper last night?"

Then teachers. Lordy, think of them all. A terrible lot of mothering has been done in this world by spinster schoolteachers. I had 'em, and I guess you did as well, right on up to college. A few of mine were a great deal better at mothering than at teaching. Just real sweet, lonely women, trying to fill the emptiness in their lives by loving the offspring of other women.

Remember Mrs. Rick? I used to have her name in the paper here sometimes, when I'd drift down onto Surfside Beach. Mrs. Rick never had a chick of her own but she was mighty free about adoption. She'd just take 'em in, off the beach, and put 'em up and care for 'em and they weren't all youngsters. Some of 'em older than she was. A mother to the general public, running a beer joint on the beach. I miss her still. I never go back to Surfside that I don't feel the great vacancy she created when she died, and she's been gone—how long? Ten years?

This Mother's Day I think I'll try to locate one of the childless mothers I've known, and give her a big hello. I might try to find Flora Mae, and see whose babies she's taking care of now.

There's a country song being played a lot on the radio now about this old boy who is always coming down with an affliction he calls honky-tonk amnesia.

It hits him when he goes out and makes all the joints. Causes him to forget that he is supposed to be at home with his ever-loving wife, and sometimes he forgets so thoroughly that he doesn't go home all night long. That naturally brings distress on the domestic front.

Honky-tonk amnesia. I wonder how many thousands of cases of that disease show up on any Saturday night. I expect it would qualify as an epidemic.

These country-and-western songs, so many of them, often strike at raw truth in a way that's really impressive, despite that they can be mighty corny.

I don't think I've ever listened to country and western as much as I have in the last year, mostly because it's the kind of music you're most likely to hit when you switch on a radio. Go from one end of the dial to the other and you'll hear C&W three times as often as any other kind. I've never been what you'd call hung on C&W but lately I've been listening to the lyrics better than I used to. They get sort of mawkish and super-sentimental but then they haul off and hit you with some basic truth, about life and love and pain and joy.

One I keep hearing says, "I overlooked an orchid, while searching for a rose."

I had to laugh the first time they ran that one past me but after I'd heard it maybe half a dozen times I got to thinking how often you see that very thing happen. Not just in courtship but in the general search all of us make constantly for things of value.

One really corny tune going round now asks the musical question, "Whattaya git when you work your fingers to the bone?" And then it answers that what you git are bony fingers.

Come on, now, ain't it the truth though? One of the awfulest things that can happen to a person is to spend his life doing hard old back-wrenching labor in which there's no reward for the spirit. We're fond of saying hard work is good for a person but it's got to be more than just work, or here's what it gets you—bony fingers.

Not many of the C&W song writers, I've noticed, will go off and leave us without a little glimmer of hope that everything is going to improve soon. Like the song about the bony fingers says, "Maybe things'll git a little better in the mornin'."

Occasionally a C&W lyric will offer a phrase that's so simple it's childish and yet so descriptive you wonder why it hasn't entered the language and earned a place in dictionaries. One I'm thinking of is in the song sung by the old boy who says to the woman, "I see the want-to in your eyes."

I think in that one the woman is married and is being asked to dance, or something, by a guy who doesn't happen to be her husband. So she refuses but shows that want-to in her eyes. Haven't you seen want-to in a thousand pairs of eyes? In children's eyes, when they look at a toy? In the eyes of dumb creatures, looking at food they can't have?

Then once in a while a C&W lyric will surprise you with what comes close to real beauty, genuine poetry. There's a couple of lines in a song called "Country Bumpkin" and they describe the birth of a child in this way: "Into a bed of love and death-like pain, into this world of wonders, one more wonder came." I think that's pretty good, despite that it doesn't rhyme.

Do you ever study people in your rearview mirror? I have become an expert rearview mirror observer, as when I am in stop-and-go traffic. I see many interesting sights this way.

I enjoyed watching a woman conduct an argument behind her steering wheel just this past Wednesday morning. She was back of me in a traffic jam for a dozen blocks or more and I think she was rehearsing.

You understand she was alone in her car. I decided she was on her way to a confrontation of some sort. Maybe with a man friend, or her boss, or perhaps one of her employees.

Anyhow it was going to be a sticky session and she needed to get herself organized for the fight, and the congested traffic provided the opportunity.

She spoke the lines of both parties. I figured that out by the way she turned her head and changed her expression once in a while, and I saw she was doing that when the other party was talking.

Then she would come back with a rejoinder and frequently it would be a brilliant and telling blow and that would please her immensely. She would pause afterward a bit, and turn her head to the left and produce a satisfied smile. The argument she was practicing has probably been had now. I hope she won. I expect she did because she was well prepared.

Sometimes I am able to figure out what two people in the car behind me are talking about. Not by lip reading so much. Mostly by gesture. And the day of the week is a hint, too.

On Monday morning, for instance, if you have two guys in a front seat they will most likely be talking football. Also on Friday afternoons on the way home.

A few football terms are fairly easy to pick up by lip reading. First down. Field goal. The word football itself. If you watch closely you will catch a guy gesturing by holding out his hands with fingers spread, like a receiver about to snag a pass, and you can get the speaker's exact words by watching his mouth: "Right in his hands and he dropped the ball!"

Last week I was in front of a couple of gents having an exchange that puzzled me for several blocks. One would talk a while, and the other would listen, grinning. Then suddenly both would erupt with laughter. Finally I saw that they were taking turns at telling jokes.

They must have been plenty funny stories, too, judging from the laughter. How I longed to hear. I have not heard a really good joke in a year.

They kept up those stories about a mile. Traffic would loosen up and we'd get separated and then I'd hit a red light and here they'd come coasting up behind me again, laughing and wiggling and bobbing in their seats, and I could see I had missed another good story.

Once I was almost certain I had heard the story that the driver was telling. I felt I caught a phrase or two, and by connecting them up with his gestures I decided he was telling the one about the presidential candidate kissing the baby. I suppose you have heard it. I certainly will not repeat it here.

Don't you imagine that people proficient at lip reading learn a great many interesting things just from watching the others of us talk? Hoo boy. A man and his wife riding in traffic together may be speaking on plenty intimate topics, and just ahead of them is a lip reader sitting there taking in every word.

We have a great army of steering-wheel singers in this town. I am one of these myself.

A steering-wheel singer sings only in traffic when he is alone in the car, and he sings along with the radio. Watch for him next time you get in a traffic jam.

People who live outside Houston in smaller places are always telling me that they simply couldn't stand driving in our traffic and they can't see how we endure it. What they don't understand is that Houston people come to terms with the traffic and it doesn't much bother them. They find things to do while they're in it. They rehearse arguments. Tell jokes. Sing along with Mitch. I know one who studies a foreign language with a tape recorder on the seat beside him.

I have become an excellent steering-wheel singer. I amaze myself. I sing with the very top performers only, and I am mighty versatile. I can sing with Floyd Tillman or with Beverly Sills. Some mornings I am better than Tom Jones. I am certainly better than Frank Sinatra.

Houston is also full of dashboard drummers who sit at traffic lights and rap out the beat with their fingers on the dash. I am not as good a dashboard drummer as I am a steering-wheel singer but I'm no bush leaguer. It pleases me the most to find a person behind me who is obviously tuned to the same station, hearing the same song, singing with it and drumming the beat on the dash.

When you perform in traffic that way, you probably figure you have no audience. But you may be getting studied closely in a rear-view mirror up ahead.

You see them in parks sometimes, and other public places where family gatherings are held in pretty weather.

Maybe there'll be five or six carloads of them, and all kinfolks. Ten adults and fifteen children. Their homes are scattered in towns fifty to seventy-five miles from the park and they have converged on this central location to observe a special occasion. Grandma's birthday, something like that.

Everybody has brought a picnic basket and they have eaten and the children have run and played and shouted and the grown-ups have done all their gabbing. So now it is time to load up and start back home.

Before they go they must perform the ritual—getting together for a group picture. Have you ever watched the taking of the group picture?

The clan is called together by the family photographer. In every gang like this there is always one party with a reputation as a taker of pictures. Generally it's a woman, who is large and has a voice like a drill instructor and a name like Emily.

Everybody in the family lets Emily boss the picture-taking because she is willing to fool with having the film developed. She also maintains the album where this group photograph will go. The truth is Emily doesn't know second base about taking pictures but it doesn't matter because nobody else in the bunch does either.

The album is already overloaded with group pictures exactly like this. You will never find Emily in any of them as she is always behind the camera, directing and producing. She prefers it this way. "I just don't take a good picture," she says. That doesn't refer to her photography. It refers to the fact that she doesn't like the way she looks in a picture.

She puts Grandma and Grandpa in aluminum lawn chairs and seats the kids on the ground in front and orders the adults to shoulder together in the back. They are all required to look directly into a flaming sun.

"Everybody close together," Emily directs, looking into her view finder and taking little backward steps. "I can't get you all in if you're not close together. Chester? Chester! Move over close to Whitley a little bit. Okay, I'm gonna snap on three. One . . . two . . . Wait a minute. Lucille, your eyes are shut. Open your eyes."

"The sun hurts 'em," Lucille complains.

"Go ahead, Aunt Emily, she *looks* better with her eyes shut." Laughter from the boys.

"All right, Billy Dean, that'll be enough of that smart mouth." A parent's voice from the back row.

"Hey, Grandpa's eyes are shut, too. Grandpa? Does the sun hurt your eyes?"

Grandpa doesn't answer.

"He's gone to sleep," Grandma says. "Alford, my law, come on and keep awake."

Emily begins the countdown again. "One . . . two . . ."

"Wait a second," somebody says, "where's Pauline? Pauline?

Jimmie Nell, go find your Aunt Pauline and tell her to come get herself in this picture."

"She's gone to the toilet," Jimmie Nell announces.

Pretty soon here comes Pauline, grinning and blushing and taking a place in the back row.

"All right—" Our director goes back to directing—"all yawl look at me now. One . . ."

"Ouch! Billy Dean you *stop* that!"

"Now what?" Emily lowers the camera.

"Billy Dean pinched me."

His father's voice: "Billy Dean, I'm gonna get me a limb and set your pants afire if you don't straighten up."

"One . . ."

"Stop wiggling, Jimmie Nell."

". . . two . . ."

"Do you want us to say cheese?"

"Say frog. Say frog instead."

"Billy Dean, shut your ugly mouth."

". . . three! There!"

"Oh my law, did you take it? You didn't snap, did you? I blinked. I know I blinked."

"Grandpa? Grandpa! Emily? Look here. You'll have to take it over. Grandpa was asleep again."

"Well, poor old thing, he missed his nap."

So Emily goes back to directing. "All right, everybody keep still, and look right here at the birdie. One . . ."

The last few years I have noticed a good many of my contemporaries sitting around talking about their funerals. They seem to enjoy it.

I am surprised that a lot of them have got their funerals all planned, and even paid for. Or else they are paying on them by the month, hoping I guess to be all free and clear by the time they check on out.

I don't mean they're just buying cemetery lots. I mean the works, the funeral itself. The casket, the hearse that will haul them in style on that last ride, even the organist playing back there behind the stiff curtain—everything paid for in advance. All the widow will have to do is call the undertaker and say "Execute Plan B" and put on something black.

Why, some guys already have their tombstones bought, and set, and their names engraved, and their birth dates. And a blank space left to be filled in with the date they finish up. I guess the tombstone man could run out there and fill in the space even before the funeral, so everything will be complete.

My own plans about leaving out of here aren't anywhere near that firm. It doesn't much appeal to me to plan an event I am not eager to see take place.

So far, my planning has been a process of elimination. I mean deciding not so much what I want as what I don't want. For example, I don't want to be pumped full of coal oil, or whatever they use now, and laid out at the undertaker's to see whether anybody will want to come soft-shoeing in to view me. Boy, I am warning you. If anybody does that to me they are going to get a haunting that will scare blood out of a ghost.

Something else I don't want is six or eight of my friends pall-bearing me around in a box. Trying to keep sad expressions. None of that.

I don't want a freeway funeral procession, either. I see them, whizzing across town. A hearse, five cars, and two cops with flashing lights. And everything going fifty-five. Quick, get out of the way, here comes a funeral.

It will be fine with me not to have any parade at all. It just messes up traffic.

But if they want to have some kind of little service, that's all right. Maybe get out under a shade tree somewhere, late in the afternoon after it cools off some and everybody's through working.

When so many of my friends started talking about funeral services I thought of asking my large buddy Wes Seeliger, get him dated up to come say a sentence or two over me. He's young enough to outlast me, and he's qualified with the Episcopalians as a preacher. Once in a motel room in San Augustine he pounded on a Gideon Bible and preached to me for two hours, so I didn't figure he'd mind doing it again for ten minutes.

Also Wes is creative, and could think of a lot of good stuff to say about me. How I fed squirrels, and loved little children if they weren't smart-mouth, and never did rob any banks, or at least none that he knows of. Nice things like that that people want to hear at funerals.

But about the time I was fixing to speak to him about it, derned if I didn't get a letter from old Wes saying he had given up pastoring churches and gone to selling insurance. Well, I don't know. I'm afraid if word got out that an insurance salesman was preaching my funeral nobody would show up.

Now on the question of what to do with remains. Where they are put away seems so important to most parties. Yet I can't see it matters much. I am personally counting on being able to ghost around, and know what is happening, and see a lot of new country. If that turns out to be right, where they deposit me won't make any difference because if I don't like it I will just move. If it turns out to be wrong, well, I won't ever know *what* they did with me, so there you are.

I hear that in these cremating places now they can work a person down to where he won't much more than fill a teacup. In that case, there might be room left to display me at Scheller's Place in Glen Flora. Say right there next to Ed Scheller's old mess kit that he carried in France in World War I.

I might even serve a purpose there. They could put up a little sign, and set out a coffee can with a slot in the lid, and take donations in my memory. Maybe help pay for a new fire truck. Now I'd like that.

Last Saturday was my birthday. I was sixty, and I celebrated fiercely.

Because I had been listening to friends who have passed sixty and they had convinced me that sixty is the beginning of the end. They call it the Big Six Oh. Beyond that mark, they said, the grade gets steeper, and you go downhill faster and faster.

I could see, then, that I had better hurry and enjoy living before somebody turned my clock off. Therefore I tried to work in all the enjoyment I could stand, on what I had begun to think of as my last day.

I drank wine. I sang songs. I told doubtful stories in mixed company. I danced with two or three young women, barely past fifty years of age. I ate red meat, and grazed on salty dips, and covered over my food with rich sauces. I downed white bread, and chocolate cake. Everything that tastes good and is bad for old men. I stayed up until about 2:30 A.M.

The next morning at 6:30, sure enough, I felt wretched. So this is what being sixty feels like. My friends were right. The Big Six Oh is dreadful. Somebody came along and asked, "Well, how do you feel, being sixty?" I said I felt like eighty.

I crept through the day, and ate broth for supper, and went to bed before dark. Monday morning at six o'clock, I felt a lot better for some reason. By noon Monday I felt almost normal. Now, writing this report on Tuesday, I feel perfectly all right again.

What it was that caused me to feel so rotten last Sunday morning is sure mysterious. I expect I was simply struck by a barrage of psychosomatic symptoms, induced by that gang of soreheads trying to make me feel punk about living six decades.

Today I feel pure-dee good. I feel better than I did on my thirtieth birthday. I can look back at my record and I see that the week I turned thirty I had something the matter with my back that I couldn't straighten up. Hey, that was thirty years ago. I thought I was already falling apart then, and here I am, still warm, and up, and about.

It may be I will like sixty better than fifty. I never did much like being fifty. I didn't like thirty, either. I loved forty. The forties were fine, but there's something too vague about being in your fifties. You're not young, but you're not really old enough to get the full benefit of being elderly.

Because there *are* benefits. People are more patient and tolerant with you when you get as old as I am. You can see them being considerate, saying, "Yeah, he forgets things, and loses his glasses, and it takes him twice as long now to get down what he used to do so quick and well. But after all, look, he's getting along. He's no yearling."

You think that hurts my feelings? No way. I like it.

Also, there are things you can do at sixty that you couldn't do at thirty. Like talk to pretty girls in public, or toss one a flower without arousing the slightest suspicion that you're up to anything distasteful.

You can even go places at sixty and be more comfortable, feel safer, than when you were forty. You can go in dim smoky dives, crowded by young people with angry eyes and a fierce resentment of invaders. And you can see them shrugging at you. "What's an old dude like that gonna do? He ain't gonna do nothin'." And they turn away. I do not go in many such places, and I never do except for special reasons, but I would rather go now, at sixty, than twenty years ago.

You want to know one of the neatest things about being sixty? You can remember so much. I amaze myself, the things I am now able to remember, and so clearly.

When I came to fifty-five, I found it astounding that I could suddenly look back and see things that happened half a century before. I am talking about significant events, such as the time my Cousin C. T. dropped the yellow kitten in a churnful of buttermilk and put the blame on me, which happened in 1926. I was five years old then.

As I passed along through my fifty-sixth year, and my fifty-seventh, and fifty-eighth, instead of growing weaker my memory improved. I remembered the day the rooster swallowed my mother's wedding ring and I was only three. I had never before remembered that but suddenly I did.

But now, entering into my seventh decade, something really exceptional is happening to my memory. I could become famous for it. It frightened me a little when it began. The first thing was, I remembered when my sisters were born, and they are both older than I am.

Then I remembered the day my father first harnessed the mule and went out to plow the garden alone, and he was only nine. That happened in 1894, or twenty-seven years before I was born. I submit that this is very little short of a marvel, and that I am the only one that can do it, and I am hoping that some way it will be worth money to me in the evening time of my life.

Think what a mark I can leave, if I make another ten years to seventy. By then I ought to the only citizen left alive who can remember the day the Declaration of Independence was signed. If I reach eighty, I might be able to recall standing on the beach to welcome Columbus when he discovered America that time.

It's now a little past nine o'clock on Tuesday morning. By the time you read this stuff on Wednesday, whatever great and good thing is going to happen will have happened. Maybe it will have happened to you.

I don't know what it's going to be but I know it's good. Maybe it will happen to us all. That would be the best. If it happens only to you, well, I just hope you have the grace to handle it, and I hope the same about myself. Because listen, this is bound to be a huge event, a magnificent happening.

So I've got to write about it. I have a lot of other stuff to write, but let it wait. I've been several days on the road, and done interviews, and taken pictures, and I intended to start doing all that this morning. But not now. It doesn't much interest me, not when this great good event is about to explode.

When I rolled out this morning, I knew this was some kind of a special day. I put in more than eight hours beneath the quilts, and I felt all rested and full of vinegar. I went out and walked around a bit.

And I passed this woman, or almost passed. She was out by her gate and she was cutting gardenia blooms off a bush, and the fragrance of them was all about. I remarked about the perfume of those gardenias and the woman cut a small bloom and handed it to me.

Of course it is not customary for women in housecoats to hand gardenias to old guys early in the morning, or any other time, but I liked getting it, and took it with me when I drove to the store to get some coffee cream.

It wasn't a big flower as gardenias go, but it was perfect, and had some of the stem left on, and a few leaves to set it off, and it smelled mighty nice.

I got into the early traffic on the way to the store. While I was stopped at a light a Jeep pulled up beside me, close, in the lane to my left, and this young woman was driving it. An old-fashioned kind of Jeep, entirely open, with no top at all. The young woman—call her a girl; she was a girl to me—was dressed up something grand, going to work in a polite office somewhere, I imagine. She had a scarf on her head to keep her hair from getting messed up as she went along in that open Jeep.

The sight of that girl, so nicely dressed, and driving the Jeep—well, I just wish it was painted into a picture, so I could put it on my wall. Because if you want to know the truth, that girl reminded me of my own daughter. She was about the right age, and was wearing a little pensive grin, waiting for the light to change, as if she was thinking about something nice.

Before I knew I was doing it I had my head stuck out the window and was telling her hello, and I asked her what she thought about the day.

She took that greeting just exactly right. She tossed her head back a little and sang me an answer. She said she thought it was a beautiful day, just perfect. So I tossed her my flower.

The range was short and I made a good pitch. The flower landed on the seat beside her. She picked it up and smelled it and tucked the stem inside her scarf, so that the bloom was close to her ear.

As the light changed, she turned my direction and switched on a smile that must have fogged film in the drugstore across the street. A smile so brilliant, it's a lucky thing it wasn't released at night, else every electric light within half a mile would have shut itself off in shame.

I was slow pulling away from the intersection, but I didn't get honked at. I have a rearview-mirror image of the guy behind me, sitting there the same as I was, grinning, because he had seen the smile, too.

What I am trying to tell you is, things like this happen on extraordinary days, days that are superior, positive, and high quality. Great and good things happen on days like this.

If you turn out to be the one that the great good thing happened to, be sure to let me know.